O For a Thousand Tongues

O For a Thousand Tongues

The 1933 Methodist Hymn Book in Context

Andrew Pratt

✛ EPWORTH

British Library Cataloguing in Publication data

A catalogue record for this book is available
from the British Library

The cartoon used on page 29 is reproduced by permission of the
Director and Librarian of the John Rylands University Library of
Manchester, and of the Methodist Church.

'O Jesus we are well and strong' (847) on page 134 is used while
efforts to trace the copyright holder have been unsuccessful.

'Friend of the home, as when in Galilee' (753) on page 163 is used
by permission of Piers Morgan.

0 7162 0589 0

First published in 2004
by Epworth Press
4 John Wesley Road
Werrington
Peterborough PE4 6ZP

Printed and bound in Great Britain by
Biddles Ltd, *www.biddles.co.uk*

Contents

Acknowledgements

I am grateful to a number of people who have made this book possible. Firstly, Professor J. R. Watson suggested the topic while the Revd Professor K. G. C. Newport supervised the study on which the book was based. Ursula Leahy read the original text and made helpful and necessary comments on it. The staff of Liverpool Hope University College and the John Rylands University Library of Manchester have been immensely helpful in finding documents, providing encouragement and support and an environment for study.

Various Methodist churches and Circuits have supported me as I have worked, while the Methodist Connexion, the Bolton and Rochdale and Liverpool Districts have aided with funding. I am grateful for all of this.

As the book began to take form the staff at Methodist Publishing House have offered consummate support in all the ways that are necessitous to the completion of a book of this kind.

Last, but not least, my wife Jackie has encouraged me, and then coped with the consequences of my responding to her encouragement, and it is to her that I dedicate this book.

Foreword

The copy of the 1933 *Methodist Hymn Book* that I most frequently use belonged to my grandfather. He was an Ipswich shopkeeper, and a Primitive Methodist. He must have subscribed to an initial offer for Christmas, because the book has his name stamped on the bottom corner of the front cover – 'G. E. Watson. Dec. 25th 1933'. It is a beautiful book, still a joy to handle and read after seventy years, the typeface sharp and clear, the binding still sound, the paper fine and clean. It is much more elegant and handsome than the words-only copy used in churches (stamped 'for the use of visitors' because a Methodist would normally have a copy), which had some of the ugliest print ever used in a hymn book; and much sharper and clearer than my own rather fuzzy later edition, given to me in the 1950s. Such a production must have been something of a miracle if, as Andrew Pratt notes, the book was still being argued about at the Methodist Conference of 1933 and still at the printer's in November.

Perhaps, fancifully, I take my grandfather's copy, and my own less attractive later one, as a metaphor for some of the processes described in this book. At the outset it was, in Andrew Pratt's words, 'the visible symbol of Methodist Union': it was a new start for a new church, a book full of new hope. As the years went by, and especially as society began to change in the 1960s and 1970s, its innate conservatism, which Dr Pratt correctly identifies as one of its principal features, became a disadvantage. By 1983, when its successor, *Hymns and Psalms*, appeared, it had begun to look not only conservative but even a bit antiquated.

For the Methodist Church, however, it was surely a great book. For fifty years, in Dr Pratt's words, it 'became inseparable from what it meant to be Methodist'. To those of us who were brought up with it, it was the rock on which our faith was built, together with the Authorized Version of the Bible. Bible and hymn book together presented living truths in some of the most powerful language the English tongue has ever known. The two texts resounded against one another, intertwined with one another, interpreted one another. And they were poetry, not prose. Prose was for the sermon, which expounded both hymns and Holy Scripture, gave understanding and illumination to what was often dark, mysterious and magnificent. The hymn book itself was, for us, full of mystery and wonder. The hymns were what Coleridge called 'the living educts of the imagination': the truths and the language that represented them, as he put it, moved 'in conjunction' and formed 'the living chariot that bears up (for *us*) the throne of the Divine Humanity'. For us as children, they held the promise of a religion of awe and wonder, sometimes incomprehensible (though not as often as the adults seemed to think) but filled with the beauty of holiness. The only exception was the children's section, which was patronising and trivial: 'God has given us a book full of stories'; 'Jesus, Friend of little children'. Even worse were the silly leaflets that were sent round for Sunday School Anniversaries: we had a very real sense of disappointment every year at being deprived of our hymn book.

Although the compilers clearly had some sense of the greatness of the material they were handling, their primary aims were more practical. They wanted a book that would unite the different elements of the Church: 'This hymn book', they wrote, 'is issued for the use of *all* British Methodists, and for not a few Methodists "beyond the seas" as well.' So they deliberately appealed to the common heritage. This can be seen in the opening paragraph of the Preface, with its magnificent first sentence: 'Methodism was born in song.' All branches of the Methodist Church looked back to John Wesley and the events of May 1738, and the Preface skilfully took its readers back to a time before there were names and sects and parties, to a time of a new birth. That new birth, which became a new church, was 'born in song' (Brian Hoare's hymn spectacularly adopts something of that excitement). The achievement of the original Church, and of its founder, was highlighted by reprinting John Wesley's own Preface to the great 1780 book, *A Collection of Hymns for the Use of The People Called Methodists*.

Everything in the two prefaces was designed to unite rather than divide. The strategy succeeded brilliantly, as Dr Pratt points out. Indeed, the outcry when the announcement was made in 1979 that a committee was to be set up to compile a successor was evidence of the way in which the book had taken hold of the hearts and minds of the Methodist people. It had succeeded in somehow accommodating most of their different kinds of worship, from the psalms pointed for Anglican-style chanting, which were clear evidence of Wesleyan practice, to the section entitled 'The Gospel Call', with its Primitive Methodist favourites, including its 'denominational anthem', 'Hark! The gospel news is sounding'. The contents were indeed what Dr Pratt calls 'a rich mix of material': although he points out, with telling detail, the predominant influence of the Wesleyan majority on the committee. However, he also shows the way in which that committee successfully resisted some of its tiresome correspondents, ready and strident with their opinions at every stage: it held its nerve, stiffened by the central core of impregnable Wesley material.

The Methodist Hymn book served the Church well, perhaps too well. Andrew Pratt's case is that it was a conservative book, one which did not engage sufficiently with the world around it: preoccupied with the needs of the Methodist Church, it did not reach out to the unchurched as *Songs of Praise* had done in 1925 and 1931. Dr Pratt sees the book as rooted in late-Victorian patterns of religious behaviour, and as ignoring the cultural and religious upheavals consequent on the First World War. I think that he is correct, although it would be a mistake to approach the book with too many twenty-first-century expectations. The compilers could not have anticipated the women's movement, the demands of post-modern theologies, or the rising tide of secularism and materialism. Even so, Dr Pratt is surely right in seeing the book as looking back rather than forward, although it did achieve some notable 'firsts': it was the first major British book to print 'Thine be the glory, risen conquering Son' (from *Cantate Domino*, 1924), and 'Praise to the living God', by Landsberg and Mann. In it Cwm Rhondda first crossed the border from Wales; and it introduced other fine tunes – Vermont, Highwood, Blairgowrie, and Anchor.

Andrew Pratt's account of the genesis and contents of *The Methodist Hymn Book*, and of the first responses to it, has helped me to understand the book, with all its strengths and limitations, much more clearly than before. I can also see why it was so beloved. In its black morocco covers, resting on pianos in almost every Methodist home in the country, it served its Church with dignity and grace, without ever becoming more than a distinguished monument to the fine nonconformist religion of its time and place. But that in itself was no small achievement.

Richard Watson

Introduction

In 1932 the Wesleyan Methodist Church, the Primitive Methodist Church and the United Methodist Church entered into union and formed the Methodist Church in Great Britain.[1] Methodism, as the cliché has it, was 'born in song' and therefore it was no accident that a hymn book was chosen to be 'the outward and visible sign of union'.[2] In any other denomination such a publication would be of transient or marginal significance. For Methodism it was salient.

While much scholarly attention has been given to the significance and the effect of the 1932 Union, the impact of the 1933 *Methodist Hymn Book* has been, largely, ignored. It is not that the importance of hymns has gone unrecognised, indeed it has been stated that 'The long-term influence of "Our hymns" must have been greater than that of Wesley's sermons',[3] yet references to it are very few and generally unspecific. Turner defined the production of the *Methodist Hymn Book* as the 'first great achievement' of the Union of 1932. He noted that it contained over 250 hymns from the original Wesleyan inheritance, an estimate which is open to dispute, depending on which Wesleyan book is being referred to, and stated that it lasted for 50

---

1 The union was enabled by The Methodist Church Union Act, dated 1929 and the uniting Conference took place at the Royal Albert Hall in London on 20 September 1932.

2 MARC 30/263. References to the Collection of the Methodist Archives and Research Centre of the John Rylands University Library of Manchester include accession numbers in brackets {-} prefixed MARC, with the exception that all references to the 1934 Hymn Book Committee Papers are listed as MARC followed by the number 29 or 30 (indicating Box File MAW MS.29 or MAW MS.30), a stroke (/) and a number indicating the reference number which I have given to the particular paper as it is catalogued. This catalogue is available at the Library. Books which are not widely available but which are contained within the John Rylands University Library have accession numbers indicated in brackets the first time they are mentioned in the text, though the edition used for the preparation of this book may be different and full reference will be quoted in the relevant footnote.

3 R. Davies, A. R. George and G. Rupp, *A History of the Methodist Church in Great Britain*, London, Epworth Press, 1983, Vol. 3, p. xxxviii.

years. He says nothing more.[4] The most useful contribution has
been made by Bryan Spinney who wrote a summary of the genesis
of the *Methodist Hymn Book* and the debate surrounding its gestation.[5]

An examination of the origin of this book and its subsequent use
within Methodism provides a new perspective on the process of
Methodist Union and the history of the first 50 years of this denomination.

No other single book would have as much influence on the history
of the Methodist Church in the twentieth century. Travelling the
length and breadth of Methodism in the United Kingdom from the late
1930s to the early 1980s, the uniting feature of Methodist worship
was the *Methodist Hymn Book*. Styles of worship varied across the
Connexion but the hymn book provided an anchor, a sense of coherence. Whether in Aberdeen or Truro, you knew the book from
which you would be singing. It was, indeed, a visible link between the
disparate congregations that made up the Methodist Church. More
than this the book lasted for 50 years before an attempt was made to
replace it, and in many places, in the United Kingdom and abroad, it
is still in use.

The book's influence for ordinary Methodists simply cannot be
underestimated. It was, and is, an important book. No other hymn
book of any denomination has lasted so long in general use. The book
provided the main resource for preachers preparing for Sunday
worship. Ordinary Methodists used its verses for private prayer. Like
John Wesley's *A Collection of Hymns for the Use of The People Called
Methodists* (1780), this really was a 'little body of experimental and
practical divinity' that would sustain the believer through difficulty
and enable praise in moments of exaltation. More than that, as John
Wesley knew so well, worshippers took the hymns away with them in
their heads and their hearts. Sermons were easily forgotten, yet hymns
provided a way by which theological insights could be remembered.
This is the strength of a book that had gained such widespread use for
such a long time. It was also a critical flaw for the denomination.
People became wedded to the book. It became inseparable from what
it meant to be Methodist. It remained in use for 50 years without any

4 J. M. Turner, *Modern Methodism in England*, 1932–98, Peterborough, Epworth Press,
1998, p. 52.
5 B. F. Spinney, *Tuned for Praise* (2nd impression), Southampton, 1999, p. 12–22.

amendment and with the publication of only one supplement, *Hymns and Songs* (1969).

While hymns can help to preserve and transmit tradition, like any other medium, they can become dated. The *Methodist Hymn Book* was published in 1933. The world had changed immeasurably by the time it was eventually replaced. In the meantime people coming new to Methodism were expected to take hold of a book which was, in many ways, an anachronism. Those who thought about it were bemused by what they found. Not as bemused, perhaps, as an onlooker from outside the denomination who might have wondered at the reality of 'hobgoblin and foul fiend' in the latter half of the twentieth century. Culturally an attempt might be made to relate the book to the Bible. But methods of reading Scripture had moved on. Critical scholarship allowed for fresh interpretations of Scripture, yet these seemed to be countered by the very tool that was supposed to enable them to be understood. Someone coming new to the faith would find little sustenance here for the coming week. An informed observer would ask why the Methodists clung to this book when, since 1950, so much new material had been written that was more fitted for worship in a modern, and then post-modern, age. In another denomination this would not have been so critical. Hymns within a prayer book tradition are neither as significant, nor expected to be so influential. In such a context singing is the prerogative of the choir rather than the congregation.

To my knowledge, no one has asked why the book lasted so long. The answers, for there is more than one, are important, not only from the point of view of history. What we learn should help to inform our action and conversation at a period in which the Methodist Church, following the signing of the Covenant, considers ways of working more closely with the Church of England. Clive Marsh argues that Methodism no longer looks to hymns for its theology and that it will not, in future, do its theology through hymns.[6] Not everyone agrees with him, but if he is right it should prompt us to ask why this denomination is discarding a tool that has been so significant in its genesis, growth and life for over 250 years. Marsh's perspective has, undoubtedly, been influenced by his contact with and use of the *Methodist Hymn Book*. The hymn books of Methodism are no longer

6 C. Marsh, *Unmasking Methodist Theology*, London, Continuum, 2004.

used in the ways in which they were in the past. It is questionable as to whether *Hymns and Psalms* ever could have taken the place of the *Methodist Hymn Book*. Whether that has been to the benefit of the Church in the latter quarter of the twentieth century will be for history to judge.

At the same time that the influence of hymns in Methodism has undergone a gradual diminution, the place of liturgical prayer book worship has become more important. This is not the place for a full discussion of this issue, but suffice it to say that Wesleyan Methodism, with its historically closer links to the Church of England and more formal styles of worship, never entirely lost touch with the Prayer Book tradition of its parent denomination. Following Union the *Book of Offices* was published in 1936. This had 96 pages. The *Methodist Service Book* of 1975 had 257 while the *Methodist Worship Book* (1999) comprises 605 pages. This simple quantitative survey gives an indication of the increasing amount of prose material that has been provided for Methodist worshippers in the last half of the twentieth century. Meanwhile there are fewer hymns authorised for use in worship in spite of the vast quantity of material that has been written since 1950. Some of this shift of emphasis can be accounted for by the process of liturgical renewal that has affected all denominations. The effect on Methodism is, arguably, greatest as it speaks of a move away from hymns to prose liturgies as the vehicle for worship and the transmission of theological emphasis.

At a time when Methodist identity and confidence has been thrown into sharp relief by conversations with those of other denominations, when the question has been asked as to whether it is even possible to think of a 'Methodist Theological System', this study throws light on that identity and its expression.[7] While Methodism contemplates the possibility of yet another hymn book, the question posed by the *Methodist Hymn Book* as to what hymnody should be authorised for the use of people called Methodists is again being raised.

The shift of emphasis that we have witnessed, and the questions that it raises, can be traced back to the time of Methodist Union and the consequent effect of the increased influence of Wesleyan culture across Methodism. To this Union and the place of the *Methodist*

---

7 B. Beck, 'A Methodist Theological System', *Epworth Review*, Vol. 31, No. 1, 2004, p. 16–22.

Hymn Book within it we must return. We need to know more about the book. Where did it come from? What was it like? What was its theological basis? How did the Church use it? Only when these questions have been answered will it be possible to make a judgement as to how significant the book was in cementing Methodist Union and shaping the Methodist Church during the half century during which it was in use.

On the way we will be provided with an insight into the practical activity of a denomination at the time of its birth, the agony and the ecstasy, and also the life of a most remarkable hymn book.

I

Division and Union:
The Methodist Hymn Book and
its Background

For those who are not familiar with the time of Methodist Union, and Methodist history preceding it, some background information is needed. What is provided here is of necessity brief. I have offered a window into the origins of Methodism, a résumé of Methodist history, and an outline of the cultural background against which Union took place, in order to provide a clearer understanding of the genesis of the *Methodist Hymn Book* and its reception.[8]

Seeds of Division

Prior to the death of John Wesley in 1791 Methodism already held within itself the seeds of division. The characters of John and Charles Wesley were very different,[9] the elder, John, having to remonstrate with this 'sprightly, rollicking young fellow, with more genius than grace'.[10] Around this time John was temporarily absent from Oxford. Charles began to receive communion weekly, a frequency unusual at this time, in Christ Church Chapel (Oxford Cathedral), encouraging others to do likewise. In all their conduct they were methodical. They

---

8 For a more detailed account of the 1932 Union see J. M. Turner, in Davies, George and Rupp, *A History of the Methodist Church in Great Britain*, Vol. 3, p. 309–61.

9 G. Lloyd, *Charles Wesley: A New Evaluation of his Life and Ministry*, unpublished PhD thesis, Liverpool, 2002, provides a new appraisal of the relationship between John and Charles Wesley.

10 D. Brook, *The Oxford Methodists*, in *A New History of Methodism*, ed. W. J. Townsend, H. B. Workman and G. Eayrs, London, Hodder and Stoughton, 1909, Vol. I, p. 139.

gained the name 'methodist'[11] as a consequence, but they were also called 'sacramentarians' or 'supererogation men'.[12] The nature of the movement, begun here, was one of seeking perfection in all things, but particularly in those things that would lead to holiness. John later defined Christian perfection as 'the humble, gentle, patient love of God and man, ruling all the tempers, words and actions: the whole heart and the whole life'.[13]

It was in John's character to organise this movement in an authoritarian manner so that those adhering to it could be enabled to conform. This is, perhaps, a satisfactory method for those in the hierarchy of the Church who seek to apply principles to their followers which should be adhered to in minute particular. It is less satisfying for ordinary Christians who lack the abstract commitment of their leaders, yet hold deep loyalties to people and to their community, forming their faith on a basis of individual freedom and fellowship, rather than obedience to an ethical code. 'The conflict between these viewpoints was intensified in Methodism'.[14] John Wesley was an autocrat who could not envisage the mantle of authority resting on anyone else. He wrote of those who 'demand a free Conference . . . wherein all things shall be determined by most votes . . . It is possible after my death something of this kind may take place; but not while I live'.[15] This autocracy was applied to everyone, even to his brother. Disunity was bound to result following his death.

Unification

At the time of John Wesley's death, because of the manner in which he had made decisions and taken judgements, many matters were left unresolved.[16] What was the relation of Methodism to the established church? Could Methodist ministers administer the sacraments? How

---

11   See R. P. Heitzenrater, *Mirror and Memory, Reflections on Early Methodism*, Nashville, Kingswood, 1989, p. 13–32, for a discussion of the origin of the name 'methodist' and its significance.

12   D. Brook, *The Oxford Methodists*, in *A New History of Methodism*, p. 145.

13   J. Wesley, *The Letters of John Wesley*, ed. G. Eayrs, London, Hodder and Stoughton, 1915, p. 83.

14   R. Currie, *Methodism Divided*, London, Faber & Faber, 1968, p. 17.

15   F. Baker, quoted by Currie, *Methodism Divided*, p. 23.

16   Lloyd, examines this in some detail. *Charles Wesley: A New Evaluation of his Life and Ministry*, p. 237–83.

was the Connexion to be governed? The majority of those people known as Methodists sought to retain links with the Church of England following John Wesley's express wishes.

The first Conference took place in 1791. William Thompson, then at Halifax, was elected President[17] and Dr Coke Secretary.

From 1797 the New Connexion (1797), the Independent Methodists (1807), the Primitive Methodists (1807), the Bible Christians (1815) and the Wesleyan (Methodist) Association (1834) appeared alongside the embryo Wesleyan Methodist Church. There were sporadic attempts at reunion,[18] but each group developed its own traditions and published its own hymn book. Division continued with the differing claims of democracy and autocracy providing rallying points within Wesleyan Methodism.[19]

A successful process of reunion began with the first Methodist Ecumenical Conference taking place in 1881. In 1906 the Bible Christian Church, United Methodist Free Churches and the Methodist New Connexion agreed to unite and the United Methodist Church[20] was formed by Royal Assent on 26 July 1907.[21]

In 1911 the fourth Methodist Ecumenical Conference took place. The process of reunion continued inexorably, if slowly.[22]

From 1918 to 1932 negotiations took place. As a result the United Methodist Church, the Primitive Methodist Church and the Wesleyan Methodist Church formed an organic union. The Methodist Church Union Act was passed in 1929, the sixth Methodist Ecumenical Conference took place in 1931 and in 1932 the Methodist Church was formed.[23]

---

17 J. M. Turner, *Conflict and Reconciliation, Studies in Methodism and Ecumenism in England 1740–1982*, London, Epworth Press, 1985, p. 67.

18 Currie, *Methodism Divided*, p. 317ff.

19 Reference should be made to R. Davies, A. R. George and G. Rupp, *A History of the Methodist Church in Great Britain*, Vol. 3, and to J. M. Turner, *Conflict and Reconciliation, Studies in Methodism and Ecumenism in England 1740–1982* for a full account of the process of the division and reunification of the Methodist Churches.

20 See F. S. Thorne, 'All together now! The United Methodist Church 1907–1932', *Proceedings of the Wesley Historical Society*, Vol. 51, Part 3, 1997, p. 73.

21 Currie, *Methodism Divided*, p. 317ff.

22 John Munsey Turner provides a detailed assessment of this period in Davies, George and Rupp, *A History of the Methodist Church in Great Britain*, Vol. 3, p. 309–61.

23 Currie, *Methodism Divided*, p. 321ff.

The Churches and their Hymns

It was inconceivable that hymns would not be central to this newly
founded denomination. John Wesley's attention was drawn to the
importance of hymn singing in worship, and its potential, during his
voyage to Georgia (October 1735–February 1736).[24] The influence on
John Wesley of the German reformed tradition, and that of Martin
Luther, in the use of hymns cannot be underestimated. Charles Wesley
wrote in excess of 6,000 hymns or sacred poems.[25] It has even been
said that Methodism was raised up by John Wesley to sing his
brother's hymns. Hymn singing had always been central and was
likely to remain so.

Each denomination had produced hymn books that gave expression to their theology, provided a vehicle for worship, a tool for outreach and a means of praise. The books were subtly different but came
from the same basic source. It was inevitable that one question, above
all others, would present itself to these praising people as they came
together: '*what* hymns should be sung?' The *Methodist Hymn Book* of
1933[26] was the answer to their question.

No book, however innovative, arrives into a vacuum. The previous
Methodist hymn books are important to our understanding, together
with others known to have been in use by Methodists at the time of
production and publication. While most attention inevitably focuses
on the books of the uniting denominations, in excess of 50 books of
hymns published since 1904 were available to the editors of the
Methodist Hymn Book. These covered a variety of styles ranging from
the *Public School Hymn Book* (1919) and the *Rydal School Hymnal*,
through *Sacred Songs and Solos* (1921, 1930 various editions),
Alexander's Hymns, various denominational books from this country
and abroad, to the Psalter in English Verse and the then recently
published *Songs of Praise* (1925, enlarged 1931).

---

24 J. R. Watson, *The English Hymn*, Oxford, Clarendon Press, 1997, p. 205.

25 F. Baker, *Charles Wesley's Verse*, London, Epworth Press, 2nd edition, 1988. By a
narrow definition of a hymn 6, 000 is an exaggeration, though Charles Wesley wrote at least
8, 990 poems.

26 Hereafter the *Methodist Hymn Book*, Methodist Conference Office, London, 1933,
is referred to as *Methodist Hymn Book*.

The Wesleyan Methodist Church

At the time of Union in 1932 the Wesleyan Methodist Church used the *Wesleyan Methodist Hymn Book* which had been published in 1904.[27] This was considered to be a lineal descendant of John Wesley's *A Collection of Hymns for the Use of The People Called Methodists*.[28] This description is interesting on two counts. First, given the description of the *Methodist Hymn Book* of 1933 as 'a lineal descendant of Wesley's collection',[29] the parallel is noted. Secondly, the *Wesleyan Methodist Hymn Book* of 1904 was closer in structure to the *Methodist Hymn Book* than to *A Collection of Hymns for the Use of The People Called Methodists*. The *Wesleyan Methodist Hymn Book*, as we shall see, was to have a profound effect on the shaping of the *Methodist Hymn Book*.

The Wesleyans had begun to recognise the estrangement, and the need, of the masses. Centres of evangelism and social amelioration, such as St James Hall in London (ancestor of Kingsway Hall), the Manchester Mission and the Central Hall in Birmingham[30] were established. In these places preaching predominated, with congregational participation limited to the singing of hymns. Choral performances took place. There was an awareness of the need of bodies and minds to be fed. 'Growth in discipleship was as vital to them as conversion.'[31] To this end the hymns that were sung were important. Wesleyan Methodists were aware that 'Hymns are the safest protection and the surest vehicle of orthodoxy.'[32]

The Wesleyan Methodist Conference of 1901 had appointed a Committee of Revision charged with the task of preparing a new hymn book. This committee took as its starting point the first edition of *A Collection of Hymns for the Use of The People Called Methodists* of 1780 but they were also cognisant of the various revisions of that

---

27 *Wesleyan Methodist Hymn Book*, Wesleyan Conference Office, London, 1904.

28 See *Works of John Wesley*, Vol. 7, *A Collection of Hymns for the Use of The People Called Methodists*, ed. F. Hildebrandt and O. A. Beckerlegge, Oxford University Press/Nashville, Abingdon, 1983.

29 *Methodist Hymn Book*, 1933, Preface.

30 Where Luke Wiseman (Chairman of the Hymn Book Committee which produced the *Methodist Hymn Book*) was to minister.

31 J. M. Turner, in Davies, George and Rupp, *A History of the Methodist Church in Great Britain*, Vol. 3, p. 312.

32 B. L. Manning, *The Hymns of Wesley and Watts*, London, Epworth Press, 1942, p. 143.

book which had taken place since its original publication. By their own admission, 'In the delicate task of removing hymns from Wesley's original book, the Committee have sought to act in a spirit of reverence towards compositions which possess a special sacredness in the eyes of all Methodists', endeavouring 'to retain all the hymns that have gained a permanent place in the affections of our people'.[33] There was a conscious attempt to 'preserve intact the clear and full expression of Methodist doctrine . . . enshrined in Methodist song'.[34] This conservative attitude did not, however, lead the compilers to retain the ordering of the original. This, together with the addition of some 300 hymns not in the Wesleyan hymn book of 1876, most of which were by hymn writers of the nineteenth century, enabled this book to be regarded as, in every sense, new.[35]

Aware of the need to reassure people in the face of change, the 1901 Committee nevertheless stated that 'The main object of those to whom the present compilation was entrusted has been to preserve the continuity of the present with the past.'[36]

In 1901 the Church was regarded as 'widely ramifying'.[37] Attention was given to the needs of children and young people, seasons and festivals of the Church and the need of 'workers in sundry departments of active service'.[38] It was not thought necessary to include a specific section for mission or evangelistic services, the indication being given that hymns for such occasions could be readily found throughout the book. The explanation was given that the book had a wider purpose than simply to furnish texts for use in public worship, echoing Wesley's intention to provide 'a little body of experimental and practical divinity'[39] that would serve its readers in their private devotions, at times of 'sickness and trial'.[40]

The volume totalled some 981 hymns. In addition there were a further eight Ancient Hymns and Canticles, the Ten Commandments and the Beatitudes. The book was produced jointly by the Wesleyan

---

33 *Wesleyan Methodist Hymn Book*, Preface, p. vi.
34 *Wesleyan Methodist Hymn Book*, Preface, p. vi.
35 F. L. Wiseman, 'Early Methodist Psalmody, with a note on Wesleyan Methodist Hymn Books', in *A New History of Methodism*, Vol. II, p. 561f.
36 *Wesleyan Methodist Hymn Book*, Preface, p. vi.
37 *Wesleyan Methodist Hymn Book*, Preface, p. vi.
38 *Wesleyan Methodist Hymn Book*, Preface, p. vi.
39 *Wesleyan Methodist Hymn Book*, Preface, p. v.
40 *Wesleyan Methodist Hymn Book*, Preface, p. vi.

Methodist Church, The Methodist New Connexion and the Wesleyan Reform Union, and in correspondence with the Methodist Church in Australasia.

Within the structure of the book worshippers first had their sights turned towards 'The Glory of God'. They were presented with the call of the gospel which sought to help sinners to return to God. Thereafter 'The Christian Life' was described. Roughly two thirds of the content of the book, 633 hymns, comprised these sections. A further 47 were devoted to 'Time, Death and Eternity', the remainder of the book having two sections, 'Family Religion' and 'Special Occasions'.

Cultural and semi-cultural interests were built around the church or hall building. This 'outreach or . . . creeping secularisation',[41] depending on how you regard it, did not ignore the young who were taught to pray, to think, to debate and to question. Hymnody, however, was largely unaffected.

> There are two ways of writing or speaking to children: the one is to let ourselves down to them, the other to lift them up to us. Dr Watts has wrote on the former way, and has succeeded admirably well speaking to children, and leaving them as he found them. The following hymns are written on the other plan: they contain strong and manly sense, yet expressed in such plain and easy language as even children may understand. But when they do understand them they will be children no longer, only in years and in stature.[42]

The Wesleyans followed this advice. Material for children was, broadly speaking, of sound literary quality written to educate them, to inculcate theological understanding, rather than simply being something that was fun to sing but of dubious merit.

Theology in the early twentieth century was largely inadequate to meet the evolutionary mood of the age, and Methodism suffered from this weakness as did all basically non-liturgical churches. Free Church Ministers were left either to compromise with it, leaving themselves

41 J. M. Turner, in Davies, George and Rupp, *A History of the Methodist Church in Great Britain*, Vol. 3, p. 314. Newton has also noted the Wesleyan concern over such secularisation voiced by the Methodist Sacramental Fellowship following Union: J. Newton, *Heart Speaks to Heart*, London, Darton, Longman and Todd, 1994, p. 70.

42 J. Wesley, Preface to *Hymns for Children*, 1790, quoted in *Works of John Wesley*, Vol. 7, *A Collection of Hymns for the Use of The People Called Methodists*, p. 132.

open to the criticism of being modernists, or to ignore it, which led to irrelevance. 'Hymns for Service and Influence' related to a Christian call with little reference to the world of work.

The commitment to meet together in a disciplined fashion was beginning to wane. The local church could no longer claim un-questioning allegiance. The sense of corporate holiness that marked earlier periods of Methodist history was in decline and class divisions of the Victorian era, rather than fading, were being perpetuated.[43] In this situation hymnody served two functions. First, 'singing together brings us together'.[44] Hymn singing enabled a sense of corporate unity to be maintained at least on a Sunday. Secondly, what was sung perpetuated the Victorian ethos of the Church.

In spite of this, Turner has asserted that no succeeding generation achieved more in terms of mission to ordinary people.[45] There was an attitude of acceptance of the authority of the Church. Along with this went a sense of being chosen, which heightened people's obligation to their local congregation and to the wider Connexion. This could give rise to arrogance. Willey recognised that respectability rather than reverence was the chief trait of the Church he remembered from the opening decades of the century.[46] The Church was both inbred and out of date.[47] Even in the 1920s this sense of estrangement from those out-side the Church remained. Bill Naughton, speaking of his experience in Bolton, related that he found the atmosphere at a midweek Method-ist meeting 'quite novel', that the preacher's appeals to avoid the evils of drink rang as half-baked, knowing as he did 'much less about them at first hand' than did this adolescent observer whose father chose 'to spend his hard earned money on beer every Saturday evening'.[48]

---

43 Turner, in Davies, George and Rupp, *A History of the Methodist Church in Great Britain*, Vol. 3, p. 315f.

44 B. Wren, *Praying Twice*, Louisville, Kentucky, Westminster John Knox Press, 2000, p. 84.

45 Turner, in Davies, George and Rupp, *A History of the Methodist Church in Great Britain*, Vol. 3, p. 316.

46 B. Willey, quoted by Turner, in *A History of the Methodist Church in Great Britain*, Vol. 3, p. 317.

47 Turner notes that in the church of Peter Fletcher's parents, once a year there would be a 'mission' with an emphasis on conversion and 'Sankeys' replacing the more sober *Methodist Hymn Book*. For Fletcher this marked the end of Christian observance, while others made their way to the Church of England (Turner, in *A History of the Methodist Church in Great Britain*, Vol. 3, p. 317).

48 B. Naughton, *Neither Use Nor Ornament*, Newcastle upon Tyne, Bloodaxe Books, 1995, p. 135f.

In spite of all this the possibility of change began to present itself through the work of ministerial training colleges. William Fiddian Moulton introduced critical biblical study at Richmond, while his son, James Hope Moulton, followed suit at Didsbury. Such work began to transform the training of ministers for the Church and offered an opportunity for renewal.[49]

The Wesleyan Church began to be able to hold together people of a broader theological and social disposition. By the time of Methodist Union the denomination was very much in need of a new hymn book and new hymns.

The United Methodist Church

The United Methodist Church, formed out of the union of 1907 between the Methodist New Connexion, the United Methodist Free Church and the Bible Christians, provided a wide and varied source of hymnody. The denominations retained their own hymn books: *A Collection of Hymns for the use of People called Bible Christians* (1889),[50] the *United Methodist Free Church Hymnal* (1889),[51] and the *New Connexion Hymn Book* (1904).[52]

The Methodist New Connexion had close links with Wesleyan Methodism and had collaborated in the production of the *Wesleyan Methodist Hymn Book* of 1904. The New Connexion used this same book under its own title and covers.

The Bible Christians had their own book, published first in 1889. *A Collection of Hymns for the use of People called Bible Christians*[53] was offered by its compilers as '"a labour of love" and even a "means of grace"'. They heartily commended it to the attention of the 'pious and intelligent in the Churches' for whose use it was particularly intended and 'to the blessing of Him Whose glory has been sought that

49 Turner, in *A History of the Methodist Church in Great Britain*, Vol. 3, p. 318.
50 *A Collection of Hymns for the use of People called Bible Christians*, London, Bible Christian Book-Room, 1889.
51 *United Methodist Free Church Hymnal*, London, United Methodist Free Churches' Book Room, 1889.
52 *The Methodist Hymn Book*, London, Methodist New Connexion Book-Room, 1904.
53 *A Collection of Hymns for the use of People called Bible Christians*; see K. Mankin, *How they sang on the way to Zion*, p. 135–51. According to Mankin, 'almost a quarter of the total number of hymns in the hymn book [belong] to the Bible Christian Tradition alone'.

He may make it the channel of instruction and comfort to multitudes, and instrumental in extending His kingdom in the world'.[54]

This last clause is characteristic and the editors of the new book noted that, while its predecessor had been 'improved and enlarged in 1838' and slightly altered in 1862, at its core had been hymns gathered together in a section entitled 'Missionary Exertion'.[55] Nevertheless the omission of some hymns, such as 'Jesus shall reign where'er the sun' was regarded as 'unaccountable'.[56] This they sought to remedy by drawing on the great hymns of the Church from all denominations, though it is recorded that 'the proprietors of *Hymns Ancient and Modern* refused to allow the use of any of their copyright hymns'. The compilers sought to provide a source of hymns that would be useful in 'The Service Song in the House of the Lord'.[57] In doing this they asserted that 'a hymn is not the best vehicle for the expression of rigorous and exact theological views, but it is often the means of conserving the highest truths in all their divine beauty and completeness'.[58] A clear distinction between the Bible Christians and the Wesleyans is demonstrated by this comment. *A Collection of Hymns for the use of People called Bible Christians* provided 53 texts for 'Evangelistic Services'. Hymns for 'Special Occasions' included 'Hospital Sunday', 'General Charities and Almsgiving' and items 'For Those at Sea'. Nine hymns were listed under the theme of 'Temperance'. The picture is one of a Church which, while holding to its roots (there are hymns for Class-Meetings), is altogether outward looking.

The Bible Christians had, perhaps, mixed motives in entering into the Union of 1907, recognising the possible protection that this would provide against loss of members brought about by migration.

The editorial committee of the *United Methodist Free Church Hymnal* of 1889 noted that 'in recent years, many hymns have been published, whose fervour and poetic power have won the approval and acceptance of nearly all sections of the Christian Church'.[59] The editors believed that many hymns in the previous collection of 1860 had become obsolete and the layout of the book did not make it easy to use.

---

54 *A Collection of Hymns for the use of People called Bible Christians*, Preface, p. x.
55 *A Collection of Hymns for the use of People called Bible Christians*, Preface, p. v.
56 *A Collection of Hymns for the use of People called Bible Christians*, Preface, p. vi.
57 *A Collection of Hymns for the use of People called Bible Christians*, Preface, p. vi.
58 *A Collection of Hymns for the use of People called Bible Christians*, Preface, p. vi.
59 *United Methodist Free Church Hymnal*, Preface, p. 1.

In preparing their new collection the committee was concerned not to remove any hymn which 'had become familiar by use' or that had 'endeared itself to our Churches'.[60] The editors were more than willing to amend otherwise useful hymns. By contrast, within Bible Christian circles hymns moved from book to book with little amendment or alteration.

In looking for new material the committee boasted that 'No collection of hymns or sacred songs of any repute has escaped attention'.[61] The criterion for inclusion was firstly spirituality, but poetry was also important. The intention was to provide a vehicle 'for the outpouring of the heart in prayer, the uplifting of the soul to nobler aims, holier aspirations and fuller consecration, and the realisation, through sacred song, of communion and fellowship with God'.[62] The hymns included were also to provide for praise and thanksgiving, the language of praise being regarded as the 'universal language of the children of God'.[63]

The committee hoped to have produced a collection which would stimulate practical Christianity and 'to supply a medium for the devout utterance of the varied emotions and experiences of the Christian life'.[64] The hymns were to speak not only to those who could praise God out of comfort, but also those who sought courage in suffering. The collection was comprehensive, the spirit catholic. It provided 45 hymns for 'Evangelistic Services' and a section devoted to 'Temperance Services'. Hymns in this book again related to the real world. 'O Lord, be with us when we sail / Upon the lonely deep' is not only metaphorical, suggesting some spiritual pilgrimage, but also provides images that seamen would recognise. The collection is altogether more earthy than that of the Wesleyans (for whom Temperance was allied to Christian Philanthropy) but the common Methodist source is not denied, Watts and Wesley (both John and Charles) being well represented. A defence was given against those who might have questioned the inclusion of certain texts which are specifically Methodist in tenor.[65]

60 *United Methodist Free Church Hymnal*, Preface, p. 1.
61 *United Methodist Free Church Hymnal*, Preface, p. 1.
62 *United Methodist Free Church Hymnal*, Preface, p. 1.
63 *United Methodist Free Church Hymnal*, Preface, p. 1.
64 *United Methodist Free Church Hymnal*, Preface, p. 1.
65 *United Methodist Free Church Hymnal*, Preface, p. 1.

The union of 1907 had formed a body from disparate parts that had sufficient resources to support a properly trained ministry, with capital for expansion and the production of literature that was capable of political influence. This new Church adopted a relatively liberal position with regard to Scripture. 'The scriptures of the Old and New Testaments through Divine Inspiration contain a revelation of the will of God to man and furnish a sufficient rule of faith and practice.'[66] Thirteen hymns in the Wesleyan/New Connexion book were devoted to the Scriptures, 15 in the *United Methodist Free Church Hymnal* and 12 in *A Collection of Hymns for the use of People called Bible Christians*. The sacraments were regarded by the United Methodists as of 'divine inspiration and perpetual obligation'.[67] A mere 15 hymns in the *United Methodist Free Church Hymnal* were allocated to sacramental services compared with 20 in the Wesleyan/New Connexion book.[68] Interestingly, 30 texts were provided by the Bible Christians and these were differentiated into Baptism of Infants (4), Baptism of Adults (2) and the Lord's Supper (24).

Many of the United Methodist Free Church societies had been almost congregational in outlook. Churches which had been involved in the disruption of the 1840s and the consequent expulsions from the Wesleyan Methodist Church were represented. What had been formed was in effect a bridge church amalgamating those who had sought a more democratic form of organisation within Methodism. The United Methodists and the Methodist New Connexion were distributed for the most part in the North, the Bible Christians in the South and West of England. This latter group, though not always financially secure, brought a virility to the wider body of the Church.

As with the Primitive Methodists, benevolent lay domination was the norm for many societies. Such leaders had pastoral, preaching and financial responsibility that provided benefits, but also dangers, and was regarded as a threat to good order by the Wesleyans. Above all these people had a shared hymnody which demonstrated itself to be

---

66 Quoted by Turner, in Davies, George and Rupp, *A History of the Methodist Church in Great Britain*, Vol. 3, p. 326.

67 Turner, in Davies, George and Rupp, *A History of the Methodist Church in Great Britain*, Vol. 3, p. 326.

68 Newton, *Heart Speaks to Heart*, p. 70. Newton's commentary implies that some Wesleyans recognised this as symptomatic of a diminished view of the importance of Eucharistic observance and a source for concern.

founded on historic Methodist tradition but also contained within it a wider spectrum of emphasis. The *New Connexion Hymn Book* was very much an ecclesial tome, the *United Methodist Free Church* offered a greater laxity in terms of literary quality, while *A Collection of Hymns for the use of People called Bible Christians* provided the denomination with a sense of enthusiasm and vitality.

The Primitive Methodist Church[69]

Free worship was championed by the Primitive Methodists, with extempore prayer being of central importance. The denomination had two hymn books, the *Primitive Methodist Hymnal* of 1886[70] and the *Primitive Methodist Hymnal Supplement* (1912).[71] This latter book was the most recent denominational hymnal available to the compilers of the *Methodist Hymn Book*.

Primitive Methodist hymnody began in revival and its first collection of hymns reflected this, being a hymnal chiefly intended for open-air meetings and evangelistic outreach. The contrast of purpose with that of Wesleyan hymnody should be noted. Hugh Bourne edited *The Large Hymn Book* in 1825 and this was superseded by John Flesher's collection in 1854.

In spite of the origins of Primitive Methodism the *Primitive Methodist Hymnal* of 1886 had no section devoted to evangelistic services and only 25 hymns for 'Missions'. A closer examination of the book indicates that a revivalist influence, rather than resulting in specific sections, is evident throughout the book. This is especially true of the section entitled 'The Christian Life', which addresses issues of conversion, justification, and regeneration as well as the possibility of a fall from grace and recovery. The section of the *Primitive Methodist Hymnal Supplement* devoted to 'Service' also has a distinctly evangelistic tone with the inclusion of texts such as 'Rescue the perishing, care for the dying'. Hymns for 'Mariners and Travellers' in this hymn book are more metaphorical than those of the *United Methodist Free*

---

69 For a description of this denomination see G. Milburn, *Primitive Methodism*, Peterborough, Epworth Press, 2002.

70 *Primitive Methodist Hymnal*, London, Primitive Methodist Publishing House, 1886.

71 *Primitive Methodist Hymnal Supplement*, London, Primitive Methodist Publishing House, 1912.

Church Hymnal. This supports Turner's assertion[72] that the denomination was closer to Wesleyanism than the more proletarian groups.

In spite of this, Primitive Methodism was characterised by a theology that went hand in hand with radical politics, and an anti-sacerdotal stance, while worship was almost Pentecostal in style. Congregational participation was encouraged. This was very different from the Wesleyan Church, and its church government was more democratic.

The *Primitive Methodist Hymnal*[73] was compiled by a committee appointed by the Primitive Methodist Conference of 1882.[74] There had been a call for a book more suitable for contemporary use and so the compilers sought 'to retain the older hymns which are endeared by many hallowed associations to the hearts and memories of Christians of every name, and to add the choicest productions of our own times'.[75] It was acknowledged that the greatest number of hymns included would still be attributed to the Wesleys and Watts but 'selections from numerous other authors and translators' were to be included.[76] Lengthy hymns were not abbreviated but lively, vigorous singing, characteristic of the connexion, was encouraged, though 'a hurried style . . . [was] deprecated'.[77] The arrangement of hymns within the hymnal was idiosyncratic. In each section they were grouped according to metre. The later *Primitive Methodist Hymnal Supplement* of 1912 continued this practice.

One would hardly expect a collection of 1,051 hymns, together with a setting of the *Te Deum* and sundry additional tunes, to require supplementing, yet the Conference of 1910 saw the need to augment this considerable collection. There was a feeling that, good though the book undoubtedly was, after a quarter of a century it might be 'no longer completely adequate'.[78] The editors were aware of the amount of new material that had become familiar to the people of the Church.

72 Turner, in Davies, George and Rupp, *A History of the Methodist Church in Great Britain*, Vol. 3, p. 328.
73 See Mankin, *How they sang on the way to Zion*, p. 123–34. Mankin comments particularly on the uniqueness of this book.
74 See K. Lysons, *A Little Primitive*, Buxton, Church in the Market Place Publications, 2001, p. 201–6.
75 *Primitive Methodist Hymnal*, London, M. T. Pickering, reprinted with the Supplement, 1912, Preface, p. 1.
76 *Primitive Methodist Hymnal*, Preface, p. 1.
77 *Primitive Methodist Hymnal*, Preface, p. 2.
78 *Primitive Methodist Hymnal Supplement*, Preface, p. iii.

There was also the necessity to address themes which had, thus far, been neglected. Consequently they felt comfortable including hymns in the Supplement simply on account of their merit or, on other occasions, in spite of their inferiority because nothing else relating to a particular theme was available. They recognised that the usefulness of a hymn does not relate solely to its literary qualities. Many popular hymns were included that with a more stringent approach might have been eliminated from consideration: 'we are taught that high poetical excellence may be but little help and its absence but little drawback'.[79] Similarly, hymns which others might regard as 'too austere, too mystical, or too subtle',[80] found their way into the collection. The committee seem to have realised that what they were presenting was new and likely to be met with resistance.[81]

Ultimately what was produced was later to be described by Turner as 'a collection which catches the somewhat exuberant and romantic atmosphere of Edwardian Methodism'.[82] This was the most recent Methodist collection prior to the production of the *Methodist Hymn Book*.

Methodist Union (1932)

Methodist Union and the background against which it took place has been documented elsewhere.[83] Churches of all denominations in this period had a declining influence.[84] At the same time the population of the United Kingdom had grown.[85]

Amalgamation of the more liberal Methodist bodies with Wesleyanism was made possible by the fundamental change which took place in 1878 when the Wesleyan Methodist Conference admitted lay representatives.[86] J. Scott Lidgett (who was to become the first President of

---

79 *Primitive Methodist Hymnal Supplement*, Preface, p. iii.

80 *Primitive Methodist Hymnal Supplement*, Preface, p. iii.

81 *Primitive Methodist Hymnal Supplement*, Preface, p. iii.

82 Turner, in Davies, George and Rupp, *A History of the Methodist Church in Great Britain*, Vol. 3, p. 329.

83 See Turner, in Davies, George and Rupp, *A History of the Methodist Church in Great Britain*, Vol. 3, p. 333–61.

84 J Stevenson, 'British Society 1914–45', *The Penguin Social History of Britain*, Harmondsworth, Penguin, 1990.

85 *Whitaker's Almanack*, J. Whitaker and Son Ltd, London, The Softback Preview, 1997, p. 112.

86 J. Kent, *The Age of Disunity*, London, Epworth Press, 1966, p. 1.

O For a Thousand Tongues

the united Church after he had already been President of the Wesleyan Conference in 1907) in 1909 regarded union as fundamentally logical:

> The theology of all branches of Methodism is identical. All attach the same importance, at least in theory, to church fellowship and offer similar means of satisfying it. All enforce the duty of unceasing evangelism, which is based on the will of God that all men should be saved and come to the knowledge of the truth. All admit the right, and enforce the duty, of the laity to take part in evangelism, and in the pastoral supervision of the church. Above all, the emphasis is everywhere laid on the importance of experimental religion, and therefore on conversion, on the possibility of the direct witness of the Spirit of adoption giving the assurance of present salvation, and on the calling to the life of entire sanctification which is brought about by the reign of perfect love in the heart.[87]

At this stage the Primitive Methodists, led by A. S. Peake, continued to consider union. Conversely Arthur Jones of the United Methodist Church asked at the fourth Ecumenical Conference (1911), 'have we not really had enough of Union to last us for a little while?' adding, 'And, further, I must frankly say that I, for one . . . do not see that we are particularly near our Wesleyan friends.'[88] Conversations, nevertheless, proceeded.

These tensions, naturally, continued in the united denomination and had an effect on the work of the committees delegated with preparing the *Methodist Hymn Book*. It is important to see that such divisions have, as it were, a human face. This can be illustrated by the attitude of one of the leading figures in the Church at that time. When statistics relating to the location of churches were sought in preparation for possible amalgamation, F. L. Wiseman, then Home Missions Secretary of the Wesleyan Methodist Church, and later Chairman of the Hymn Book Committee, wrote to Aldom French saying that he did not have such information. His letter gives a clear indication of his feelings: 'The work of compilation would be enormous', and 'the utility of the whole is not obvious to me'.[89] Wiseman seemed to lack an understanding of the necessary work required for reunion to take

---

87 J. S. Lidgett, in *A New History of Methodism*, Vol. I, p. 421.
88 Currie, *Methodism Divided*, p. 248.
89 Currie, *Methodism Divided*, p. 250.

place smoothly and even seems to be offering some passive resistance. This is pertinent, for he was then charged with the task of unifying a disparate group of people into a working committee, and demonstrating a commitment to the unity that the hymn book was expected to represent.

The rationalisation of places of worship had a clear practical value but the process was threatening to all the participants. Ultimately, even after Union in 1932, such changes were difficult to achieve. Those societies which were threatened with closure perceived themselves as defending a bastion, not only of their religious and theological heritage but also of a cultural, political and societal nature. This was to reflect on the process of union and the reception, if not the production, of the *Methodist Hymn Book*.

The First World War brought a change of tone. Movements that drew people together, such as the League of Nations, and a desire within the Church of England for a renewed Church to serve all classes, became popular. Such a spirit was threatening to the Wesleyans, a denomination which preserved a sense of hierarchy and order, of inherent conservatism. It was easier for the Free and Primitive Methodists to accept. This cultural difference would be another source of tension for the Hymn Book Committee.

Nevertheless, the social distinction between the Wesleyan Methodists and the free Methodist denominations had begun to reduce, so that in 1924 stipends of ministers across the three denominations approximately equated. This did not prevent a charge of snobbery being made against the Wesleyans, but a difference of preference as to styles of communion service and theology was more deeply rooted than any class distinction.[90]

J. Ernest Rattenbury, a Wesleyan and eminent hymnodist, stated that 'There is a clearer kinship between many Wesleyans and Anglicans than with either of the junior Methodist Churches.'[91]

Ultimately the Methodist Church Bill was passed in 1929 with each of the uniting denominations holding its final Conference in the summer of 1932. The Uniting Conference took place on 20 September 1932 at the Royal Albert Hall. The Deed of Union was signed and three Wesleyan Methodists were elected to office: John Scott Lidgett as

---

90 Kent, *The Age of Disunity*, p. 6.
91 Currie, *Methodism Divided*, p. 250f.

President, Sir Robert Perks as Vice-President and Robert Bond as Secretary.

The membership of the denominations at the point of Union was as follows:[92]

Denomination	Membership	Ordained ministers	Local preachers
Wesleyan Methodist	517,551	2,510	18,785
Primitive Methodist	222,021	1,131	12,896
United Methodist	179,527	729	5,232

The union was an uneasy one that did not address the issues that were presented by society or the church. The amalgamation did not provide a source of new ideas about church organisation but, rather, an uneasy compromise.[93] At least they would sing from the same book, the outward and visible sign of their unity, although this would not be published until December of 1933.

---

92 R. Davies, A. R. George, and G. Rupp, *A History of the Methodist Church in Great Britain*, Vol. 4, London, Epworth Press, 1988, p. 648f.

93 Turner, in Davies, George and Rupp, *A History of the Methodist Church in Great Britain*, Vol. 3, p. 340.

2

From the Idea to the Book[94]

On Tuesday 5 November 1929[95] representatives of the uniting Methodist Conferences assembled to consider whether a new Hymn Book was needed.[96] A cursory examination of the membership of this group shows that, from the outset, the bias of representation was Wesleyan, male and ordained. In 1930 a report to the Conferences of the three denominations gave an indication of the make-up of a proposed committee, viz., 'Wesleyan Methodist, eighteen members; Primitive Methodist, nine; United Methodist, nine'. A footnote added that 'The Joint Committee, including Ex-Officio members, totals 48, with two representatives of the Wesleyan Reform Union'.[97] The Chair of the Committee, F. Luke Wiseman (1858–1944), was a Wesleyan and is remembered as an autocrat.[98] There was a clear bias of representation on the committee.[99]

The resolution of these discussions was positive and a plan was

94 The difficulty in providing an account of the origin of the *Methodist Hymn Book* (1933) has rested on the disordered sources which have to be examined in order to provide such a picture. In addition to published hymn books, some of which are not easily available, there are 411 individual items contained in the archive of the Hymn Book Committee held in the Collection of the Methodist Archives and Research Centre of the John Rylands Library of the University of Manchester. These were left in no particular order but they have now been examined and catalogued. Many of the papers were undated but I have attempted to work out a chronology from those that were, using informed guesswork where necessary with those that were not. What follows is, as far as can be ascertained, an accurate account of the history of the compilation of the book.

95 MARC 29/61.

96 MARC 29/70.

97 MARC 29/61.

98 Personal conversation with Roger C. Driver, 1 December 2001.

99 This bias has been reflected 50 years on in the compilation of the *Dictionary of Methodism in Britain and Ireland* ed. John A. Vickers, Peterborough, Epworth Press, 2000. Of the 50 members of the Committee listed only 25 are mentioned in the Dictionary. Nineteen of the 23 Wesleyans are noted, 5 of the 13 Primitive Methodists (one only receiving a brief sentence, the article being about his son) and one of the 12 United. Members of the Wesleyan Reformed Union are not mentioned at all. Doubtless part of the reason for this

decided upon whereby all the members of the committee 'should individually do the necessary preliminary work'.[100] They met again, in
retreat, at Digswell Park Conference House, Welwyn North, on 7–9
April 1930.[101]

Prior to the meeting each member of the committee made a preliminary examination of the denominational hymn books being used
by the churches. The committee then considered this material in full
session. At this meeting one sub-committee was appointed to deal with
hymns to be edited and reconsidered.[102] Another sub-committee was
convened to consider the plan and arrangement of the new book and
the classification of the hymns.[103] The fact that sub-committees were
formed within the main body of the Hymn Book Committee[104] meant
that the bias that has already been observed was exaggerated and at a
later date, as we shall see, this gave rise to conflict.

By the time of reporting to the 1930 Conferences of the different
denominations the committee had not reached a stage at which a first
draft of the book could be presented. Their report included terms of
reference and at this point the examination of the hymns under consideration still required to be completed. The task ahead was viewed
as 'an arduous one'.[105] The committee sought re-appointment with a
mandate to present a first draft of the new hymn book to the
Conferences of 1931. At this stage it was noted that work within the
committee had been amicable and that voting had not followed
denominational lines. A 'spirit of unity and fellowship . . . has
pervaded all its sessions . . . and every member has been enriched by
our consideration of the Methodist heritage in Hymns that are
common to us all'.[106] It is doubtful whether this is an entirely true
representation of what was actually happening, and the length of time
taken for the task suggests that all did not run smoothly. There is
evidence of interchanges between members of the committee which
supports this assertion.

In July 1930 a letter was sent out to members of the committee

---

is because the people who received preferment after union were predominantly Wesleyan,
and the Wesleyan Methodist Church was the majority denomination. The President, Vice-
President and Secretary of Conference at Union were all Wesleyans and it was some years
before a non-Wesleyan was elected President.

100 MARC 29/61, p. 2.   101 MARC 29/66 and others.
102 MARC 29/70.   103 MARC 29/61, p. 2.
104 Arguably it would be difficult to progress the work in any other way.
105 MARC 29/61, p. 2.   106 MARC 29/61, p. 2.

asking for hymns to be nominated for consideration for inclusion in the new hymn book. Along with this was sent a list of hymn books published since 1904 so that their contents could be evaluated.[107]

A Continuation Sub-Committee met on 22 September 1930. The minutes of its meeting included reference to the need to decide on a manner of retaining 'Methodist phraseology'. The question was raised whether this should be achieved through the retention of headings, the character of hymns, or by some other method. It was agreed that the Historical Hymns of Methodism should be distinguished by a descriptive note.[108] By September 1930 a Scheme of Contents had been drawn up.[109] Procedures were adopted for the preparation of the Hymn Book.[110] By October 1930 1,507 texts had been considered.[111] Clearly the task was immense.

Already, it seems, the outline of the book had been formed and it was nearer in layout to *Wesleyan Methodist Hymn Book* than to any of the other denominational books. The confidential nature of proceedings meant that matters of layout and projected production were well founded by the time that anything was made public. It would have been difficult to promote any resistance to this from outside the committee.

The layout was critical as it held within it, among other things, the premise that evangelistic mission was something to be sustained by the whole body of hymnody contained within the book, and not identified in one or more sections. This was inherently different from the expectation of the United Methodist Free Church and Bible Christian elements of the United Methodist Church. A similar distinction was evident in relation to Temperance. From one perspective it would be easy to assume that these matters were deemed unimportant and so could be omitted.

A further Retreat at Digswell Park Conference House took place in October. At this meeting matters relating to the draft contents of the book and to particular hymns were considered. A request had been received from the Independent Methodist Churches asking that they might be represented on the committee. It was recorded that the committee itself did not have the power to co-opt and that, in any case, preparation was so far advanced that new members would find it

107 MARC 29/74.   108 MARC 29/91.
109 MARC 29/87.   110 MARC 29/94.
111 MARC 29/144.

difficult to be integrated.[112] In many other ways, as work proceeded, the committee assumed authority of action which suggests that the argument against co-option covered another agenda. This underlines the autocracy of the committee and perhaps, in this case, animosity to a group long separated from the uniting denominations.

In November W. T. Davison and J. C. Mantripp provided a draft Table of Contents.[113] This was presented to the Continuation Sub-Committee which also appointed groups to advise on 'Hymns for Little Children', and for 'Social Service'.[114]

Early in December a circular letter was sent to members of the committee together with schedules listing nominated hymns.[115] On 24 December, J. Alfred Sharp (the convenor) found it necessary to send out letters admonishing those who had not returned schedules of hymns.[116] By 17 January 1931 Sharp was tackling members individually over this matter.[117] The pressure at this point is indicated in a humorous fashion by a cartoon bearing the inscription: 'Weary editor heaves sigh of relief! – Sec. sighs also – & goes on!'[118]

Seeds of the inconsistency of editing which we have already seen in the book were being sown. It is also reasonable to assume that from this point tensions, which had hitherto been submerged, began to surface within the committee. Humour is often a safe way of defusing, or giving expression to, such tension. It is interesting that it is Sharp's admonition, that of the professional (he was the Wesleyan Book Steward from 1911 to 1932) over the amateurs, but also the Wesleyan over the 'junior' denominations, that first gives a hint of the irritation which was present.

In April 1931 the committee met again at Digswell. The minutes of the meeting indicate that a sub-committee was appointed to draw up recommendations for the Conferences relating to the Tune Book. Reports of the Sub-Committees on Hymns for Little Children and National and Social Service were received. Hymns in various schedules were examined and a statistical analysis of the results was presented.[119]

The Editorial Committee met on 21 May and considered the scope of the work to be undertaken. The decisions of this meeting can be summarised as follows:

112 MARC 29/144. 113 MARC 29/147. 114 MARC 29/149.
115 MARC 29/150. 116 MARC 29/151. 117 MARC 29/152.
118 MARC 29/155. 119 MARC 30/347.

1. It was agreed that all current forms of each hymn should be examined.

2. The original form of the hymn and any alteration or divergence or deletion that may have occurred in its subsequent history should be examined, and a full report with recommendation should be submitted to the committee.[120]

3. The committee considered that the terms of reference gave it power to shorten a hymn, when necessary.

4. The committee also agreed that it had authority to decide

   a) the question of titles
   b) explanatory notes to certain hymns
   c) the insertion of the first line of the original in certain translations.

5. The subject of the Metrical Versions of Psalms and the use (in prose) of Psalms and Canticles for chanting appeared to be outside this discussion. The matter was being dealt with by a sub-

---

120 Such reports are not extant within the archive.

committee appointed by the full committee, viz. Dr W. T. Davison and J. C. Mantripp.

6. The subject of Hymns 'chiefly for private devotion' seemed to lie outside the work allotted to the Editorial Committee. This was seen as largely a matter of indexation and would be dealt with at a later stage by the full committee.

7. The question as to whether the Editorial Committee was to deal with minute, but very important questions, such as spelling, use of capitals and so on was addressed. It was recognised that editing might unconsciously affect doctrine. J. C. Mantripp was requested to draw up a memorandum on these points for the guidance of the committee.

8. It was understood by the Secretary that the important subject of the order of hymns within each subsection was reserved. This would be dealt with by the full committee at a later stage.

9. Hymns marked for comparison were to be sent to a sub-committee consisting of Henry Bett, MA [Wesleyan], Arthur S. Gregory, MA [Wesleyan], and S. G. Dimond, MA [United], as also were the hymns that were translations.

10. The question was discussed of bracketing those verses in hymns which might be retained but not sung.

11. Members of the committee were asked to notify verses suitable for Doxologies, the close of a meeting, etc., such verses to consist either of one verse of eight lines or two verses of four lines.

12. The Secretary was requested to supply each member, as soon as possible, with a number of hymns already provisionally selected, so that the work of editing might proceed.[121]

In a letter dated 19 June 1931, from Sydney G. Dimond to Edgar C. Barton (Secretary of the New Hymn Book Committee), the concern was expressed that, at that time, in the description of hymns provided by the committee, texts that were in more than just the *Wesleyan Methodist Hymn Book* were only indicated by 'W'. Dimond suggested that it would be diplomatic to add other sources in order that the draft might gain a wider acceptance.[122] It is notable that the sub-committee of which he was a part was, again, dominated by Wesleyans.[123] The

---

121 MARC 30/224.
122 MARC 30/239.
123 Bett and Gregory were Wesleyan, while Dimond was a United Methodist.

bias here, in a group charged with making decisions between different versions of hymns, is extraordinary, particularly when it is realised that one of the contributory denominations of the United Methodist Church (of which Dimond was representative) was close enough to the Wesleyans to share in the compilation of the *Wesleyan Methodist Hymn Book* of 1904. In addition Bett was recognised to be extremely conservative, preferring texts that were scholarly rather than popular, while Gregory was from the Catholic wing of the Wesleyan tradition.[124] In the light of the concern expressed over the possible effects of editing on doctrine (7 above) such an imbalance was critical. What is then surprising is the prominent role assigned to J. C. Mantripp (Primitive Methodist) though, as we shall see, the amount of influence resulting from this seems to have been minimal. The appointment was, while not denying Mantripp's ability, token if not diversionary. Mantripp had, hitherto, been involved in drawing up lists of contents and in offering direction as to the use of Psalms and Canticles. These matters were important and substantive and indicate the use to which this Primitive Methodist's expertise was, initially, being put. The delegation of responsibility for punctuation and associated matters would have given him much work and, of necessity, reduced the time that he would have had to apply his critical skills to the overall work of compilation and decisions relating to the content of the book.

The progress which had been made by the New Hymn Book Committee was reported to the Conferences of 1931.[125] It indicated that the books then being used by the three denominations had been examined, and listed additional sources that had received attention.[126]

The report gave an insight into the method that the committee adopted to carry out its task. Recommendations of members were tabulated by the Secretary, and the results made available to the full committee. To facilitate its work the committee had met twice in extended session at Digswell Park Conference House.[127] This information was less likely to give rise to criticism than the actual results of their efforts might have done. The report did not contain a draft copy

124 J. Newton, *Heart Speaks to Heart*, p. 71. A. S. Gregory became a member of the Methodist Sacramental Fellowship and his cousin, also a Minister, later joined the Roman Catholic Church.
125 MARC 30/343 passim.
126 MARC 30/343, p. 1.
127 MARC 30/343, p. 1.

of the proposed book but detailed what had been achieved since the previous Conferences. There seems to have been a great reticence in making public the actual proceedings and decisions of the committee.

To determine which hymns to include from the current books it was decided not to reject any hymn in present use 'except upon a decisive vote'.[128] The report does not give any indication of what would constitute 'a decisive vote'. The current books of the three denominations contained a total of 2,159 different hymns. The committee accepted 786 of these and rejected 1,185. A further 188 were reserved for further consideration.[129] Very frustratingly the reasons for inclusion and exclusion and an indication of which texts were concerned were not provided. All that was made available were numerical statistics.

Hymns not included within these collections were also examined but for these the criterion for acceptance was a decisive vote for inclusion.[130] Again, no definition is provided as to what might be considered a 'decisive vote'. In addition to these sources a few manuscript hymns had been submitted. Altogether 749 hymns not available in the four Methodist books were nominated for consideration. At the time of writing the report the committee had examined 500 of these and provisionally accepted 148. It was recorded that 'these hymns will greatly enrich the new Book, especially in "Hymns of Adoration", "Hymns for Social Service", "Hymns for the Young", and "Hymns for the Seasons of the Christian Year" '.[131] It would be interesting to know the names of authors who had submitted texts, which were deemed acceptable or unacceptable, and what were the criteria that were being applied in the process of selection, but this information has not been preserved.

The committee reported that 'The many great Evangelical Hymns of our tradition needed no defence for there was no-one to question', while 'A certain number of Chorus hymns which have proved specially serviceable in Missions and Special Evangelistic Services' had been included. Again, one is prompted to ask what is meant by 'a certain number'? Such reporting allowed for the 'sober' influence of material from the *Wesleyan Methodist Hymn Book* of 1904, noted by later commentators, to be maintained.[132]

128 MARC 30/343, p. 1.   129 MARC 30/343, p. 1.
130 MARC 30/343, p. 1.   131 MARC 30/343, p. 2.
132 Davies, George and Rupp, *A History of the Methodist Church in Great Britain*, Vol. 3, p. 317.

It was noted that a draft table of contents and a suggested classification of nominated hymns had been prepared. The committee stated four future objectives:[133]

1. to complete the examination of submitted hymns;
2. to carry through the very large amount of editorial work;
3. to attend to copyright and similar matters;
4. to make the final selection, reducing the number to near the suggested limit of 1,000, and to determine finally the Table of Contents and General Arrangement.

The hope was expressed that a draft of the new Hymn Book would be able to be presented to the three Conferences of 1932, and that the book itself would be available for the United Conference in 1933. Clearly it was intended to present the book to Conference with the minimum possible opportunity for the committee to be challenged over its decisions. While this would have made the task of the committee much easier, it also offered them great power in modelling the most effective instrument for theological education and doctrinal catechesis that would be available to the new denomination and, unknown to them, for the next 50 years of Methodist history.

It was suggested that the time was right to appoint a Tune Book Committee 'consisting of twenty members in the proportion of ten Wesleyan Methodists, five Primitive Methodists and five United Methodists – together with eight members appointed by the New Hymn Book Committee from their own number, and F. Luke Wiseman, BA (Chairman of the New Hymn Book Committee) an ex-officio member'. It was noted that a representative of the Wesleyan Reform Union would be invited to attend the meetings of the Tune Book Committee. [134] The constitution of this committee did not gain universal acceptance, being regarded as unfairly weighted,[135] and lacking in Welsh representation,[136] though an article in the *Methodist Recorder* expressed support for it stating that it had a denominational, geographical and competency mix and included the 'technical expert and amateur'.[137] The original committee was continuing to seek to put its own particular stamp on the proceedings. A conservative influence was being maintained.

133 MARC 30/343, p. 2.   134 MARC 30/343, p. 2f.   135 MARC 29/136.
136 MARC 29/112.   137 MARC 29/175.

At the meeting of the full committee which took place on 9–11 September 1931 it was decided that if, in the judgement of the Editorial Committee, a hymn was considered to be below the level of the standard required, such a hymn should be starred for further consideration by the full committee. It was felt that this course of action would materially assist the full committee when the time arrived for the final selection of hymns. No indication of the criteria for such a standard were provided.

The Report of the Sub-Committee on Ancient Hymns and Canticles was submitted. At this stage the following statistics were recorded relating to hymns from all sources: [138]

Hymns accepted	1,043
Hymns rejected	1,082
Hymns to be reconsidered	123
Total	2,248

It is surprising that, even within the Hymn Book Committee Archive, there is no list of accepted and rejected hymns from this stage of the process. Were such lists destroyed to prevent any examination which might allow for a critique of the process of the committee? Members with an eye to maintaining a historical record of such an important process would surely have recognised the value of such documents. Items of much less significance have been retained.

On 14 September the New Tune Book Committee met. It asserted its independence and discussed the appointment of a musical adviser.[139] This latter debate was not decisive and there is evidence in the archive of a private conversation,[140] and individual[141] and circular letters[142] relating to this topic before a minute records the nomination of M. L. Wolstenholm in this role.[143] One would have expected such a crucial role to be that of a Conference appointment[144] rather than a simple matter of co-option. The fact that it was not is, perhaps, evidence of the autocracy of F. Luke Wiseman noted earlier.

Reports of the first meeting of the New Tune Book Committee, and that of the New Hymn Book Committee, were carried by the press on

---

138 MARC 30/298. 139 MARC 29/143.
140 MARC 29/159. 141 MARC 29/141.
142 MARC 29/157. 143 MARC 29/128.
144 Or at least open to scrutiny by Conference.

17 September.[145] These indicated that Psalms for chanting would be included in the New Book,[146] that no more new hymns could be received from the general public,[147] and that the general quality of new material was regarded as being inferior to that already in use.[148] This last point was demonstrated by the fact that of the original hymns submitted especially for airmen and passengers by air, not one text was thought to be 'of sufficient merit for inclusion'.[149] The evidence of the conservatism of the committee continued to present itself.

The full committee took the opportunity to appoint eight members to the Tune Book Committee.[150] One can only assume that, at a time of Union, the Conference officials of the uniting churches had more pressing matters with which to deal than ensuring that the production of the new hymn book was undertaken in a representative manner.[151]

There is evidence of the weight of work which the committee members were being asked to undertake in the need to appoint an assistant for J. C. Mantripp to relieve him of most of his normal Circuit duties;[152] and a letter from Arthur S. Gregory to Edgar C. Barton complains that the 'pace is altogether too hot!', as additional meetings had been called necessitating attendance on five consecutive days in one week just before Christmas.[153] Part of this pressure had been caused by the Ecumenical Conference, a matter that Barton 'would rather explain than write about', implying that things might be said in relation to union that it would be wiser not to record. In his reply to Gregory he concludes, 'I hope you will survive.'[154]

In addition to Committee attendance, work was being done by individuals in their own time and then communicated via the Secretary.[155] The Archive contains on-going correspondence with individuals relating to the book as a whole and to individual texts; for example,

---

145 e.g. MARC 29/160.
146 MARC 30/322.
147 MARC 30/322.
148 MARC 30/322.
149 MARC 30/323.
150 MARC 30/322.
151 Such issues of representation do not seem to have exercised greatly those in authority in the church at this time. Personal conversation with Roger C. Driver, 1 December 2001.
152 MARC 30/286.
153 MARC 30/240.
154 MARC 30/241.
155 MARC 30/242.

W. W. Thackray wrote to Wiseman referring to the need for hymns on the duty of the forgiveness of enemies, the duty and blessing of peace-making and children obeying and honouring parents.[156] There is evidence from outside the Archive that some material was sent out to individuals who were not on the committee and that what came back was accepted uncritically.[157] Alfred Taberer has indicated that James Bradburn, a minister and personal friend, drew up a list of 28 hymns, which duly appeared, without alteration or emendation, at Nos 311 to 338.

On 17–18 December 1931 the Editorial Committee met and, among other things, appointed a sub-committee to deal with punctuation.[158] It is surprising that criteria for punctuation were not set earlier in the editorial process in order that texts could be provided in as near to final form as possible.

The cost of the book was something that from time to time exercised the committee. The first evidence of this (10 December 1931) comes in a resolution of the Longton Circuit Meeting to make available a popular or 'cheap' edition of the new hymnal.[159] This was followed by a memo to the New Hymn Book Retreat (meeting on 5–8 January 1932) outlining a Special Notice of Motion proposed by Mr E. C. Early that 'In view of the need to keep the price of the new Hymn Book as low as possible, and since the number of congregations using the Psalter is comparatively small, and for these separate books of Psalms are available, the Committee decide to omit the Psalms from the Hymn Book.'[160] Part of a letter from J. Alfred Sharp to Clement Gerrard reads: 'When I tell you that the work of the Committee has already cost a very large sum, and that before the Hymn Book is even set-up there will be some thousands of pounds spent on it you will see how carefully we should move.'[161] It is clear that Sharp was conscious of the constraints within which he and the committee were having to work, and the likelihood of criticism.

In the meantime the Tune Book Committee, through the efforts of the Irish representative, Major Johnson, had ascertained that, other than the main denominational hymn books, *Alexander's Hymns No.*

---

156 MARC 30/403.
157 A. A. Taberer, personal correspondence, 6 March 2000.
158 MARC 29/118.
159 MARC 30/216.
160 MARC 29/120.
161 MARC 29/171.

3, *Redemption Songs*, Sankey, the *Crusaders' Hymnal*, the *People's Hymnal* and about 14 other tune books were in use in church meetings.[162] It seems likely, from the final cast of the book, that not much notice was taken of this information. There is also evidence that people in the provinces were asked to provide local information, though the nature and extent of this involvement is not apparent from the archive.[163]

The Tune Book Committee began to organise its work by allocating tunes, sorted according to metre, to groups of people for examination and report.[164] By the end of 1932 the committee had received 2,500 unpublished tunes for consideration.[165] On 14 December 1931 a Tunes Selection Committee met[166] and reopened the debate that had been initiated by the appointment of the Tune Book Committee, giving rise to protracted correspondence between the convenor, J. Alfred Sharp, and Clement Gerrard. The constitution of the Selection Committee was indicated as being seven Wesleyan including the chairman, two Primitive Methodists and two United Methodists. From this it can be seen that, compared with the main Hymn Book Committee, the proportion of the Wesleyan membership was increasing. Gerrard pressed for additional Primitive Methodist representation.[167] Sharp responded that, in his view, 'The Chairman . . . is understood to represent all phases and all churches.' He continues:

Personally I do not care for this adjustment for Churches. What we want are the best men for the work, and as the Committee chose the men I assume they regarded them as the best men to do the work which needs to be done. More and more am I convinced that in dealing with a lot of these matters we shall have to cast aside the ideas of balancing of representation . . . To increase the number of members in the committee would seem to me to be folly.[168]

Gerrard responded by continuing to argue for additional representation:

It is quite true that efficiency ought to come before the balance of representation, but it is a question whether we are getting greater

162 MARC 29/180.   163 MARC 29/185.   164 MARC 29/125.
165 MARC 29/104.   166 MARC 29/176.   167 MARC 29/170.
168 MARC 29/171.

efficiency, and as the principle of balancing has so far been followed, I personally think it should have been followed in this case.[169]

He contended that there had been no real choice in the appointment of the Selection Committee: 'The Convenors were fixed up at head-quarters and thus when we met last Monday it was the easiest way out to follow the suggestion that they be appointed to the Selection Committee.' Gerrard sympathised on the question, which Sharp had also raised, of cost but felt that the addition of two members would not greatly increase the expense. He concluded:

> I am influenced in the attitude I am taking by the fact that one of our very best men, R. W. Callin, who on the grounds of qualifications certainly ought to have been on, has not even been considered.[170]

Sharp responded:

> You forget that there is one other on the Selection Committee that is not Wesleyan. He represents the Wesleyan Reform; so that comes to five and five with the exception of the Chairman and the Musical helper, Mr Lightwood.

It was pertinent that the Wesleyan Reform Union was not part of the uniting Church. Sharp was not allowing this to cloud the issue. He pressed the point that all work done by the Selection Committee would come before 'the groups'; so that every group would have a share in the work of the Selection Committee, and each member in the group would have the opportunity of expressing his or her view in respect of every hymn. Sharp refers to Callin but suggests that it would not be possible to have every competent man on the committee, that Mr Callin 'will have the opportunity of putting his views when the group meets to consider the work of the selection committee'. Sharp concludes that he is sure that nothing of what has passed is of a personal nature and that Gerrard 'would do whatever . . . [he] felt

---

169 This response might be deemed charitable given the imbalance noted from the outset.

170 MARC 29/172.

right as graciously as it could be done'.[171] Sharp's role as Secretary seems to have allowed him to win the day. The influence of particular denominations is clear.

As work on the book progressed, it was decided that certain matters relating to its production should remain confidential to the committee or, at appropriate points, to members of Conference. Papers issued were marked 'Private and Confidential'.[172] This led to a dispute which appears to have been initiated by the press, illustrated by an article in the *News Chronicle* of 26 February 1932 which reported under the headline '1,185 Hymns to Go – Secret Decision of Methodists', that

> Every member of the committee is bound in honour to maintain secrecy concerning the old-fashioned hymns which have been excluded and the modern ones that take their place. From another source the 'News Chronicle' learns, however, that some of the less popular of Charles Wesley's hymns have been omitted.

The article goes on to report that there had been a fear that a 'new theological balance' was to have been introduced but that the committee had sought to retain the 'favourites of former days . . . while enriching the Hymn Book with the hymns in use in other churches'.[173] The question of the authorship of Wesley hymns raised by Bett,[174] and later by Baker,[175] does not seem to have exercised the committee. *Joyful News* (the newspaper published by Cliff College), reporting on 7 April, sought to refute this by stating:

> The foolish story in the daily press that members of the Committee were sworn to secrecy is of course without foundation. Naturally the inclusion or exclusion of certain hymns has not been bruited abroad.[176]

The article was initialled by W. H. H. If, as seems likely, this is William H. Heap, a Wesleyan member of the committee, then it is

---

171 MARC 29/173.
172 E.g., MARC 29/186.
173 MARC 30/285.
174 H. Bett, *The Hymns of Methodism*, 3rd edition, London, Epworth Press, 1945, p. 21–33.
175 F. Baker, *Charles Wesley's Verse*, p. 102–15.
176 MARC 29/250.

understandable why the report has this acerbic tone. The committee
papers and the availability of information tell a different story from
W. H. H.

At the beginning of 1932 it became clear that if deadlines were to be
met extra meetings would be needed.[177] Between 5 and 8 January the
full committee met again in retreat, this time at Westminster Training
College,[178] though on this occasion *The Methodist Leader* reported
that London members went home each night which detracted from the
'retreat' nature of the gatherings.[179] Various matters were considered
relating to authors' names, the heading of hymns, contents, the form
of presentation to be made to the Conferences, hymns for private
devotion, and the Notice of Motion suggesting the omission of Psalms
from the main book.[180] A number of texts were examined.[181] By the
middle of January lists of hymns with their sources were being prepared.[182]

In the press hints continued to be given as to the nature of the book
that was expected,[183] while individuals were more specific as the
correspondence between W. W. Thackray and F. Luke Wiseman indicates. Thackray sought hymns which addressed the duty of forgiveness of enemies, the duty and blessing of peacemaking, and children
obeying and honouring their parents.[184] At this time the question of
peacemaking and the claims of pacifism were regularly finding a
prominent place in the columns of the *Methodist Recorder*.

During 1932 it was reported that, because of his 'experience in dealing with manuscripts and the technique of printing and binding', J. C.
Mantripp had been delegated to deal with the practicalities of the production of the book.[185] Mantripp continued to be occupied in areas
where he would have little influence over the content of the book, yet
this was done in such a way that the officers of the committee could
argue that they were demonstrating a lack of bias in the appointment
of a non-Wesleyan to this role. This could be interpreted as having a
political intention.

By now the work of the Editorial Committee had become more
focused and a letter, dated 21 January, calling members to a meeting

177 MARC 30/234.   178 MARC 29/301.
179 MARC 30/291.   180 MARC 29/171.
181 MARC 30/293.   182 MARC 29/197.
183 MARC 29/290.   184 MARC 30/403.
185 MARC 30/286.

on 3–5 February indicated the source books which members would need to bring with them. The selection had narrowed considerably.

Throughout the early months of the year the process of considering both texts and tunes continued. From 5 to 8 April the full committee met again in 'retreat', at Digswell, in spite of having received an invitation from H. B. Workman to come to Hunmanby with the added offer of 'separate bedrooms, beautiful grounds, and . . . [being fed] like turkey cocks'.[186] The minutes of the meeting contain a tribute to J. Alfred Sharp who had died. It was then recorded that it had been decided not to have a separate Youth Index but to indicate such hymns by a sign in the index. An index of the first lines of all verses was to be included, while an index to subject and text would be put in a new linear index. The Index of Authors and Translators was to follow the pattern adopted by the compilers of the *United Methodist Free Church Hymnal*. This was a small token of recognition of the input of this denomination.

Translated hymns would be preceded by the first line printed in the original language. The hymns presented for the use by little children were agreed. F. Luke Wiseman was asked to write the Preface and 'The New Methodist Hymn Book' was decided upon as the title. A scheme of contents was approved. At this point 967 texts had been accepted.[187] The atmosphere appears to have been more relaxed, with some members of the committee enjoying 'bouts of squash rackets'.[188]

From 4 to 6 May the Tune Selection Sub-Committee met.[189] Lists of hymns were compiled for which tunes needed to be selected.[190] From 6 to 8 June the sub-committee met again, this time giving consideration to a Memorial from the Carlisle District Synod suggesting that consideration should be given to setting tunes at a lower pitch to enable improved congregational singing and that older, more familiar tunes should be retained alongside new tunes. A list of tunes and sources was prepared.[191]

On 3 June the Editorial Committee met and edited a number of hymns. They also appointed a Single Verse Sub-Committee comprising F. Luke Wiseman, J. C. Mantripp, and Arthur S. Gregory, together with Edmund S. Lamplough and Edgar C. Barton as

---

186 MARC 29/191.
188 MARC 30/252.
190 MARC 29/52.

187 MARC 30/270.
189 MARC 29/53.
191 MARC 29/68.

Convenor.[192] The Wesleyan influence was perpetuated and Lamplough was the only lay-person represented.

The 'Sources of Hymns Listed in the Draft Scheme of Contents of the *Methodist Hymn Book* Presented to the three Conferences of 1932' was substantially the same as that presented to the Conferences of 1931.

On 23 June the *Methodist Recorder* carried an article relating to the Report to Conference which was 'strictly private and confidential', for the information of the members of the Conferences only. The article compares the Table of Contents of the new book with that of Wesley's book of 1780. The author notes that the section on the Holy Scriptures has a new place compared with that of the (Wesleyan) book of 1904 and with that which it occupies in the *United Methodist Free Church Hymnal*. The rest of the article is statistical or descriptive, summarising the writer's view of the report. It concludes that 'when the Committee has given the book its final touches, it will be generally acknowledged to be the "best yet" – catholic[,] comprehensive, characteristic – a worthy hymnal for the praises of a united Methodism'.[193] On 14 July in a further article note was made of 'losses and gains'. It was remarked that the section on

'The Sacraments' is nearly doubled, and the number of hymns of Adoration and Worship, and on the Saviour's Ministry on earth are considerably increased, and rightly so. The author concludes: 'It *is* a good book – isn't it?[194]

Clearly there was bias in the writing.

On 21 July 1932 the *Methodist Times* and the *Methodist Recorder* carried reports on the Conference debate on the 'New Hymn Book Report'. It was noted that 'Dr Kirtlan objected that in the list of suggested hymns there were only three' [on Death and Judgement]. There had been, he said, in recent years a weakening of the doctrine of sin, of the necessity of an agony of repentance, of the terrible reality of retribution. In making this statement he sought to bind the committee by a resolution to attend to the matter of Passion hymns and the 'Death and Judgement' section. F. L. Wiseman said that while he was disposed to support this objection, the general standard of the book

192 MARC 30/266.   193 MARC 30/264.   194 MARC 30/263.

had to be taken into consideration, and while there were many hymns they might like to have in the book now, 'would they like to retain them ten years hence?' Spinney, reflecting on the fact that ultimately the section on 'Death, Judgement and the Future Life' had been cut from 37 to 19, as compared with the *Wesleyan Methodist Hymn Book* (though there were another five hymns in the 'Funerals and Memorial' Section), regarded this as significant in a post-war era.[195]

Wiseman was reported as hoping 'they would not proceed by detailed resolutions of that sort, as any member of Conference might feel moved'. At the same time Conference might rest assured that every attention would be paid not only to the remarks now made, but to any others which might be presented to the committee. Effectively the book was being presented as a *fait accompli*.

Dr Kirtlan responded: 'Sometimes Committees promise to do things and don't, but on the word of honour of Mr Wiseman I will not press the matter further.' At this Wiseman was seen to bow. The President reaffirmed this commitment.[196]

By this time 'The Committee had provisionally accepted 960 hymns, and they hoped that the stream of original hymns sent in for consideration would now diminish'.[197] The Tunes Selection Sub-Committee meeting on 29 July considered 133 tunes 'selected by Mr Lightwood from upwards of 2,000 original compositions submitted'.[198] During August a letter came to the committee from Australia making reference to seven copies of a list of hymns and suggested tunes.

During the autumn correspondence relating to the hymn book and its contents seems to have reached a peak. Frederick H. Mills wrote to F. Luke Wiseman referring to the arrangement of the 'New Hymn and Tune Book'. He cited the example of the 1925 *Psalter & Church Hymnary* of the Presbyterian Church in Ireland, and suggested that the layout of this was better than that of the current Methodist Book, presumably the *Wesleyan Methodist Hymn Book*. He goes on to say that his own idea is better still.[199] The letter, he had been informed, had been passed on to Edgar C. Barton, who later had no record of having received it, but who agreed to give the Irish book consideration.[200] Clearly it was too late in the process for such an assurance to

---

195 Spinney, *Tuned for Praise*, p. 20.
196 MARC 30/261.
197 MARC 30/261.
198 MARC 29/46.
199 MARC 30/307.
200 MARC 30/308.

have any validity. In October J. A. Lewis wrote to F. Luke Wiseman in heated terms:

> Can you get back some of the fine finials to Chas. Wesley's hymns that the blundering bricklayers have snapped off . . . He generally ended, if he could, on the top note . . . e.g.,
>
>> Into a saint exalt a worm
>> A worm exalt to God.
>
> Put it back, worm and all.[201]

The letter ends with a postscript praising a tune of Wiseman's. People were still suggesting possible hymns for inclusion in the book, as a letter, dated 11 October 1932, from Chas. Taylor to Mr Hirst indicates,[202] and a letter from Hugo A. Bernard to the Methodist Publishing House suggested that a pocket edition of the book would be welcome, as would a book bound jointly with the prayer book.[203]

The Editorial Committee met on 11 November to attend to the editing of texts.[204] It met again from 22 to 25 November when F. Luke Wiseman was confirmed as Chairman.[205] The Tunes Selection Sub-Committee assembled concurrently[206] and considered a number of tunes, the minutes of this meeting running to six pages of typescript.[207] The full committee listed, accepted and omitted hymns, and made corrections and additions to the book. The index of Children's Hymns, the absence of Temperance hymns and the Single Verse Section were addressed. Accepted chorus hymns [9] were listed. In the case of the pointing of Canticles and Psalms it was decided to follow the New Cathedral Psalter. General approval was given to the Preface[208] prepared by John Telford (and not F. Luke Wiseman as had previously been decided).[209] Telford and Mantripp were delegated to prepare a biographical index. It was decided that 'Amen' was to be used 'with discrimination'. The date of publication was expected to be

---

201 MARC 30/306. 202 MARC 30/408.
203 MARC 30/309. 204 MARC 29/42; 30/312.
205 MARC 29/40. 206 MARC 29/38.
207 MARC 30/386.

208 Four pages of a typescript copy of the Preface, with a note in handwriting at the top of the first page in blue/black ink: 'presented to Hymn Bk. Com. Dec 1932', is present in the archive. MARC 30/313.

209 MARC 30/270.

the autumn of 1933, missing the Uniting Conference. The question of how the book might best be introduced to the Methodist public was tabled by W. R. Maltby.[210]

An undated press cutting (probably from December 1932), for which the source is unspecified, indicated that perhaps only one further meeting of the full committee would be necessary. The article stated that 'The Committee has cause for gratification at the reception accorded to its work by the three Conferences'. The article remarked on the paucity of hymns on the judgement – 'The omission of the section is not the proper way to treat the subject' – and acknowledged that this was being addressed.[211] Judgement was a subject which had become less acceptable than it had been to a previous generation not scarred by war.

The *Methodist Times and Leader*, reporting on 1 December 1932, indicated the hope that the book would be ready for the following autumn. It was noted that 'Suggestions from the Australian Hymn Book Committee, and various groups, including the men at Didsbury and Richmond College, were also considered, as well as Professor Bett's plea for a reconsideration of certain Wesley hymns.'

On the same date the *Methodist Recorder* stated that 'The Committee expressed gratification at the reception given by the three Conferences to the Draft submitted to them.' It also related conversations on the Judgement Section and the selection of 'chorus hymns' and anticipated that publication would be not later than Christmas 1933.[212] Time was moving on!

The Tune Selection Sub-Committee met on 18–20 January 1933 to consider tunes selected by the different groups.[213] On 6 February the Editorial Committee met[214] and was presented with an amended copy of the Preface.[215] At this meeting it was decided unanimously that the title for the book should not be 'The New Methodist Hymn Book' as had been suggested in April 1932,[216] but the *Methodist Hymn Book*.

The minutes of the meeting included notes on the scheme of contents, details of the order of hymns in sections, lists of deleted hymns, and matters relating to copyright. It was decided to use the Authorised Version for the Psalms and further revision of the Preface

210 MARC 30/258.
212 MARC 30/257.
214 MARC 29/29.
216 MARC 30/270.
211 MARC 30/255.
213 See, e.g., MARC 29/32.
215 MARC 29/26.

was suggested. Wesley's Preface to the 1780 Hymn Book was to be printed separately. The single verse section (prepared under the auspices of Wiseman and Maltby) was examined and the index of hymns for young people was referred to a sub-committee of Wiseman, Maltby and Telford for revision. It might be asked why Lilian Cox,[217] with her expertise, was not included in this sub-committee. A cross-index of hymns for children was to be prepared by Mantripp. Again, why not Lilian Cox? Correspondence had been received from W. H. Heap and N. Paul Abraham and this was referred to a small sub-committee.[218] Another copy of the minutes[219] makes reference to the sympathetic reception of a letter from Sir Walter Essex.

On 28 February F. Luke Wiseman received a letter from R. Lee Cole of the Methodist Church in Ireland relating to a detail in the text of 'Abide with me'.[220] Correspondence in the *Methodist Recorder* suggested that 'Abide with me' should read 'in life, in death' not 'in life and death'.[221] A note from Wiseman makes the cursory observation that it would be retained as it stood already in the text prepared for the book, and this was indeed 'In life, in death'.[222] Such detailed critique was still being offered very late on in the editorial process.

From 14 to 16 March, and again from 17 to 19 May, the Tunes Selection Sub-Committee met.[223] On this latter occasion the minutes noted the resignation due to ill health of the Musical Adviser (Dr M. L. Wolstenholm) and the nomination of C. F. Brockless as his successor.[224] This again took place as a co-option. Another copy of the minutes indicated that the Preface to the Tune Book would be prepared by F. Luke Wiseman,[225] in spite of Telford's involvement, which has already been noted.

On 25 May a letter was despatched calling together a joint meeting of the Hymn and Tune Book Committees.[226] On 8 June the Tune Book Committee met[227] and then on 9 June both the Tunes Selection Sub-

---

217 Lilian Cox's expertise was in the area of hymns for young people. She wrote an article entitled 'Youth and the New Hymn Book' for the *Methodist Recorder*, 8 February 1934, p. 9, and had written at least one hymn in use by the Girls' League.

218 MARC 30/225.

219 MARC 30/246.

220 MARC 29/27.

221 *Methodist Recorder*, 18 August 1932, p. 15.

222 MARC 30/14.   223 MARC 29/28.

224 MARC 29/25.   225 MARC 30/375.

226 MARC 30/374.   227 MARC 29/16.

Committee[228] and the Joint Hymns and Tunes Committees met.[229] The minutes of the Joint Committee noted the deletion of hymns and the approval of the single verse section. It was decided that the word 'Amen' was to be omitted except when required by the text. It was agreed that the Psalms would be retained in spite of suggestions for their deletion or a reduction in their number. The Preface was presented and, after some changes had been made, was adopted. The Chairman was accorded a standing vote of appreciation.

It was decided that Conference would be asked to discharge the full committee and to appoint a Continuation Committee comprising the Revds Wiseman, Barton, Harrison, Maltby, Rattenbury, Telford, Swinden, Mantripp, Fisher, Smith, Squire, Metcalfe, Sir Walter Essex, and Messrs Lamplough and Early. Of these three were United Methodists, two Primitive Methodists, one Wesleyan Reformed and the remainder Wesleyans. According to this list Wesleyan control had increased, there were no women and only three laymen. A correction to the minutes records the proposed members of the Continuation Committee as: Wiseman, Bett, Dimond, Gregory, Harrison, Maltby, Mantripp, Strong, Swinden, Telford, Barton, and Mr Lamplough,[230] increasing the proportion of Wesleyans further and reducing the lay representation to one. The London members of the committee were delegated to deal with the report to Conference.[231]

The Editorial Committee met on 19 June. The minutes recorded the death of Dr Brook. Approval was given for the Report to Conference. A few texts were edited. Other notes related to canticles, the index of young people's hymns, the order of the scheme of contents, continuous numbering throughout the book, the place of 'Blake's Hymn' in the single verse section, and the adoption of the Preface with a few minor alterations.[232]

The Tune Book Committee found it necessary to meet again on 26 July,[233] the Continuation Committee meeting on 18 September. The Agenda indicates that the work of the Chant Book Committee and tunes were addressed.[234] No final publication date was indicated in the archive but it is clear that committee business continued into the autumn of 1933. The most recent document in the archive is a photo-

---

228 MARC 29/17.
230 MARC 30/245.
232 MARC 30/244.
234 MARC 29/9.

229 MARC 29/23.
231 MARC 30/368.
233 MARC 30/410.

graph, inscribed on the back '1934 Hymn Book Committee'.[235] The book was finally published in December 1933.

When it was nearing completion the new *Methodist Hymn Book* was regarded by those who had been charged with reporting on its production as 'a Book of Praise which, while true to the traditions of Methodist Song, has gathered treasures, new and old, for our worship in all its phases, and both for young and old'. The appreciation by the committee of the part played by F. Luke Wiseman was expressed in a standing vote. It was noted that though in the work of the committee, 'the strain [on the secretary, Edgar C. Barton] had been severe . . . it has been borne with unfailing urbanity and wise forethought'.[236]

235 MARC 29/2.
236 MARC 29/14, p. 2.

3

What was the Methodist Hymn Book like?

If someone were to take a copy of the *Methodist Hymn Book* from a shelf and begin to look through it what would they think? Not all hymn books are the same. A reading of the content and layout gives not only an indication of the agenda of the editors, but also offers a window into the culture of those who produced it. The literary and historical impression given by a book is important. The feel of a book is not always consonant with the time of its production. Then again, hymn books do not exist in isolation. At the time of production of the *Methodist Hymn Book*, *Songs of Praise* (1925, 1932) and the *Church Hymnary* (1927) were immediately contemporary.

So a number of questions are posed by a reading of the book. How would it compare with other hymn books? If the date of its production was not known, if you had not been brought up singing from it, when in history might it be placed? What was its historical and literary context? It is to these issues that we turn.

Historical Picture

A Wesleyan Hymn Book?

From the outset the book demands to be seen not just as a Methodist book but as a Wesleyan book. It opens with 'O for a thousand tongues to sing' (1)[237] which had been the first hymn in each of the previous

---

237 Hymns in the *Methodist Hymn Book* will be indicated by a bracketed number (*) in the text corresponding to the number of the hymn in the book.

Wesleyan books[238] but, though present, not the first in the other contemporary Methodist hymn books.[239] Of the first 35 hymns in the *Methodist Hymn Book*, 21 were found in the *Wesleyan Methodist Hymn Book* of 1904. There seems to have been a conscious attempt on the part of the editors to make the book feel Wesleyan. This assertion, though bold, is supported by statistical evidence. Sixty-one per cent of the content of the *Wesleyan Methodist Hymn Book* was retained. This compares with 46 per cent of *A Collection of Hymns for the use of People called Bible Christians* and 42 per cent of the *Methodist Free Church Hymnal*. The picture with regard to Primitive Methodism is more complex. If the *Primitive Methodist Hymnal* and *Primitive Methodist Supplement* are taken together 57 per cent of this corpus was preserved in the *Methodist Hymn Book*, but it is rare for a supplement to gain the same circulation as the normative collection. If the *Primitive Methodist Hymnal* alone is taken then a mere 42 per cent was retained. What is clear from the outset is the number of hymns from the extensive Primitive Methodist corpus that were omitted.

In addition, the Preface to the *Methodist Hymn Book* refers firstly to Wesleyan Methodism[240] and then to the other branches of the denomination, and this same pattern is followed in the Preface to the Edition with Tunes.[241] The choice of listing was clearly not alphabetical! When books were published to accompany the new hymn book, the emphasis was maintained.[242] Telford begins *The Methodist Hymn-Book Illustrated* with a 'Table of Wesley's Original Editions',[243] which notes that 'Other collections' were issued in 1875, 1904 and 1933, these, with the exception of the last, being the dates of publication of Wesleyan collections. This is followed by a list of 'Other Hymn Books' where those books used by the Primitive Methodists, the Methodist New Connexion, United Methodist Free Churches and Bible

---

238 Berger states that 'Practically every Methodist hymn book since [*A Collection of Hymns of the Use of The People Called Methodists*] has opened with this hymn.' T. Berger, *Theology in Hymns?*, Nashville, Kingswood, 1995, p. 74.

239 With the exception of the New Connexion book of 1904 which, as has been noted, was the same as the *Wesleyan Methodist Hymn Book*.

240 *Methodist Hymn Book*, London, Novello, 1933, p. iii.

241 *Methodist Hymn Book*, p. x.

242 See J. Telford, *The Methodist Hymn-Book Illustrated*, London, Epworth Press, 1934.

243 Telford, *The Methodist Hymn-Book Illustrated*, p. vi.

Christians are cited. This could be justified in terms of the size of the uniting churches but this factor should not necessarily have influenced the editing of the hymn book.

The overall appearance of the book suggests that Wesleyan influence was dominant in terms of both its structure and its layout, though on this point alone it would be unwise to make a judgement. The book was likely to mirror the pattern of one of the contributory denominations. The choice was, nevertheless, of great importance for it determined, in part, the hymnody that was seen as worthy of consideration for inclusion.

These factors having been stated there was one unifying factor. There was a unanimous intention to stamp the book as Methodist. Eighty-two per cent of the texts in the first section of the book were present in contemporary Methodist books. Priority was given to hymns composed by the Wesley family (269 items), and Charles Wesley in particular (243 texts). Twenty-seven per cent of the material in the book came from these authors. This was a reduction over their representation in previous books[244] but was still substantial. Methodism was not to be denied Charles Wesley's magnificent rendition of Psalm 150, 'Praise the Lord who reigns above' (14), nor the enigmatic 'None is like Jeshurun's God' (68), which assumes a scholarly understanding of Scripture, referring to Deuteronomy 33.26 from which it takes its theme. The zenith of incarnational hymnody is represented with Charles Wesley's 'Glory be to God on high' (134) and 'Let earth and heaven combine' (142). Alongside Charles Wesley's passion hymns we find Samuel Wesley's 'Behold the Saviour of mankind' (193), a single inclusion from this author, while John Wesley's translations of German texts are found throughout the book. 'Father of all! whose powerful voice' (47) illustrates the willingness of the editors to explore their own heritage. Though written by John Wesley it was not extant in any of the contemporary Methodist sources.

In summary, what had been produced was a book that, if handed to a Wesleyan, would be recognised as being clearly representative of the denomination. It would not have been as familiar in feel to members

244 The *Wesleyan Methodist Hymn Book* had over 45 per cent.

of the other Methodist churches, those styled 'junior'[245] or, less pejoratively, 'smaller'[246] by the Wesleyans.

The Influence of the Wesleys

What place did the Wesleys' hymns have within the *Methodist Hymn Book*? The Wesleys dominate certain parts of the book. Turning to the section on 'Faith and Regeneration', we find that the logically structured progression is carried initially by six texts of Charles Wesley in succession. Indeed, only seven texts out of 21 are not by Charles Wesley and two of these are translations by John Wesley. 'The Communion of Saints: Christian Fellowship' is one of the most cohesive and logically structured sections of the book, again owing not a little of its consistency to the predominance of Charles Wesley's texts, these comprising no fewer than 11 out of 14.

The retention of hymns by Isaac Watts (44 items) as well as the Wesleys will be seen to be characteristic of a collection that is conservative in relation to Methodist tradition. It was agreed by the editors of the *Methodist Hymn Book* that the 'Historical Hymns of Methodism would be distinguished by a descriptive note',[247] and certain texts, for example 'Where shall my wondering soul begin' (361), are indicated by a preceding phrase or sentence in italics.

Methodism began as much with preaching as with song. It is not surprising then that the section on 'Ministers and Teachers' had all of 16 texts compared with 18 on the Lord's Supper. Ministry and teaching were imperative and characteristic of the denomination, while the Lord's Supper was seen, historically, to have been a sacrament of which Methodists should avail themselves in the denomination within which Methodism developed, the Church of England. Such a sweeping statement does, of course, have to be set alongside the fact that the Church of England of their day itself did not emphasise the importance of this sacrament, while John and Charles Wesley urged people to observe communion frequently, providing hymns specifically for the

---

245 Currie, *Methodism Divided*, p. 250f.
246 J. E. Rattenbury, *The Eucharistic Hymns of John and Charles Wesley*, London, Epworth Press, 1948, p. 151.
247 MARC 29/63.

occasion.[248] Nevertheless the Eucharist remained, for many Methodists, a sacrament secondary in significance to the 'sacrament' of preaching. This lack of emphasis on the Eucharist was a point of contention for some Wesleyans and the spur for the formation of the Methodist Sacramental Fellowship.

The competing calls of the uniting denominations and the unifying need to include material from the Wesley corpus appears to have left the editors with little room for additional material. The *Church Hymnary* and *Songs of Praise* provided some. The lack of items dating from after the Great War is noticeable.[249] Occasional items from outside of Methodism have been justified by Telford in *The Methodist Hymn-Book Illustrated*. For instance, he expressed the opinion that George Herbert's texts were made accessible for public worship through the attention paid to him by John Wesley,[250] six of his poems having been adapted for singing in *The Charles Town Hymn Book*,[251] and over 40 appearing in *Sacred Hymns and Poems*.[252] This looks like a conscious effort to allow for the inclusion of texts that had not received the imprimatur of consistent inclusion in the Wesleyan corpus. Communication with world-wide Methodism during the production of the book seems to have been limited. There is, for instance, little if any correlation with *The Methodist Hymnal*[253] of 1932 produced by the Methodist Church in the United States of America, though the book was available to the editors of the *Methodist Hymn Book*, and Rattenbury provides an Addendum on 'The American Orders' in his account of the eucharistic hymns of John and Charles Wesley.[254]

What the *Methodist Hymn Book* seems to offer, then, is a collection in which items from the Wesleys are present in significant numbers, but their influence had lessened with the passing of time. The book was not entirely dictated to from beyond the grave. Valuable texts had been written by other authors and some of these warranted inclusion.

---

248 See Rattenbury, *The Eucharistic Hymns of John and Charles Wesley*, which includes the texts of the hymns from the 1745 collection.

249 Spinney, *Tuned for Praise*, p. 15.

250 Telford, *The Methodist Hymn-Book Illustrated*, p. vii.

251 J. Wesley, *A Collection of Psalms and Hymns*, printed by Lewis Timothy, Charles Town, 1737.

252 Telford, *The Methodist Hymn-Book Illustrated*, p. 10.

253 *The Methodist Hymnal*, The Board of Publication, of the Protestant Methodist Church, Nashville, The Methodist Book Concern, 1932.

254 Rattenbury, *The Eucharistic Hymns of John and Charles Wesley*, p. 159.

Devotional Literature

Looking further through the book we begin to see its purpose.
Historically Methodists have regarded hymns as a devotional
resource[255] as well as for public worship. The section of the *Methodist
Hymn Book* entitled 'God' gives pause to reflect on this heritage.
Having begun by stressing the creative power of God, the texts move
through from the recognition of God as creator, to the providence of
God and the implication of divine love drawn from these observations. In another book the texts might have been arranged in alphabetical or metrical order, but here the primary consideration seems to
be devotional. The editors structured the hymn book to be used also as
a prayer book.

The book is a devotional resource. All that is lacking is a section
actually designated as 'Devotional',[256] and Mantripp was later to produce a book to enable the devotional use of the *Methodist Hymn
Book*. Reading through each hymn, one after another, in the section
'His Sufferings and Death', is a profoundly moving experience. It is as
though Jesus' death is held up like a crystal, turned this way and that,
one moment in shadow, the next in gleaming light. Understanding
deepens as we progress. Even without music we are brought
metaphorically to our knees, 'lost in wonder, love and praise'. We are
reminded of John Wesley's 1779 preface to the collection of 1780,
included after the preface to the *Methodist Hymn Book*, in which he
aspired to provide a 'little body of experimental and practical divinity'[257] for readers as much as for singers. This aspiration clearly
informed the editors of the *Methodist Hymn Book*. This same section
also shows that the material that was acceptable to the hymn book
committee was catholic in nature, by no means deriving from only one
Church tradition. Contributions by John Mason Neale, Edward
Caswall, and Frederick Faber are evidence of this fact. Texts of a popular nature are few and far between, those of Elizabeth Cecilia
Clephane (197), Elizabeth Rundle Charles (198) and Frances Jane van
Alstyne (199) being significant.

---

255 Ivor Jones has pointed out the difficulty that this imposes on those selecting and
assessing hymns for use in public worship. 'Pastoral Poetry and Hymnody', *Methodist
Recorder*, 19 September 2002, p. 15.

256 MARC 30/202.

257 *Methodist Hymn Book*, Preface, p. vii.

An entire section was provided for 'Home and Family Worship'. Devotional, home and family use of hymns was not anticipated by the editors of the contemporary *Standard edition of Hymns Ancient and Modern* (1922), the *English Hymnal* (New Edition) (1933) or *Songs of Praise* (1926, 1932), if the structure of the books is any guide. This is also true of the *Baptist Church Hymnal* published in the same year as the *Methodist Hymn Book* (1933).

A Victorian Hymn Book?

If the book was Wesleyan, in the denominational sense, influenced by the Wesleys and devotional in nature, where is it most comfortably placed from a cultural perspective?

Ian Bradley, examining the use of Victorian hymns in the twentieth century, notes that between the publication of the *Methodist Hymn Book* and *Hymns & Psalms* fewer Victorian tunes were lost than is apparent from an examination of other denominational sources.[258] He relates this to a renewed interest in Victorian hymnody in the 1980s. What is clear here is Bradley's lack of critical attention to the *Methodist Hymn Book*. He castigates *Songs of Praise* as being 'aggressively anti-Victorian',[259] while the *Methodist Hymn Book* emerges unscathed with barely a mention. Given Bradley's agenda, that of reclaiming the Victorian hymn, this implies that the *Methodist Hymn Book* was sufficiently aware of the heritage of Victorian hymnody to avoid his criticism.

Was the *Methodist Hymn Book*, in essence, a Victorian hymn book?

Texts relating to 'His Kingdom, Present and Future' illustrate a tension evident within the collection. Walter John Mathams' 'God is with us, God is with us' (252) with its sonorous triumphalism speaks of an age when 'men were men':

> 'God is with us, God is with us,'
> So our brave forefathers sang,
> Far across the field of battle,
> Loud their holy war-cry rang;

---

258 I. Bradley, *Abide with me*, London, SCM Press, 1997, p. 229.
259 Bradley, *Abide with me*, p. 224.

Never once they feared nor faltered,
Never once they ceased to sing –
God is with us, God is with us,
Christ our Lord shall reign as King!

Great the heritage they left us,
Great the conquests to be won,
Armèd hosts to meet and scatter,
Larger duties to be done,
Raise the song they nobly taught us,
Round the wide world let it ring:
Chorus

Speed the cross through all the nations,
Speed the victories of love,
Preach the gospel of redemption
Wheresoever men may move;
Make the future in the present,
Strong of heart, toil on and sing:
Chorus

Soon the struggle will be over,
Soon the flags of strife be furled;
Downward from his place defeated,
Shall the enemy be hurled;
Onward, then, with ranks unbroken,
Sure of triumph, shout and sing:
Chorus

This is the hymn of the public school boy who would fear nothing in
the face of the foe. Over against this the sensitive words of Dora
Greenwell (259) exhibit an understanding and interpretation of
Freudian psychology that, at the time of compiling the book, would
have been regarded as quite *avant garde*. The fourth verse speaks of
repressed emotions:

Each heart's deep instinct, unconfessed;
Each lowly wish, each daring claim;
All, all that life hath long repressed,
Unfolds, undreading blight or blame.

What is more surprising is the fact that this hymn was published as early as 1869.[260]

'Raise the Psalm: let earth adoring' (16) demonstrates the acceptability to the editors of the Victorian world-view that Mankin has described.[261] There is a mood of empire in which Britain and Christianity are synonymous and the movement is inexorable, for 'God is working His purpose out' (812). We read of a world brought under the jurisdiction of Christianity in which 'each kindred, tribe, and tongue' would 'Raise the new accordant song' (16). This authority would be sustained until the 'day of doom':

> Tell it out beneath the heaven,
> To each kindred, tribe, and tongue,
> Tell it out from morn till even
> In your unexhausted song:
> Tell that God for ever reigneth,
> He, who set the world so fast,
> He, who still its state sustaineth
> Till the day of doom to last.

In the Romantic Period and to some extent in the Victorian era which followed it, 'Doom' was not seen as a negative expression, but rather an indication of the end to which all creation was proceeding, this image being used somewhat more clearly in the third verse, which refers to 'righteous doom'. Even in the 1930s it is likely that this would have required explanation.[262]

The change in attitude following the First World War, which brought society to an understanding that spawned the League of Nations and fostered a view of universal fellowship throughout the world, seems not to have been understood. Many of the hymns within the collection derive unashamedly from the Victorian age when religion and colonial imperialism were closely bound. There is a tension illustrated here. Sometimes the book offers a contemporary world-view, at others a reactionary hankering after what had been prior to the Great War.

---

260 R. Watson and K. Trickett, *Companion to Hymns & Psalms*, Peterborough, Methodist Publishing House, 1988, p. 255.

261 Mankin, *How they sang on the way to Zion*, p. 14–34.

262 C. Annandale, *The Student's English Dictionary*, London, Blackie, 1911, already related 'doom' to 'an adverse issue'.

The historical setting of the origin of the book, between two world wars, and the experience, or lack of it, of active involvement of committee members in the Great War, seems significant. The poignancy of Elgar's Cello Concerto owes much to the effects of the war and it contrasts greatly with those pieces that the composer had written earlier. There is a sense of despair at the destruction of Edwardian values and culture that so epitomised much of his work. It is this that is lacking in the *Methodist Hymn Book*. The section concerned with 'Trustfulness and Peace' provides texts that explore the reality of those things that might disrupt our peace, but they are weighted towards the spiritual rather than the temporal. The *Methodist Hymn Book* feels Victorian, or at most Edwardian.

Only occasionally does sensitivity to the aftermath of the dissipation and carnage of the war appear. 'Lord God, by whom all change is wrought' (55) recognises that God brings about movement. In a time which had been undermined by traumatic change, this must have been particularly pertinent. 'Darkness and dread we leave behind' would have meant something different for the author, but the shadow of the second decade of the century might well have been in the minds of the editors. The hopefulness which characterises the hymn was appropriate to the inter-war years. This assured, optimistic note is echoed by the next text, 'Sweet is the memory of Thy grace' (56). 'In all my vast concerns with Thee' (57) originates from Psalm 139 and continues the theme.

The section on 'The Church in Prayer', reflecting the spirit of the Victorian church, is dangerously guilt-laden and lacking in any affirmation of human potential that might have been expected had the influence of Darwinism been allowed to influence the choice of texts.[263]

In spite of this, 'From glory to glory advancing' (30) from *Songs of Praise*, and attributed to the Liturgy of St James, offers a different though rare perspective. Here is a reflection on the path of sanctification which has the inexorable feel of a world bowled over by the claims of Darwinism that was beginning to feed the optimism of Victorian England.[264] Progress to a higher plane was unstoppable: 'Ever fit us by service on earth for / Thy service on high'.

---

263 Entering the twenty-first century, Patricia Williams has demonstrated where this process was leading. Patricia A. Williams, *Doing without Adam and Eve, Sociobiology and Original Sin*, Minneapolis, Fortress Press, 2001.

264 This contrasts with Mankin's observation that nineteenth-century Methodist

'Hymns for Week-Day Services' are extremely limited. Given the dominance of the Protestant work ethic and the prevalence of Methodist weekday activities this paucity is hard to explain, unless it reflects a decline in this form of association following the First World War.

The section on 'School and Work' is brief. It is logically placed between sections dealing with 'Children' and 'Home and Family Worship'. It presumes a Christian context for education in which education prepares for life, not just for work. A line like 'For Pisgah gleams of newer, fairer truth' assumes knowledge of, or leads to questions about, a biblical text.

> We bless thee, Lord, for all this common life
> Can give of rest and joy amidst its strife;
> For earth and trees and sea and clouds and springs;
> For work, and all the lessons that it brings;
>
> For Pisgah gleams of newer, fairer truth,
> Which ever ripening still renews our youth;
> For fellowship with noble souls and wise,
> Whose hearts beat time to music of the skies;
>
> For each achievement human toil can reach;
> For all that patriots win, and poets teach;
> For the old light that gleams on history's page
> For the new hope that shines on each new age.
>
> May we to these our lights be ever true,
> Find hope and strength and joy for ever new,
> To heavenly visions still obedient prove,
> The Eternal Law, writ by the Almighty Love!

Without such information the hymn (872) makes little sense. These are texts for the educated yet, at the same time, they provide a subtle means of social control as tempers are subdued and pupils sing themselves into a state of malleable acceptance of authority.

---

hymnody showed no reaction to the scientific challenge of the theory of evolution. Mankin, *How they sang on the way to Zion*, p. 204.

Day by day we magnify thee,
Not in words of praise alone;
Truthful lips and meek obedience
Show thy glory in thine own.

Day by day we magnify thee,
When for Jesu's sake we try
Every wrong to bear with patience,
Every sin to mortify. (867)

This is, again, a sign of Victorian, or class defined, cultural influence.
The section addressing 'Home and Family Worship' has a nine-teenth-century feel to it. The home is held in prayerful obedience even unto death.

Thou gracious God, whose mercy lends
The light of home, the smile of friends,
Our gathered flock Thine arms enfold,
As in the peaceful days of old.

Wilt Thou not hear us while we raise,
In sweet accord of solemn praise,
The voices that have mingled long
In joyous flow of mirth and song?

For all the blessings life has brought,
For all its sorrowing hours have taught,
For all we mourn, for all we keep,
The hands we clasp, the loved that sleep:

The noontide sunshine of the past,
These brief, bright moments fading fast,
The stars that gild our darkening years,
The twilight ray from holier spheres:

We thank Thee, Father; let Thy grace
Our loving circle still embrace,
Thy mercy shed its heavenly store,
Thy peace be with us evermore. (873)

Home is happy and idealistically presented as the cradle of God's children.

> O happy home, whose little ones are given
> early to thee, in humble faith and prayer,
> to thee, their Friend, who from the heights of heaven
> dost guide and guard with more than mother's care! (875)

There is an underlying assumption not only that the family will pray and read the Bible together but that they will sing together.[265]

Life is depicted as a battleground through which the Christian proceeds to heaven. In this battleground the temptation to sin must be overcome while, simultaneously, the believer copes with human suffering. The imagery is again Victorian or pre-Victorian, the language, largely, archaic. This is not to deny the power of the selected texts but more to make a comment on their dislocation from the human experience of those who were contemporary to the production of the book. Again we sense that the editors were living in a world that was detached from that around them. Nostalgia and comfort seem to have been greater motivating forces than relevance.

Francis Turner Palgrave demonstrated in his anthologising that he had an ear for that which was both popular and lasting in its appeal to the English poetry lover. He also demonstrated, in his text 'Thou say'st: Take up thy cross' (158), a skill in writing. The words would have been compatible with Pre-Raphaelite culture, seeking a more perfect artistic archetype from the past, though the vision that Palgrave seeks is that of Jesus. The language owes itself, like that of Frederick Faber, to the Romantic Movement, yet the whole tenor of the text is Victorian. In 1933 this would have provided a comfortable echo of a lost age.

Of all the sections of the book that are of a time before the Great War none is more so than the part of the section for 'National and Social Life' entitled 'King and Nation'. While some of the material here looks back on a nation's history to find a reason for faith (878, 885), much of what is presented finds its roots in empire and an unhealthy patriotism which, at times, passes through chauvinism to

---

265 A sense which has been preserved anachronistically in Cradle Rocking ceremonies in certain parts of the Methodist Church in Lancashire to the present day. Such a ceremony was observed accompanying a Baptism in Orrell Methodist Church, Wigan in 2002.

jingoism. The tenor is that of a triumphal nation in which others will find salvation. Britain is, as it were, God's ambassador. The words reflect an ethos in which it was appropriate, or seen as necessary, to engender nationalistic fervour.

In spite of the date of its production the *Methodist Hymn Book* is incontrovertibly a product that owes its ethos to a late Victorian culture. In part this culture is beginning to demonstrate a change mirroring that which took place as Edward VII came to the throne. There are some signs of optimism, some brighter facets. What is largely lacking is evidence of the profound change of perspective that came about as a consequence of the Great War.

After the War

Poetry written after the First World War reflected a sea change in the attitude of a generation. It left Europeans with 'an urge to see that war of that kind should be abolished from the earth'.[266] The inclusion of 'Behold the mountain of the Lord' (904) in the *Methodist Hymn Book*, with its stress that

> No longer hosts, encountering hosts,
> Shall crowds of slain deplore;
> They hang the trumpet in the hall,
> And study war no more.

though from an earlier generation, encapsulated the spirit of that age. To some it made way for nihilism with an overthrow of familiar structures. Those who had passed through this experience were never to be the same again, yet those who were too young or too old to share would never fully understand.

Lionel Adey has observed that: 'Without doubt late Victorian and Edwardian hymnody, notably for the young, encouraged the improper veneration of the nation-state.'[267] He continues:

Between the wars patriotic hymns declined in proportion and suffered a change of tone and focus. The nation, its confidence

---

266 E. Routley, *Christian Hymns Observed*, Oxford, Mowbray, 1983, p. 79.
267 L. Adey, *Class and Idol in the English Hymn*, Vancouver, University of British Columbia Press, 1988, p. 222.

eroded by the slaughter and subsequent unemployment, ceased by degrees to presume itself either self-sufficient or divinely sanctioned to rule and evangelise vast regions of the earth. In the quickly established Remembrance Day convention, hymns and prayers commemorated fallen members not so much of the nation as of the social community.[268]

'Turn back, O man, forswear thy foolish ways' (Bax) (912) begins to show evidence of an awareness of a changed attitude to war. The text calls humanity back to 'hear the inner God'. Empires are regarded as 'tragic' and sleep is 'haunted'. There is recognition of the need for all the world's people to be one that is contemporary in spirit with the formation of the League of Nations in 1920. The hymn was written in 1918.[269] 'God of our Fathers, known of old' (889) was criticised by Adey for its 'idolatrous use [of] the Old Testament myth of the Chosen People',[270] in suggesting that 'Dominion over palm and pine' had been given to Britain. The Old rather than New Testament provides the theme but the language is otherwise contemporary. In spite of this there is an underlying understanding that humanity is under God's justice; the author pleads for 'Thy mercy on Thy people, Lord!' While Bax had moved fully into the post-Passchendaele experience, Kipling, nevertheless, has an understanding that war is not all glory and that penitence must go along with praise.

The *Methodist Hymn Book* was influenced, to some degree, by the moral imperative that had been presented by the Great War. This can be demonstrated by an examination of the content of the section entitled 'National and Social Life'. The opening hymn is Isaac Watts' interpretation of Psalm 90, 'O God our help in ages past' (878). The first thing that must be noted is the choice of first line. The text originally began: '*Our* God our help . . .' The editors were in line with public preference (with the *Church Hymnary*, *English Hymnal*, and *Songs of Praise*) in avoiding words which might seem exclusive. The choice of text, however, broke no new ground for Methodists in that the *Primitive Methodist Hymnal* and the *Wesleyan Methodist Hymn Book* both used this version.

---

268 Adey, *Class and Idol in the English Hymn*, p. 222f.
269 Adey, *Class and Idol in the English Hymn*, p. 219.
270 Adey, *Class and Idol in the English Hymn*, p. 216.

From another perspective Goodwin has suggested that in the after-math of war there was a revival of religion (manifest particularly in 1923–26).[271] If the hymn book was sparsely equipped to provide material for this renewal, it is questionable as to how suitable the book was to meet the needs of worshippers during the inter-war years. Portraying 'Citizenship and Service' the editors sought to walk a tight-rope between the contemporary world vision for renewal of those like William Temple, and the intensely patriotic hymnody that saw citizenship in terms of duty to country which overrode all other claims. Amidst this it was natural that some of the material chosen would be humanistic in tenor, some clearly coming from Unitarian sources.

The collection moves naturally to a consideration of 'World Peace and Brotherhood'. The roots of hope are acknowledged as present in the Old Testament and, while a few texts call on God to bring peace, there is a healthy recognition of the part that people play, both in failure and in those actions that are likely to establish peace. Ebenezer Elliott's text 'When wilt Thou save the people' (909), though written before 1850 appears to be particularly redolent of those emotions brought about by the experience of the First World War.

> When wilt Thou save the people,
> O God of mercy, when?
> Not kings alone but nations;
> Not thrones and crowns, but men!
> Flowers of Thy heart, O God, are they;
> Let them not pass, like weeds, away,
> Their heritage a sunless day.
> God save the people!
>
> Shall crime bring crime for ever,
> Strength aiding still the strong?
> Is it Thy will, O Father,
> That man shall toil for wrong?
> 'No,' say Thy mountains; 'No,' Thy skies;
> Man's clouded sun shall brightly rise,
> And songs ascend instead of sighs:
> God save the people!

---

271 C. H. Goodwin, 'The Revival of Religion 1923–1926', *Proceedings of the Wesley Historical Society*, Vol. 51, Part 1, 1997, p. 11.

When wilt Thou save the people,
O God of mercy, when?
The people, Lord, the people!
Not thrones and crowns, but men!
God save the people; Thine they are,
Thy children, as Thine angels fair;
From vice, oppression, and despair,
God save the people!

Wakefield has commented that this section contained mainly pre-war (First World War) hymns. This fashion was followed by a reaction against humanism and the pendulum swung back.[272] The emphasis which we can see in the *Methodist Hymn Book* is as likely to have been caused by a hankering after past security, as much as any reaction against humanism.

John Greenleaf Whittier's poem 'Immortal Love, for ever full' is presented as two hymns, though neither is included in the section on 'World Peace and Brotherhood'. The first utilises this first line, and the second begins: 'O Lord and Master of us all' (103). The words have a modern sense of inclusiveness that is characteristic of the philosophy of the author and his heritage in the Society of Friends.

The section devoted to 'His Kingdom, Present and Future' has evidence of the social perspective of the gospel message. 'Hail to the Lord's anointed' (245) speaks of help being offered to the 'poor and needy'. 'He hath opened a door / To the penitent poor' provides a negative view of poverty. It is viewed as something to despise, and is allied to sin. This is an image that would have found a contemporary resonance among those editing the book and yet, by the time of its publication, in a context of depression and unemployment, was exceedingly unhelpful. This apart, the contents of the section are evangelistic and triumphalist rather than social in nature (unless the inclusion of 'My Heart and voice I raise' (115), included in the additional hymns, is noted). The texts look forward rather than picturing a realised eschatology. Such a theological perspective was not foreign to Methodism at this time. Berger has shown the presence of a thread of realised eschatological in Charles Wesley's hymns pointing to a

---

272 G. S. Wakefield, 'The Hymnody of the Past Fifty Years', *Bulletin of the Hymn Society of Great Britain and Ireland*, Vol. 6, No. 12, 1968–69, p. 240.

'heaven below'.[273] Perhaps this is a sign of the millennialist influence that is noticeable whenever there is a turn of century.

Both secular and religious poets responded to the effects of the Great War, as did artists and musicians. In contrast a reading of the *Methodist Hymn Book*, and compared with the *Wesleyan Methodist Hymn Book*, suggests that nothing as cataclysmic as the First World War had taken place between the production of one and the compilation of the other. The tenor of each is much the same and the changes in content that can be discerned are not in any way indicative of what has happened. The impression is of an evolving corpus that seems to have developed in isolation from the world, from reality.

Signs of Pressure

The *Methodist Hymn Book* is a catholic collection. The Editorial Committee does not seem to have pandered to the pressures of either the formal or less formal wings of the uniting denominations. The *Church Hymnary*, which was published in 1930, is very similar to the *Methodist Hymn Book*, suggesting that it had an influence on the editors or that the context in which the two editorial groups were working resulted in similar decisions being made. The content of the *Methodist Hymn Book* is evenly balanced between the Methodist denominational sources though, overall, the collection exhibits a strong Free-Church bias that largely mirrors the Wesleyan corpus.

What is surprising, is the very uneven editing of the book. Much of it proceeds in a sensible and well-ordered fashion with individual items effectively edited. This is not true of all of the book. For example, when addressing Christmas the editors did not follow the pattern of the liturgical calendar. The Epiphany hymn, 'Brightest and best of the sons of the morning' (122) precedes 'While shepherds watched their flocks by night' (129). There is evidence of poor editing of individual texts within this section. 'Give heed, my heart, lift up Thine eyes' (126) does not make logical sense as it stands. 'It came upon the midnight clear' (130) might have been more appropriately placed in the section 'National and Social Life – World Peace and Brotherhood'.

This could be accounted for by insufficient time being available for

---

273 Berger, *Theology in Hymns?*, p. 137–9.

the compilation of the book, a contention supported by contemporary evidence.[274] In addition the editors had to contend with the differing expectations placed on them by the denominations they represented and by factions within the individual churches.

The book was published late. Methodist Union had taken place. What should have been used as the hymnal at that Union was not even at the printers. There is evidence that the Editorial Committee had put in much extra work, that some choices were delegated to people outside the committee and that the Secretary had worked over the Christmas period in previous years. Examination of the hymn book suggests that the pressure under which the committee was working resulted in corners being cut.

A Literary Picture

Having looked at the book from a historical point of view, the question which must now be answered is: what literary impression does the book give?

Contemporary with the *Methodist Hymn Book*, Henry Bett wrote a critique of the hymns of Methodism (1913, 1920 and 1945).[275] For the most part Bett took as his source the hymns of the Wesleys. This study addressed the language of the hymns and their literary associations. Rattenbury examined the theological basis of Charles Wesley's hymns from the perspective of their evangelical doctrines[276] as well as providing a study of the eucharistic hymns of John and Charles Wesley.[277] Telford provided a largely uncritical commentary on the *Methodist Hymn Book*.[278] These books offer a contemporary perspective of the hymns, both included and excluded, from the hymn book.

Learned and Popular Texts

Firstly, within the book there is a distinct contrast between learned and popular texts. This distinction has been defined by Adey.[279] Wren

---

274 MARC 30/165.

275 Bett, *The Hymns of Methodism*, 1945.

276 J. E. Rattenbury, *The Evangelical Doctrines of Charles Wesley's Hymns*, London, Epworth Press, 1941.

277 Rattenbury, *The Eucharistic Hymns of John and Charles Wesley*.

278 Telford, *The Methodist Hymn-Book Illustrated*, passim.

279 Adey, *Class and Idol in the English Hymn*, p. x.

has observed that the style of hymns and religious songs is often a reflection of their purpose. He warns that an analysis of what is 'popular' or 'art' can become both patronising and damaging.[280] An examination of the *Methodist Hymn Book* shows that the tension of which Wren is aware has had its effect on the compilation of the book. It was reported in the *Methodist Recorder* that when it was seen fit to include chorus hymns the comment was made that 'the canons of literary merit used for the rest of the book' were suspended.[281] What, then, were these canons? Are they hinted at by the book itself? The John Wesley Preface which is reproduced in the *Methodist Hymn Book* states that:

1. In these hymns there is no doggerel; no botches; nothing put in to patch up the rhyme; no feeble expletives. 2. Here is nothing turgid or bombast, on the one hand, or low and creeping, on the other. 3. Here are no cant expressions; no words without meaning. Those who impute this to us know not what they say. We talk common sense, both in prose and verse, and use no word but in a fixed and determinate sense. 4. Here are, allow me to say, both the purity, the strength, and the elegance of the English language; and, at the same time, the utmost simplicity and plainness, suited to every capacity. Lastly, I desire men of taste to judge, (these are the only competent judges) whether there be not in some of the following hymns the true spirit of poetry, such as cannot be acquired by art and labour, but must be the gift of nature. By labour a man may become a tolerable imitator of Spenser, Shakespeare, or Milton; and may heap together pretty compound epithets, as 'pale-eyed', 'meek-eyed', and the like; but unless he be born a poet, he will never attain the genuine spirit of poetry.[282]

There is no evidence that this Preface provided guidelines for the editors and, even if it did, much interpretation would have been necessary in order to derive from it a workable set of standards by which to select and edit texts.

---

280 Wren, *Praying Twice*, p. 134.
281 *Methodist Recorder*, 1 December 1932, p. 14.
282 *A Collection of Hymns for the Use of The People Called Methodists*, London, Wesleyan Methodist Church, 1889, Preface.

An article carried by the *Methodist Recorder* (14 November 1929) expressed the hope 'that in the choice of new hymns every care will be taken to maintain the high level of literary expression to which Methodists have from the first been accustomed'.[283] Again, we do not know what the nature of such a standard might have been. Invariably such criteria are hard to define as the matters that they seek to measure are often subjective. Nevertheless, certain basic criteria could have been set but there is no contemporary evidence of this relating to the editing of the *Methodist Hymn Book*.

What can be discerned from the book itself? Robert Bridges' place as Poet Laureate, but also as an eminent hymnodist, provided an influence that was not lost on the editors. His contribution to hymnody was provided by the *Yattendon Hymnal*. The editors of the *Methodist Hymn Book* listed this as one of their original sources. Eight of Bridges' texts appear in the current volume. Two other Laureates, Nahum Tate and Alfred Lord Tennyson, had three texts each included, while John Dryden had one. The use of poetry as hymnody is not always effective, but some poets have written great hymns and these authors set the literary standard by which other writers are to be judged.

Against this benchmark writers of pure hymnody may sometimes fall short. Hymns are different in kind from unsung poetry. As an example, Nicol Macnicol's translation of Narayan Vaman Tilak's text 'One who is all unfit to count' (159) begins clumsily but taken as a whole gives humble expression to a sense of awe-filled adoration. The weakness and unworthiness of the author is contrasted with his Lord such that 'e'en the dust upon thy feet / Outweighs me utterly'. It is, perhaps, better poetry than hymnody. The purpose of hymns is that they should be sung and that requires an immediate recognition of purpose and clarity within the text, which is not needed in a poem that may be easily re-read. In addition, a hymn must be able to fit a tune. To this end not only metre but stress are important, the same pattern being followed from verse to verse.

The inclusion of George Herbert's texts is evidence of the pressure to provide 'good' poetry within the corpus. Watson's comment on Herbert is enlightening: 'His religious poetry is among the most moving and affective in the English language, though much of it is too

---

283 MARC 29/44.

complex and witty for hymn singing.'[284] Four of Herbert's texts were included.

Set against these writers John (as a translator) and Charles Wesley[285] fare well, as does Isaac Watts. The Wesleys and Watts are not alone. George Wither's 'Come, O come, in pious lays' (20) was adopted from the *Public School Hymn Book*. The language of these hymns seems to be responding to the hope expressed in the *Methodist Recorder* referred to above.

Translations from Latin, representing some of the best material of the Tractarian Movement, together with Catherine Winkworth's translations, continue this standard. John Mason Neale's translation of '*Vexilla Regis prodeunt*', 'The royal banners go forward' (184) is illustrative of this scholarly strand. The text had long been extant in the Christian tradition, though not in Methodism. A similarly erudite translation, by Edward Caswall, of a Latin text, '*Stabat Mater dolorosa*', is included as 'At the Cross, her station keeping' (185). Catherine Winkworth's translation of Joachim Magdeburg's '*Wer Gott vertraut, hat wohl gebaut*', 'Who puts his trust / In God most just' (495) ends with a bold affirmation of confident trust and a plea for renewal and peace.

Samuel Longfellow's poem 'Holy Spirit, truth divine' (288) echoes the theme of 'Come down, O Love Divine' (273) but the metre is not so extended, being 7.7.7.7, and the consequent expression less florid. Here is an economic and tightly woven text which uses a highly effective repeated but developing device in the first line of each verse, 'Holy Spirit, truth Divine', 'Holy Spirit, love Divine' and so on. It calls on the Spirit to enable the author to live a Christian life even though that life may, at times, seem to be lived in the context of a spiritual desert. The text is at once scholarly, yet accessible.

The editors seem to have chosen texts that were written by people whose poetic virtuosity and academic learning was self-evident. Poets Laureate and competent translators abound. In this company it is not surprising to find the poetry of Anne Bronte (352, 591, 592).

What do these examples tell us? It seems that it was more difficult

---

284 Watson and Trickett, *Companion to Hymns & Psalms*, p. 581.

285 The debate as to the authorship of Wesley hymns did not seem to exercise the committee. This is not surprising. What was of greater concern was the competition of one text against another for inclusion rather than who wrote what. Henry Bett was certainly cognisant of the question. See Bett, *The Hymns of Methodism*, p. 21–33.

for the editors to deal with material which was contemporary or taken from contemporary sources that were, as yet unattested. The lack of established criteria made it impossible for such material to be assessed in anything but a subjective manner. This is perhaps why the influence of Percy Dearmer and *Songs of Praise* is more limited than it might have been. In spite of the fact that *Songs of Praise* was the second most frequently used source outside of the Methodist corpus, Dearmer's ideas did not heavily influence, let alone constrain, the editors of the *Methodist Hymn Book*. An instance comes from the section of the book dealing with the incarnation. Here we might expect the editors, if they were adopting Dearmer's selections as definitive, to turn to the *Oxford Book of Carols*. Carols here are defined as 'songs with a religious impulse that are simple, hilarious, popular and modern' and it is noted that 'some of the English tunes were used by the excellent Methodists of the eighteenth century to preach their favourite doctrines'.[286] Clearly, though carols are not only associated with Christmas, many are and their inclusion within the section entitled 'His Incarnation' might have been expected. Only seven texts out of 27 included in the *Methodist Hymn Book* are also in the *Oxford Book of Carols*. The intention of the editors appears to have been to include hymns rather than carols, the distinction being the capacity of a hymn to explore and state theology over against a carol's generally celebratory nature. If the editors did not adopt Dearmer's work wholesale, neither were they omitting it entirely uncritically. Carols 'enjoy' Christmas whereas the selection presented here by the editors affirms the fact of incarnation and explores the consequence of that event. The criteria that the editors of the *Methodist Hymn Book* seem to have used were theological rather than literary, as might be expected. Altogether their approach is scholarly, though not without joy. This is ironic in that the work of the editors of the *Oxford Book of Carols* has also been deemed scholarly, and the content of this section of the *Methodist Hymn Book* was described as one of 'jolliness'.[287] The strength of the texts presented in the *Methodist Hymn Book* is indicated by the fact that, in spite of their origins, they have become popular. At this point, whatever their reasons, the editors of the

---

286 P. Dearmer, R. Vaughan Williams and W. Shaw, *The Oxford Book of Carols*, London, Oxford University Press, 1928 (23rd impression 1956), p. v.
287 *Methodist Recorder*, 8 December 1932, p. 2.

Methodist Hymn Book succeeded in choosing material that would last. Perhaps the human propensity to look back longingly to festivals of childhood was working in their favour.

The proportion of 'learned' or 'popular' material within the *Methodist Hymn Book* varies from section to section. In the opening part of the book the style of the majority of the texts is 'learned'; they are 'highbrow' but, for the most part, also 'singable'. Few are 'popular', of the style of a 'mission hymn', most exhibiting a sound poetic structure and being devoid of emotionalism. J. S. B. Monsell had commented on the reserved manner in which praise was offered to God[288] and 'O worship the Lord in the beauty of holiness' (9) sought to offer an antidote to this. The words are not lacking in dignity yet speak powerfully of the praise of God.

Within the section on the 'Gospel Call' there is a greater prevalence of 'popular' texts, though there are still a good number of more scholarly contributions, most notably from Charles Wesley and the single contributions of Frederick William Faber and John Mason Neale. Chorus hymns of a revivalist style feature prominently, many demonstrating the influence of Ira D. Sankey as an anthologist and populariser of texts.

Here is a swathe of texts that were chosen to which the implied criteria of the committee do not seem to have been applied. There is evidence that this section was edited by an individual outside the committee to whom the work was delegated. The pace at which the editors were working perhaps necessitated this.

Differences in literary taste across the denominations can also be discerned within the *Methodist Hymn Book*. Comparison of 'O God, my strength and footstool' (24) from the *Wesleyan Methodist Hymn Book* with 'Round the Lord in glory seated' (25) from the *Primitive Methodist Hymnal* and *A Collection of Hymns for the use of People called Bible Christians* illustrates different ways of exploring the nature of God. The first, a setting of a text by Thomas Sternhold from the sixteenth century, is an exploration of the care and providence of this awesome God. The latter, from the eighteenth century, lacks literary excellence ('Thus unite we to adore Him, / Bid we thus our anthem flow'), and is accompanied by a chorus providing, no doubt, a rousing sing, but little interpretation of Isaiah 6. 'Ye holy angels

---

288 Telford, *The Methodist Hymn-Book Illustrated*, p. 11.

bright' (26), however, demonstrates the poetic excellence to which some members of the Editorial Committee clearly aspired. 'Angels holy, high and lowly' (27) is altogether more fanciful, more Romantic in its theme. As the angels have praised God so all creation is bid to 'praise ye God the Lord'. Some of the rhymes are repetitive, gushing/rushing and winging/singing occurring in consecutive verses, yet, for all its imperfections, the hymn stimulates the imagination and then harnesses the thoughts produced in praise of God.

We move from this to Charles Silvester Horne's 'Sing we the King who is coming to reign' (116), based on a Christian interpretation of Isaiah 11.1–9. The words were written for C. H. Gabriel's tune 'The Glory Song' (an alternative tune by C. Luke Wiseman never gained great acceptance) and popularised by inclusion in Sankey's *Sacred Songs and Solos*. The whole tenor of the composition is revivalist and popular in its appeal. Wren points out that the structure of such hymnody allows those who have little grasp of written English the opportunity to participate by singing a memorable refrain.[289] A chorus also serves to underline the truth that the author has elaborated in greater detail in the intervening stanzas. 'Low in the grave He lay' (211) is a similar example. Its strident chorus no doubt added to its popularity. Wren's point serves to remind us that literary and theological criteria are not the only ones that are important when compiling a collection of hymns. The editors, however grudgingly, seem to have conceded this fact by including simple chorus hymns among those of greater literary stature. Nevertheless, hymns with repetition need not be vulgar, as Robert Walmsley's text 'Come let us sing of a wonderful love' (314) illustrates. Through the elegant use of four-syllable lines interspersed between longer lines, he gives a rhythmic feel to the hymn which serves the same purpose as a chorus, though only one phrase, 'Wonderful love', is actually repeated. The text is well matched to Wiseman's tune composed especially for it. Such is the depth of contrast seen within this collection.

The criteria that the editors have used in relation to the literary quality of the whole of the collection, as far as they can be inferred from the book, are as follows:

---

289 Wren, *Praying Twice*, p. 104.

1. To accept texts of which the literary merit had already been established, for instance, those of Poets Laureate and the Wesleys.
2. Overlaying such criteria was the need to represent theological interests that were not always provided for in pieces of recognised literary merit.
3. In addition the requirement of mission and evangelism, that of the repetition of truths in order that they might be reinforced, worked against the literary criteria that the editors would otherwise have wished to apply. In these instances the criterion of suitability to purpose, regardless of literary quality, was used in the selection of texts.

The Effectiveness of Language

The editors of the *Methodist Hymn Book* were faced with choices between literary quality and popularity, and also in relation to theological intent and the purpose of the hymns that they were selecting. What language was regarded as appropriate for these purposes? What evidence is provided by the hymns that were included in the final publication of the *Methodist Hymn Book*?

Metaphor, skilfully used, can enhance a text. That of sensory impairment and subsequent recovery is a common one used to represent conversion. William Tidd Matson used blindness, deafness, the inability to speak and death in his text 'Lord, I was blind! I could not see' (373). Blindness makes way for recognition of beauty, deafness for the thrill of music, speechlessness for the utterance of praise and death for life. The final stanza provides a summary. The editors exhibit no expression of sensitivity here to those who experience literal impairment.

The exacting nature of Catherine Winkworth's translations would appeal to those who sought for clarity of expression and intellectually sound poetry. 'Now thank we all our God' (10) was taken from her translation in *Lyra Germanica* (second series).[290] Rawson's 'With gladness we worship' (11) lacks the lyrical flow that Winkworth had achieved. Telford refers to Rawson's 'chaste and graceful language'[291] but, in this text, his use of rhyming couplets does not offer the sense of grandeur that the theme demands.

---

290 Watson and Trickett, *Companion to Hymns & Psalms*, p. 332.
291 Telford, *The Methodist Hymn-Book Illustrated*, p. 13.

The editors were balancing competing pressures of popularity and competence of lyrical construction. 'Come, let us all unite and sing' (22) has a light, joyful feel that would have resonated well with those who sought for 'hymns of wide popularity and proved spiritual helpfulness'[292] which were, nevertheless, not found within the Methodist corpus. 'King of glory, King of peace' (23) by George Herbert is of an entirely different school, demonstrating well the attempts which the editors made to encompass a range of material acceptable to those of widely differing tastes.

'All creatures of our God and King' (28) is a fine text, the repeated 'Alleluia' enabling the hymn to sustain a sense of praise from beginning to end. The language of 'All things praise Thee, Lord most high' (29) is vivid and evocative while it is poetically less effective. The enjambment of lines in verse two, 'All things praise Thee; night to night / Sings in silent hymns of light' and 'All things praise Thee; day to day / Chants thy power, in burning ray', interrupts the natural flow of the text, while the inverted word order in verse five, 'Omnipresent Spirit, *now*',[293] is unhelpful. This again provides evidence of the way in which certain material was included that might have been resisted by some members of the committee on literary grounds.

Oliver Wendell Holmes' 'Lord of all being, throned afar' (32) examines the theme of wonder and awe engendered by the created order. The author relates human experience to the perceived presence or absence of God, and his observation of nature to a biblically motivated understanding of God's activity. The text moves away from plain description to an interpretation of faith as illustrated within creation. Through awe the singer is drawn to petition and then dedication. It is no wonder that such a text should have found its way into all the contributory Methodist hymnals. His use of language is skilful.

A text need not be long or elaborate to be effective, as 'This, this is the God we adore' (69) illustrates. Simple language like that used by Christina Rossetti for 'In the bleak mid-winter' (137) can utter profound truths. Such writing requires great care. In spite of the discernment of the committee, a text like 'Jesus who lived above the sky' (146) that has rhymes that have descended to the level of clichés was included.

---

292 MARC 29/44.
293 My italics.

A continued examination of the *Methodist Hymn Book* shows that in almost every section texts are juxtaposed that exhibit on the one hand sensitive, and on the other bathetic, that is trite or trivial, use of language. Biblical texts are placed firmly in present reality by skilful writing such as that of John Hampden Gurney in 'We saw Thee not when Thou didst come' (148). The author may not have seen Jesus during his earthly ministry, 'We did not . . .', 'We stood not . . .', and so on, but he is convinced of the veracity of the witness of those who did. Some language appears contemporary but much is Victorian in manner and allusion. On occasion words can be used in a rather archaic, if not anachronistic manner. Singers of 'Hail the day that sees Him rise, Alleluia!' (221) need to be cognisant of the fact that the word 'pompous' at the time of the text's authorship meant 'magnificent'.

'To the name of our salvation' (93), John Mason Neale's translation of a fifteenth-century text, is overlaid with nineteenth-century images. The world is framed as 'this vale of misery'. This is all the more strange as other archaic turns of phrase are excised, for instance 'He that with a piteous eye / Looked upon our misery', this stanza having been omitted from 'Let us with a gladsome mind' (18).

The place of women writers is illustrated by the only hymn by Jean Ingelow to be included in the book. A minor poet of the nineteenth century, Ingelow's inclusion is significant for one stanza:

> Come, lest this heart should, cold and cast away,
>   Die ere the Guest adored she entertain –
> Lest eyes that never saw Thine earthly day
>   Should miss Thy heavenly reign.

Taken from 'And didst Thou love the race that loved Thee not' (149),[294] 'Die ere the Guest adored *she* entertain' speaks unashamedly of the author's own spirituality. Modern criticism, while acknowledging the cultural milieu in which the book is set, would wish to ask of it 'does it collude with or challenge a patriarchal perspective?' At this point the anticipated emendation of the text has not occurred. This is insufficient in itself to deem the book radical but it should not go unnoticed.[295]

---

294 J. Ingelow, *Poems*, 6th edition, London, Longman, Green, Longman, Roberts & Green, 1864, p. 30.

295 It is noteworthy that C. Ryder Smith had written in 1923 on the 'Bible Doctrine of Womanhood'.

An intrinsically conservative hymn by Francis Turner Palgrave, himself an almost exact contemporary of Ingelow, is also included in the book. 'Thou say'st: Take up thy cross / O man, and follow me' has a post-Romantic, Victorian mood. In the context of the *Methodist Hymn Book* this feels comfortable. At the time of publication it would have provided an encouraging and comforting remembrance of a lost (and longed-for) age. At the time these texts were written there was much female artistic talent available. Later in the book it is clear that the majority of the material coming from women is popular in nature and taken largely from Methodist Free Church or Primitive Methodist sources.[296]

A cursory reading of the *Methodist Hymn Book* shows that the language of the texts is sometimes plain and simple, at others florid. Imagery is often vivid. 'Jesus! the name high over all' (92), for instance, pictures fetters broken and Satan's head bruised.

There is a rich mix of material here. The language is varied. Frequently it was anachronistic, even at the time of editing, but passed without amendment. Sometimes it seems that hymns have been included on account of popularity rather than literary excellence. The process by which the members of the committee made their decisions is enigmatic. Questions of language and literary merit clearly provided many challenges for them and solutions to the problems that were raised inevitably led to compromise.

Hymn books are anthologies and, as such, are bound to have varied content. Nevertheless, the inconsistencies of editing and literary quality exhibited here are far wider than would be expected, and compare unfavourably with a book such as *Songs of Praise*. To some degree this is the inevitable consequence of the editing of the *Methodist Hymn Book* having been carried out by a committee instead of an individual.

With foresight it would have been possible to set specific criteria to enable members of the committee, sub-committees and individuals to work towards specific goals. The varied quality of the book, from hymn to hymn and section to section, suggests that such criteria were not established and this contention has been borne out by the account of how the book came into being.

---

296 See for example nos. 197, 198 and 199, which are present in a section that is largely scholarly in content.

4

The Hymn Book and
Methodist Worship

Having examined the way in which the *Methodist Hymn Book* came into being, and what it was like as a book, it now makes sense to look at the way in which it was of service to the Church. To what degree did it truly represent Methodist theology? How effectively did it meet contemporary needs?

When a hymn book is compiled those who edit it are subject to various expectations and constraints. Those who appoint the editors and those who are likely to use the book express their opinions. Members of an editorial panel come with their own expectations, hopes and prejudices. Not all of these will be written down but they are, nevertheless, real. The end product emerges having been subject to these pressures, but also constrained by various factors. Many factors influence the final form of a book. The time allotted for preparation, the skill and background of those involved in editing, the culture and historical setting in which the enterprise takes place, literary fashion, financial considerations and theology all have a part to play and must be considered. At the outset the structure of the book must be decided. This, together with many other factors, will influence the choice of contents.

In the case of the *Methodist Hymn Book* certain specific issues can be easily identified. The book needed to be clearly Methodist. This raised the question of theology. The task was not easy: Methodism held together those who took a literary-critical view of scripture[297] and those who were conservative evangelical; those who put into practice the priesthood of all believers and those who had a high Church view

---

297 The Revd W. T. Davison had faced a heresy charge in 1890–91 for promoting the adoption of modern critical methods.

of ordination; those who were pre-eminently sacramentalist and those who were not. Under-girding this was the recognition of theological themes that had permeated Methodism from the beginning, giving the movement its own particular shape and character. In the twenty-first century, as ecumenical ties are again being forged, Methodists might ask what theology they would wish to preserve in the hymnody they would share with the Church of England.

Secondly, the degree to which the book gave clear and visible representation to each of the uniting denominations had to be addressed. Again, in our contemporary context, the question raises itself as to what, if anything, is characteristic about the hymnody of the Church of England? In 1933, and still today, this narrower sense of ecumenism is set against a wider question. To what extent should a book be catholic, allowing for a greater variety of sources, and to what extent sectarian?

At a practical level choices had to be made between language which was seen as 'high brow' over against what was regarded as 'singable'. Which should be chosen? This also raised the question as to how to deal with 'popular material'[298] of questionable quality. The fact that such criteria were used by the 1933 Hymn Book Committee is testified to by the admission that literary standards were suspended when chorus hymns were being considered.[299] So we are faced with a conundrum. The editors themselves seem to have set standards. They never committed them to paper and they suspended their application when it suited them or, if we are charitable, when pressures caused them to suspend them. In effect they could include or exclude any material at all.

The manner of the working of the committee was determined by the attitudes of those who served on it and whether they had come from a tradition which was authoritarian or more democratic. All of this was set against the back-drop of a society recovering from the Great War, which Routley regards as having 'left an *affective* trauma: a sense of shock and profound suffering',[300] on those involved in it.

---

298 The distinction between learned and popular texts has been discussed in depth by Adey, *Class and Idol in the English Hymn*, p. x.

299 *Methodist Recorder*, 1 December 1932, p. 14.

300 Routley, *Christian Hymns Observed*, p. 79.

A Theological Picture

The structure adopted for the book is the first indication of the theological perspective that had been taken by the Editorial Committee. The contents follow the outline of a traditional preaching service. God is adored, Jesus is worshipped, his life and work is described, the Holy Spirit is invoked, the gospel is proclaimed and the people respond. The goal of this progression is a future life that is accessed through death and judgement. To reach this point takes one through 658 hymns. The intent is practical. The remaining third of the book is effectively a set of appendices addressing worship as a subject, prayer, sacraments, mission, the place of children, social interaction and times and seasons. This is a theology based on worship. For Methodists there is a precedent. Teresa Berger has identified a similar relationship between the theology of hymns and worship based on her study of *A Collection of Hymns for the Use of The People Called Methodists.*[301]

It is frustrating that the Hymn Book Committee left no papers that give a hint as to how the final structure of the book was arrived at. Reading through the material that has been preserved it becomes apparent that a draft list of contents was drawn up. The steps that were taken to arrive at this point are not clear. It is only possible to read back from the material to hand, and in this way to postulate what might have been the pressures that caused choices to be made. A brief comparison of the uniting denominations' hymn books with that of the *Methodist Hymn Book* shows where the *Methodist Hymn Book* is following one or other source and where it is in any way novel. It is from this sparse information that the reasons for particular choices, and the theological persuasion which prompted them, must be found.

What alternatives were open to the editors of the *Methodist Hymn Book* and why was this particular structure chosen? To begin with, the pattern that had been chosen by John Wesley for *A Collection of Hymns for the Use of The People Called Methodists*[302] was abandoned. This is not surprising as John Wesley had constructed his book as a tool for evangelism, and the deepening of faith. It was to be used by a movement *within* a church. The remnants of the influence of

---

301 Berger, *Theology in Hymns?*
302 *Works of John Wesley*, Vol. 7, *A Collection of Hymns for the Use of The People Called Methodists*, ed. F. Hildebrandt and O. A. Beckerlegge.

that book are apparent in the sections of the uniting denomination's hymn books related to the Gospel (entitled 'Man' in the *Primitive Methodist Hymnal*). During the nineteenth century Methodism had moved beyond the confines of Anglicanism and needed to provide not just a supplement to the worship of a mother church, but a resource for the whole of it. This development led to the provision of many books.[303] The structure of these books varied from a Supplement to John Wesley's book to completely new collections. By 1912 each denomination had its own collections that were to be the starting point for the new book. Even the Wesleyans had, by now, abandoned John Wesley's original format.

The structure adopted by each of the uniting denominations for their hymn books is related to the purpose to which those hymns were put and the theology they sought to express. A comparison of the contents of the books is provided in the Appendix.[304] What is clear from this comparison is the closeness with which the *Methodist Hymn Book* follows the structure of the *Wesleyan Methodist Hymn Book*.

The differences are worthy of comment:

1. the addition in the *Methodist Hymn Book* of a sub-section entitled 'Week-day Services', not present in any of the uniting denominational hymnals;
2. the addition of a considerable number of hymns for children in a section in their own right;
3. the addition of separate sections for 'School and Work', Home and Family Worship' and 'National and Social Life'.

The nature of society, and the Church set within that society, was changing. Wealth built by the imperial expansion of Victorian England had enabled the developing middle classes to have time for occupations other than work. Philanthropic employers extended this advantage to their workers. The Edwardians discovered leisure. The nature of Sunday was altering.

Following the First World War the sense of close association felt by

---

303 Telford lists 15 books which had afforded a resource to the uniting denominations from the time of John Wesley's death to the point of union. This is a minimal list. Telford, *The Methodist Hymn-Book Illustrated*, p. vi. See Mankin, *How they sang on the way to Zion,* for a study of these books.

304 See Appendix 1.

those returning from the trenches, together with the reduction in class distinctions, led to the formation of many groups within society designed to bring people together. The Churches, as part of that trend, were now, more than ever, actively trying to provide holistically for the life of their adherents, offering weeknight evening activities of an organised nature as well as worship on Sundays. The compilers of the hymn book sought to facilitate these meetings. Children were being viewed differently than in Victorian England. They were no longer miniature adults and now called for recognition in their own right. Hymns for children had been written before, and included in hymn books, but the need for a separate section was recognised. The arrangement of the *Methodist Hymn Book* reflected all these changes.

It now becomes clear that the place of the *Methodist Hymn Book* is in lineal progression from the *Wesleyan Methodist Hymn Book*. Even in the way that the book has been arranged, one can see that its purpose is to provide a book primarily for worship rather than an evangelistic tool. The nature of God, while clearly Trinitarian, is understated in a manner which presumes that people are being reminded of what they know, rather than being taught from first principles. The book is 'meat' rather than 'milk'. Judgement is something that will be part of the process of death and is not placed in an early, dominant position within the collection where it might influence thoughts of repentance or conversion. The Christian is viewed, for the most part, as a person enabled by God to be a good citizen, rather than one striving to emulate Christ. We are to be 'changed from glory into glory' by God. Consequently our relationship to the world and our commitment to change the world is secondary. The book is not particularly radical. It is for those with a 'love that asks no question [. . .] the love that pays the price'.

There is a paucity of hymns on the Judgement and no section on Temperance or Evangelism. Texts for such as back-sliders are well hidden. The feel of the book is that of 'church' rather than 'chapel'. It has a Wesleyan stamp.

This is a very brief overview of the structure of the *Methodist Hymn Book*. It is necessary now to look in more detail to determine the way in which theological and other choices influenced its genesis.

The Nature of God

The understanding of God espoused by the Methodist Church of all denominations was of a God of power and authority. This was an almighty God, a God who inspired awe. What was lacking was the sense of reprobation associated with Calvinism. John Wesley had been restrained in his critique of Calvinism, Charles less so.[305] What neither of them had accepted was double predestination.[306] They believed in universal grace. Such grace prevented the condemnation of those who accepted salvation through faith. While the reality of judgement was never underestimated by the Wesleys, the potentially universal nature of salvation that could ensue led to what some would regard as compromise when it came to this issue. Such a conclusion would be an unfair assessment of the Wesley brothers but it was to cause tension within the new Methodist Church. The issue of popular Calvinism had, however, been put to rest long before Union.

God was a creative and providential deity. God was Trinitarian working out, through the action of Jesus and the Holy Spirit, a salvific purpose in creation. It is now necessary to look at the way the *Methodist Hymn Book* allowed for this understanding of God and sought to resolve the tensions inherent in it.

The book opens with 'O for a thousand tongues to sing' (1).[307] The faithful are called to worship. This is the purpose of humanity as stated in the Westminster Confession. The following texts (2, 3, 4, 6, 7 and 8) provide vehicles to elicit awe in the presence of God. 'Let all the world in every corner sing' (5) makes it clear that such worship is a universal expectation. The theme of praise is 'Too high . . . For mortal tongue' (26), capturing the essence of transcendence, yet this God can be worshipped in gladness (11) and thankfulness (10) as well as awe. 'Praise to the living God!' (15) was a new introduction to British Methodism:

305 Rattenbury, *The Evangelical Doctrines of Charles Wesley's Hymns*, p. 120.

306 John Wesley presented predestination as a doctrine full of blasphemy: 'The grace or love of God, whence cometh our salvation, is free in all and free to all . . . The doctrine of predestination is not a doctrine of God . . . [it] tends to destroy the comfort of religion, the happiness of Christianity . . . this uncomfortable doctrine also destroys our zeal for good works . . . [the doctrine of predestination] hath also a direct and manifest tendency to overthrow the whole Christian revelation'. A. C. Outler, *The Works of John Wesley*, Vol. 3, Sermons III, Nashville, Abingdon, 1986, p. 544–59.

307 Numbers in brackets indicate the numbering of hymns within the *Methodist Hymn Book*.

Praise to the living God!
All praise be to His name,
Who was, and is, and is to be,
For aye the same!
The One Eternal God
Ere aught that now appears:
The first, the last, beyond all thought,
His timeless years!

Formless, all lovely forms
Declare His loveliness;
Holy, no holiness of earth
Can His express.
Lo, He is Lord of all!
Creation speaks His praise,
And everywhere, above, below,
His will obeys.

His Spirit floweth free,
High surging where it will:
In prophet's word He spoke of old,
He speaketh still.
Established is His law,
And changeless it shall stand,
Deep writ upon the human heart,
On sea, on land.

Eternal life hath He
Implanted in the soul;
His love shall be our strength and stay,
While ages roll.
Praise to the living God!
All praise be to His name,
Who was, and is, and is to be,
For aye the same!

The text had been published in the *American Union Hymnal* (1885). Translated from a Jewish Doxology, '*Yigaddel Elohim chay weyishtabach*', the text focuses on the eternal nature of God but also refers to Platonic philosophical ideas of form and perfection.

Most of the novel material in this section comes from *Songs of Praise* and the *Church Hymnary*. Not all the new material is scholarly. 'Come, let us all unite and sing' (22), though not having a chorus, relies on the repetition of 'God is love!' no less than 12 times in four stanzas. This hymn was taken from the *Christian Endeavour Hymnal*. The influence, albeit weak, of the evangelical parts of the new denomination can be seen.

God's claim is universal: 'Before Jehovah's awful throne' acknowledges that

> Wide as the world is Thy command;
> Vast as eternity Thy love;
> Firm as a rock Thy truth shall stand,
> When rolling years shall cease to move. (3)

This is a text indicative of the Arminian theology of historic Methodism. Throughout this section the hymns chosen provide a sense of wonder and awe engendered by the created order. Such reflection can lead towards Deism or Pantheism. The former is not altogether avoided. 'The spacious firmament on high' (44) reflects John Addison's persuasion that 'faith and devotion naturally grow in the mind of every reasonable man, who sees the impressions of divine power and wisdom in every object on which he casts his eye'.[308] This is, nevertheless, a fine text invoking awe by the cosmic compass of its imagery derived from the first three verses of Psalm 19.

This sense of grandeur is maintained by the inclusion of William Kethe's 'My soul, praise the Lord' (45). This text was adopted from the *Oxford Hymn Book*. The hymn draws us from reflection on the immensity of the cosmos to cornfields and vineyards that provide sustenance and joy offering to 'gladden' the singer's 'heart with good wine'. The text encompasses all living things of the earth and the seas. The fierceness of 'the wild waters' and 'rude wind' do not pass unnoticed. All of these point to the greatness of God.

Isaac Watts's 'I sing the almighty power of God' follows. The text is structurally less complex yet, through Watts's skill, is still imbued with a sense of awe and magnificence in spite of the choice of Common

---

308 J. Addison, quoted by Telford, *The Methodist Hymn-Book Illustrated*, p. 38.

Metre for the setting. Watts, characteristically, takes us a step beyond meditation and praise as he reflects on God's providential care.[309]

Charles Wesley's translation of '*Te Deum laudamus*', 'Infinite God, to Thee we raise' (33), characteristically ranges through the scriptures demonstrating the body of praise with which the Christian joins when offering oblations to God. Patriarchs, prophets, martyrs and apostles uphold the strain glorifying the 'Father of endless majesty'. The section concludes by praising God: 'For the beauty of the earth' (35).

The purpose of the editors is clear, and consonant with the under-standing of natural theology that would have been acceptable across the uniting denominations. The excesses of Unitarianism are avoided as the manifestations of God perceived in the created order are placed firmly alongside the revelation of Scripture.

Having acknowledged God as Father the book now underlines emphatically that it is portraying faith in a Trinitarian God. Reginald Heber's 'Holy, holy, holy, Lord God Almighty' (36) is poetically economical yet conveys a sense of awe which elicits worship, as does Charles Wesley's 'Hail! Holy, holy, holy Lord!' (37). Each is Trinitarian in content. 'Father of Heaven, whose love profound' (38) is penitential and, like the two following hymns in the book, has a Trinitarian structure, focusing on different persons of the Trinity as it builds from verse to verse.

The needs of the Bible Christians to have a clear and unambiguous expression of Christian Doctrine are being met in these texts. The texts are strong enough in scriptural and literary terms to provide 'meat' for the believer. Equally, they offer a sound pedagogical basis for ground-ing the newly converted in a Methodist perspective of what it means to be Christian.

God is active in creation and providence, yet this same God is immutable. 'God is a name my soul adores' (41) records the manner in which creation changes while 'no succession' is known to God.[310] Mortals live as part of the created order but cannot approach or look upon the light that is God. The transcendent view of the nature of God continues to be reinforced.

In spite of this God is not remote and the care of God continues to be acknowledged. 'Father of all! whose powerful voice' (47) illustrates

---

309 See also Isaac Watts's 'Nature with open volume stands', *Hymns & Psalms* 174.
310 *Methodist Hymn Book*, 41, verse 3.

that God is a guardian in times of temptation and provides for the needs of his children not only in a physical but also in a spiritual sense. The allusions in the hymn are scriptural: 'Thou cloth'st the lilies of the field, / And hearest the young ravens cry'. The sense of the saints being God's 'peculiar charge', is also emphasised by Isaac Watts's 'High in the heavens, eternal God' (48). The theme is continued by other texts. An evangelical imperative is provided by Charles Wesley's hymn, 'Thy ceaseless, unexhausted love' (49), for this care is not exclusive but something into which all people should be drawn. Anti-Calvinist polemic is established while the images that in other authors pointed to God are now used as metaphors for the attributes of God. God's love is providential. A number of texts inspired by Psalm 23 are offered. God is perceived to be present for the believer in times of difficulty.

The strength of this section of the book perhaps points to the need to affirm the providence of God following the Great War. Up to this time it was relatively easy to speak of God's providence. It is human to die. All families were familiar with death. What the Great War did was to bring the fact of death in war home to the masses. This was partly due to the gross nature of the carnage that was experienced; hardly a family was left without loss. Mass communication was in its infancy but newspapers and the writings of poets such as Wilfred Owen and Siegfried Sassoon served to underline the horror. In the light of this, material that was realistic, yet at the same time comforting, was necessitated. In spite of this the section is shorter than its equivalent in the *Wesleyan Methodist Hymn Book*. It is also worth noting that the number of texts that underline judgement and damnation (collected elsewhere in the book[311]) reduced and that this brought complaints from the floor of Conference, particularly from Dr Kirtlan.[312]

The theme of God's providence and care is further underlined by hymns which follow. 'The Lord Jehovah reigns' (58) provides a peroration and is a summary of all that has gone before. The glory of God is underlined, wrath and justice are balanced by love, truth and grace. The deity is regarded as self-evident in creation and having dominion over the 'powers of hell'. This same God, it is implied, be may regarded as both Father and friend. The appropriate response is

311 Hymns 639–658.
312 *Methodist Times*, 2 July 1932.

indicated in the closing lines: 'I love His name, I love His word, / Join all my powers to praise the Lord'. Such a God would be expected to pardon sinners and to seek their redemption. Charles Wesley's hymn of universal mercy and love, 'Good Thou art, and good Thou dost' (59), sets the scene. The expansive nature of God's love is delineated for 'Millions of transgressors poor / Thou hast for Jesu's sake forgiven' and yet 'Millions more Thou ready art / To save, and to forgive'. The thrust of the text is gracious and personal for the author wishes to be included: 'Tell me now, in love divine, / That Thou hast pardoned me'.

The picture of God presented by the *Methodist Hymn Book* is one of awe and wonder yet this is not overlaid with the sense of judgement that had pervaded previous collections. We search in vain for a section of hymns entitled 'Judgement', which was present in the *Primitive Methodist Hymnal*. Gone are hymns such as Isaac Watts's 'How sad our state by nature is!' which was present in the *Wesleyan Methodist Hymn Book*:

> How sad our state by nature is!
> Our sin how deep it stains!
> And Satan binds our captive minds
> Fast in his slavish chains.
>
> But there's a voice of sovereign grace
> Sounds from the sacred Word –
> Ho! ye despairing sinners, come,
> And trust upon the Lord.
>
> My soul obeys the almighty call,
> And runs to this relief;
> I would believe Thy promise, Lord;
> O help my unbelief!
>
> To the dear fountain of Thy blood,
> Incarnate God, I fly;
> Here let me wash my guilty soul
> From crimes of deepest dye.

> A guilty, weak and helpless wretch,
> On Thy kind arms I fall;
> Be Thou my strength and righteousness,
> My Jesus and my all.

Here we are more likely to sing

> How happy every child of grace
> Who knows his sins forgiven!
> This earth, he cries, is not my place,
> I seek my place in Heaven,
> A country far from mortal sight;
> Yet O by faith I see
> The land of rest, the saints' delight,
> The Heaven prepared for me! (627)

The tone is more optimistic. The human condition is filled with promise and this is reflected in the image of God's attitude towards humanity. God's claim is universal: 'it never passed by one' (77). The understanding is Arminian, though three items by John Cennick (who had parted from John Wesley's preachers over this doctrine) are included.

In all of this there is nothing entirely new but the emphasis has clearly moved. Experience of a world war had confronted people with their own mortality. They were, perhaps, less self-righteous. From such a circumstance we are less likely to judge others, for judgement is invariably presented from a position of supposed moral certitude. The *Primitive Methodist Hymnal* began with 'Eternal power whose high abode / Becomes the grandeur of a God'. Utilising images from Isaiah 6 the vision is of a remote and awe-inspiring God. 'Before Jehovah's awful throne' (*Methodist Free Church Hymnal* No. 1) states the case more clearly. The editors of the *Methodist Hymn Book* follow the *Wesleyan Methodist Hymn Book* in placing 'O for a thousand tongues to sing / My great redeemer's praise' (1) as the first text. The God they seek to worship is at once approachable, but worthy of such praise that human tongues need to be assisted by the divine (26), a conviction given expression by 'Ye holy angels bright', a hymn new to Methodism, though published first in 1627,[313] taken from the *Church*

---

313 Watson and Trickett, *Companion to Hymns & Psalms*, p. 47.

Hymnary. Praise is enabled by texts ranging from an interpretation by Charles Wesley of the '*Te Deum laudamus*' (33) to 'Praise to the living God' (15) taken from a translation attributed to Max Landsberg and Newton Mann, both of whom died in the 1920s.

The attributes of God which are emphasised are those of creativity, providence and mercy. The nature of God's being, as understood by the editors, is firmly Trinitarian. Again this is nothing new and reflects the foundation of Methodist theological understanding. This, however, did not prevent some texts of Unitarian origin, such as those of Samuel Longfellow, F. L. Hosmer and Edmund Hamilton Sears,[314] finding their way into the corpus.

The editors of the *Methodist Hymn Book* chose texts that engender a sense of awe and enable worship without, for the most part, alluding to the fearful characteristics of the Godhead. This God is a shepherd who is caring and approachable, even if seated on an 'awful throne'. God will judge the 'quick and the dead' but there is an understanding that the judgement will be enacted with mercy. Following the Great War such a picture is to be expected. There had been sufficient temporal horror without compounding it with horrendous eternal expectations. The impression is given that salvation is the end that God wants for his people. In the meantime worship in elegant hymns of praise is to be the order of the day.

Incarnation

For Methodists Jesus was the 'Son of Thy Sire's Eternal Love'[315] (found in the *Methodist Hymn Book* and *Hymns & Psalms* as 'Eternal Son, eternal love'). The sense of mercy that was attributed to God continued with a theology that required the love of God to be incarnate in Jesus. What was anticipated was a 'philanthropy divine',[316] a sense of the overwhelming love of the Godhead toward humanity finding expression in human form. John Wesley, in commenting on John 1.14, had expressed it like this:

---

314 It must be noted that not all these texts arrived without amendment.

315 Bett, *The Hymns of Methodism*, p. 86. Henry Bett, who wrote first prior to Methodist Union and then revised his work after the Union, underlined the centrality of the works of Wesley in any hymnody that deserved the name 'Methodist' and derived his theology as much from those hymns as from John Wesley's sermons or notes. His Wesleyan position was held even more tenaciously than that of Wiseman, but he also valued the literary qualities of Wesley's hymns.

316 Bett, *The Hymns of Methodism*, p. 91.

. . . in order to raise us to this dignity and happiness, the eternal Word, by a most amazing condescension, was made flesh, united Himself to our miserable nature, with all its innocent infirmities.[317]

This was allied with an understanding, already noted, of universal grace so that this person, Jesus, would become the saviour of all humankind.

Incarnation, redemption and salvation are bound up in one and, as a consequence, the hymns here speak not just of Christmas but also of the whole of salvation history and, in doing so, serve this theological understanding well.

The kenotic giving of God to the world is central. Charles Wesley's 'And can it be' (271) suggests that: 'So free, so infinite His grace – [God] Emptied Himself of all but love'. There is no evidence of debate within the committee over the inclusion of this text, though a text with a similar quotation,[318] 'High above every name', found in the 'Incarnation' section of the *United Methodist Free Church Hymnal*, has been omitted. Redemption, as has been noted, is dependent on the incarnation and the theme is strongly represented. 'Hark! The herald-angels sing' (117) speaks of 'the incarnate Deity' who mildly 'lays His glory by' and is born, 'Offspring of a virgin's womb! / Veiled in flesh'. In this way people will receive 'second birth', 'Light and life to all He brings, / Risen with healing in His wings'. The closing lines work so well there is a suspicion that they might be contrived, until it is recognised that the 'Sun of Righteousness' is that figure spoken of in Malachi 4.2. The text recounts the triumph of salvation anticipated in the incarnation for this will result in 'Peace on earth' with 'God and sinners reconciled'. 'O come all ye faithful' (118) speaks of the one who is adored as 'Begotten, not created', 'Word of the Father, / Now in flesh appearing'. An uncharacteristically clumsy translation of this text, by John Ellerton, to be found in the *United Methodist Free Church Hymnal*, has not been included. Clearly the editors had an eye to elegance of expression as well as the integrity of theology.

The incarnation is announced by messengers from heaven. 'Angels from the realms of glory' (119) pictures angels, who were present at creation, proclaiming the birth of Jesus. This epiphany is for the

---

317 J. Wesley, *Explanatory Notes upon the New Testament*, London, Epworth Press, 1976, p. 304.
318 'Emptied of all but love', *United Methodist Free Church Hymnal*, No. 69.

shepherds in the fields (129) and for the 'Wise men seeking Jesus' (862). This latter text was adopted from the *Wesleyan Methodist School Hymnal* of 1911. The pastoral allusion of verse 6, 'Every peaceful village', is anachronistic for people living in an increasingly industrial society. The season has a universal significance. Believers are expected to celebrate the event: 'Christians awake, salute the happy morn' (120).

The context in which Methodists were to enjoy Christmas was unexpectedly Catholic. Edward Caswall was an Anglican who followed Newman into the Roman Catholic Church. His hymn, 'See, amid the winter's snow' (124), begins with an allusion to the Victorian picture of Christmas but soon begins to explore the incarnation narrative and to give expression to its consequences. It is God who is born. It is God who calls forth the praise of shepherds and angels. Such a child must 'teach us to resemble Thee, / In thy sweet humility'. While his text is acceptable thus far, the editors saw cause to omit the seventh verse of the original:

> Virgin Mother, Mary blest,
> By the joys that fill thy breast,
> Pray for us that we may prove
> Worthy of the Saviour's love.[319]

To call on Mary in this way was theologically unacceptable for Methodists.[320]

The text had already found its way into the *Church Hymnary*, from which it was adopted along with the preceding item, 'Still the night, holy the night' (123). The editors did not avoid sentimental Victorian pictures of Christmas.

While Caswall's Marian verse had been expurgated the place of Mary was clearly defined elsewhere. Charles Wesley's 'Behold the servant of the Lord!' (572), retaining as it does a very human view of Mary, was altogether more acceptable. To apply to this text any sense of feminist allusion would not only be revisionist but also wrong, for although Mary is depicted as able to be God's servant, this is no more than Scripture warrants and the picture painted is submissively sub-servient rather than strong.

319 Watson and Trickett, *Companion to Hymns & Psalms*, p. 101.
320 Newton, *Heart Speaks to Heart*, p. 87.

Editing of texts is not only apparent in relation to references to Mary. 'It came upon the midnight clear' (130), written by the Unitarian Edmund Hamilton Sears, was amended when first published in England in 1870[321] to remove a humanist reference to the return of an 'age of gold'. Such a reference had been pertinent in the context in which it had been written and offered a suitable foil to materialism. While it might have been expected that this reference would be reinstated, being in line with the pessimism immediately following the Great War, the humanist allusion was, perhaps too great for the editors to accept. The ethical strength of the hymn, based on the song of the angels (Luke 2.14), is self-evident. The presence of hymns by Unitarian authors is something that some members of the Editorial Committee would have undoubtedly found suspect. Unitarians were, by definition, doctrinally unsound. Wesleyans had previously got round this issue in published hymn books by not printing the author's name after a text. This was the pattern followed in the *Wesleyan Methodist Hymn Book*. Clearly this was not a prejudice held by all the committee, as Martineau's *Hymns of Praise and Prayer* was listed as one of the sources that was used in compiling the *Methodist Hymn Book*. Following Martineau they seem to have conceded that

> the dogmatic phraseology and conception of every church constitute the mere dialect in which its religious spirit is expressed; and to change the technical modes of thought peculiar to any portion of Christendom into a different or more comprehensive language, is but to translate the intellectual idioms of one religious province into those of another.[322]

While Martineau would have seen his action as universalising, consonant with Unitarianism, such a process would have seemed less amenable to more dogmatic Methodists who deemed that doctrine was enshrined in precision of language. It can only be assumed that the editors were pressed to inclusion by the popularity of the material that was before them and that necessary amendments met with their approval.

---

321 *Hymnal Companion to the Book of Common Prayer* (1870); noted by Watson and Trickett, *Companion to Hymns & Psalms*, p. 96.

322 J. Martineau, *Hymns for the Christian Church and Home*, London, Longmans, Green and Co., 1887, Preface, p. xi.

Although, overall, this hymn book is more for those already in the fold than for those outside, the evangelistic imperative is not entirely lost. 'Cradled in a manger meanly' (127) moves beyond the personal plea for God to enter the singer's heart by asking that the message of Christmas might go to those who never listened, 'Who have winter but no Christmas / Bringing them Thy peace on earth'. The weight of this would not be lost to the Bible Christian representatives whose predecessors had spoken of 'Missionary Exertion'[323] and of 'mission to the heathen'.[324] It is this theological and ecclesiastical imperative which makes the section more than simply a collection of carols, though a rather inelegant text, 'Bright and joyful is the morn' from the *Primitive Methodist Hymnal*, which calls for people to 'worship at his feet' and to yield 'Homage due to God alone' has been omitted, presumably on literary grounds. The editors have improved on the approach found in the older Methodist hymn books by being willing to incorporate texts from a wide selection of sources. Some of these were more recent, though no item was being published for the first time.

The whole thrust of the section which addresses the incarnation is summed up in four texts, the first of which is a traditional carol, 'A Virgin most pure, as the prophets do tell' (128). Taken from the *Oxford Hymn Book*, and also present in the *Oxford Book of Carols*, it is presented in the original form in which it had been published in *Some Ancient Christmas Carols with tunes to which they were formerly sung in the West of England* but set to a tune from Sandys' *Christmas Carols Ancient and Modern* of 1833.[325] The text retells the narrative of the incarnation from the time of the Annunciation to the acclamation of the angels and the visit of the shepherds.

'Glory be to God on high' (134) provides sound Wesleyan theology from beginning to end. The use of the name 'Jesus' rather than Christ[326] serves to emphasise the concept of God's kenosis and self-investment in humanity. The theme continues, for this is the King who is 'Emptied of His majesty'. Wesley recognises the immensity of the subject on which he is exhorting us to reflect:

---

323 *A Collection of Hymns for the use of People called Bible Christians*, Preface, p. v.
324 *A Collection of Hymns for the use of People called Bible Christians*, Preface, p. vii.
325 Watson and Trickett, *Companion to Hymns & Psalms*, p. 87.
326 Cf., 'Stupendous height of heavenly love' – 'God did in Christ Himself reveal', which is much less affective.

> Of His dazzling glories shorn,
> Being's source begins to be,
> And God Himself is born!

Language is almost insufficient to expound humanity's response to this act of grace, but it must be penned:

> We, the sons of men, rejoice,
> The Prince of Peace proclaim;
> With heaven's host lift up our voice,
> And shout Immanuel's name.

Wesley now removes to Philippians 2.10 to continue this peroration, this catalogue of human amazement. The mix of sound theology and emotion, together with the poetic balance of the text (the rhyme scheme is consistent, with only the rhyming of 'am' and 'name', and 'man' and 'contain' showing any kind of strain to modern ears), makes for a hymn which must rate as one of the most elegant and profound within the compass of this subject.

'To us a child of royal birth' (141) emphasises the stature of the Christ child for he is 'The Son of man, the God of Heaven', 'The Christ, by raptured seers foretold', 'Prophet, Priest and King', 'The Lord of hosts'. 'Let earth and heaven combine' (142) is magnificent in its simplicity and stunning in its profundity. 'Our God contracted to a span [is] / Incomprehensibly made man'. This is why

> Angels and men agree
> To praise in songs divine
> The incarnate Deity.

The section is considerably larger than that of the same title in the *Wesleyan Methodist Hymn Book*. It takes time for popular material to find its way into mainstream hymn books and the popularisation of Christmas, begun in Victorian times, had made its impact too late to be reflected in the collection of 1904. By 1933 it had penetrated the cloisters of Methodism necessitating the inclusion of a greater number of texts. It is interesting, however, to note the omission of 'Arise, my soul, arise / Thy Saviour's sacrifice' with its strongly incarnational emphasis. There is no indication in the archive as to why this should be. Speculation leads to the assumption that this was probably no more than a necessary matter of choice. The text is no better or worse than others included and some preferences needed to be exercised when faced with such an abundance of material. In this book 16 texts disposed of the subject while the *Collection of Hymns for the use of People called Bible Christians* had 13, offering 'The race that long in darkness pined' (139) to uniting Methodism. The *United Methodist Free Church Hymnal* included 17 hymns and the *Primitive Methodist Hymnal* ten. The *Primitive Methodist Hymnal Supplement* omitted the section. The *United Methodist Free Church Hymnal* included Advent with Incarnation, and so the birth of Jesus was mixed with texts of preparation such as 'Hark, the glad sound, the Saviour comes' (82). The *Primitive Methodist Hymnal* was similar.

In the *Methodist Hymn Book* 26 texts were required to address the incarnation, evidence, perhaps, of the wide range of material which had become available during the reign of Queen Victoria, and which now demanded inclusion because of its popularity. This, far more than any critical biblical criteria, seems to have influenced the choices made by the editors. These texts came, nevertheless, largely from scholarly sources, and a close examination reveals that the editors chose to use what might be styled Christmas hymns at this point. The overall feel is of that of the *Wesleyan Methodist Hymn Book* expanded, while the book is more sharply focused than that of the other denominations.

When a choice was forced on the committee it seems to have been made on criteria relating to elegance of language, rather than as a consequence of any theological bias. This could also be indicative of the extensive work of Percy Dearmer and others in researching carols, though the contents of the *Oxford Book of Carols* offers little to the *Methodist Hymn Book*. In passing, it is interesting to note that the editors of the *Methodist Hymn Book* seem to have gauged popular taste better than Dearmer. More of the material they included here has survived in use to the present day.

The *Methodist Hymn Book* provides a clear window into the incarnational theology of Methodism. Such theology, as has been indicated, derived from the Wesleys and had been sung by each of the uniting denominations. The editors had, in one sense, an easy task at this stage, that of deciding which were the most elegant texts available within the corpus. What they chose to do took the task onto another plane. The expansion of the section allowed choices to be made from outside of Methodism, and history has shown those choices to have been appropriate. Texts of strong and clear theology have gained popularity with Methodist people and many have continued in use beyond the long life-time of the *Methodist Hymn Book*.

Jesus' Life, Humanity and Death

The goal of Jesus' life, humanity and death, as viewed by the editors of the *Methodist Hymn Book*, might best be summarized by the opening verse of 'Lord, as to Thy dear cross we flee' (512):

> Lord, as to Thy dear cross we flee,
> And plead to be forgiven,
> So let Thy life our pattern be,
> And form our souls for heaven.

The pattern of Jesus' life rather than his teaching is the informing principle. This life is described by the hymns.

The birth of Jesus, from a liturgical perspective, follows Advent. For the editors of the *Methodist Hymn Book*, Christ's advent and the triumphal entry into Jerusalem appear to be immutably linked. The section on 'The Lord Jesus Christ – His glory, name and praise' mixes temporal and eschatological images of Jesus. It moves from Palm Sunday to Advent with economic fluidity but little sense of direction. Theologically this is understandable but from the point of view of the hymn book it leads to some confusion.

'Hark the glad sound! The Saviour comes' (82), 'Of the Father's love begotten' (83) and 'All glory, laud and honour' (84) follow in quick succession. Charles Wesley's doctrinal hymn of salvation, 'Jesus comes with all His grace' (87), built around the theme of Palm Sunday, is found within this section. It is all rather disordered.

Ralph Wardlaw's 'Christ, of all my hopes the ground' (89) is sentimental but, more importantly, anticipated the preoccupation with millennialism which would rise later in the century in which it was written. The style of writing enabled the text to survive the decline in interest in that movement which was to be marked after 1925 in America and somewhat sooner in the United Kingdom, an interest which has, in some quarters, revived.

It is difficult to follow logically through these texts, though they underline the place of Christ both within and transcending history. The pre-eminence of Jesus, and the call to that acknowledgement by all of creation, led Edward Perronet to write 'All hail the power of Jesu's name' (91). The words satisfactorily hold in tension the understanding of Jesus' humanity signified by the use of the name 'Jesus' rather than the title 'Christ', and the eschatological expectation of his reigning in glory.

The editors' understanding of the nature and person of Jesus is implied by the texts they chose. Often this understanding is expressed metaphorically. Psalm 84.11 provides the starting point for 'Jesus, Sun and Shield art Thou' (95). Jesus becomes, successively, 'Bread and Wine', 'Love and Life', 'Peace and Joy' and 'Song and Strength' in this selection from Horatius Bonar's verses. Isaac Watts's 'Join all the glorious names' (96) shows Jesus as wisdom, love, power, Redeemer, Great Prophet, Counsellor, Shepherd, High-priest, almighty Lord, Conqueror, King and Captain. Similarly, Charles Wesley explores the attributes of his saviour in 'O filial deity' (97) which in conclusion enable him to say '. . . by faith I stand, / Strong in Thy omnipotence'. The strength of that faith is underlined. This God is Wesley's 'all in all' (98).

Horatius Bonar writes confidently:

> His Cross dispels each doubt:
> I bury in His tomb
> Each thought of unbelief and fear,
> Each lingering shade of gloom. (112)

The end of Jesus' life raises questions relating to the atonement. The time of the genesis of the *Methodist Hymn Book* was one of theological exploration.[327] The committee would have needed to be brave to echo such reflection in their choice of texts. For the most part they took a line that was safe and conservative. Samuel Crossman's meditative 'My song is love unknown' (144) is a fine illustration of the point. It is personal and introspective, as well suited to private devotion as to public worship. As the text unfolds the author reflects on the life of Christ from the point of incarnation to his tomb. The meditation leads to the conclusion that

---

327 See section on Soteriology below, p. 105.

> This is my friend
> In whose sweet praise
> I all my days
> Could gladly spend.

Jesus' life is described and people are called to emulate his example but, in spite of its elegance, the text has little to say on Jesus' teaching. This is true of this section and the book as a whole. In this the editors have followed the pattern of the *United Methodist Free Church Hymnal*. 'Jesus, Thee Thy works proclaim', from the *Wesleyan Methodist Hymn Book*, could have been included. It is assumed that the clumsy opening line precluded this. The teaching of Jesus was not unimportant within the uniting churches, and the absence of hymns can only be attributed to a lack of suitable texts available to the editors or that, on balance, other matters seemed of greater consequence, as Wootton would argue.[328] The only additional text that might have been included from the existing Methodist hymnals, 'How sweetly flowed the gospel sound', found in the *Primitive Methodist Hymnal*, points to a paucity of suitable texts. Its author, John Bowring, was a Puritan so this would not be a reason for exclusion. Was the hymn omitted because it was unduly sentimental or as a consequence of its doubtful soteriology?

> How sweetly flowed the gospel's sound
> From lips of gentleness and grace;
> When listening thousands gathered round
> And joy and reverence filled the place.
>
> From heaven He came, of heaven He spoke,
> To heaven He led His followers' way;
> Dark clouds of gloomy night He broke,
> Unveiling an immortal day.
>
> 'Come, wanderers, to my Father's home;
> Come, all ye weary ones, and rest.'
> Yes! gracious Saviour, we will come,
> Obey Thee, love Thee, and be blest.

---

328 J. Wootton, *Introducing a Practical Feminist Theology of Worship*, Sheffield Academic Press, 2000, p. 10.

The evidence of the *Methodist Hymn Book* contents suggests that the editors were particularly concerned with the response that might be made to Jesus' teaching, rather than the teaching itself. This allowed the consideration of some Unitarian texts, as observed above, that are often deist in nature, over against the strongly expressed Trinitarian tradition of Methodism.[329] Subsequently some Methodists have felt the need to reassert the orthodox nature of their faith.[330] In current discussions about the nature of authorised hymnody within Methodism this provides a useful lesson. The Report of the Board of the Methodist Publishing House to the Methodist Conference of 2004 states that there have been authorised hymn books in Methodism since the earliest days. The report goes on to argue that: 'If a hymn or song is included in an authorised collection, leaders of worship are entitled to assume that it is consistent with our doctrines and most congregations use authorised hymn books as their normal book.' The report concludes that 'to dispense with authorised or recommended hymnody would be a major break with our tradition and should not be entertained without serious and lengthy consideration'. If we believe exactly the same as other denominations then there is no problem, but if that were so we would not be Methodists. So the distinctive nature of what we believe is important.

The response of the Christian to Jesus' example is explored in hymns like 'Dear Master, in whose life I see' (163). This echoes Romans 7.21–25 illustrating the constant tension of the Christian life, that 'what I dream and what I do / In my weak days are always two'. The wanted transformation of the disciple's life is depicted in Theodore Monod's 'O the bitter shame and sorrow' (170). Stanza by stanza we witness commitment deepening as the text moves from 'All of self, and none of Thee!' to 'None of self, and all of Thee'. The progress of the text is compelling.

It is surprising then that when a theme like the transfiguration is tackled the end point is that of mystical wonder rather than earthly response. 'Lord! It is good for us to be' (168) is competent in its description of the event itself. It is here where 'the son of thunder

---

329 It is interesting in this light to realise that Martineau found space for Bowring in his collections.

330 J. B. Taylor, for example. Various lectures while he was a lecturer at Queen's College, Birmingham during the period 1979–82, and more recently at an Anglican Methodist Synod in Liverpool, 2002.

learns / The thought that breathes, the word that burns', here where the disciples are 'entranced, enwrapped, alone with Thee'. Yet, at the conclusion of the hymn they are still on the mountain top. Theologically this event is a mid-point affirmation of the nature of Jesus, but there is no sense in which Arthur Penryn Stanley grapples with their return from the heights and the movement towards Jerusalem. There is no evangelical imperative deriving from Jesus' sense of wishing to move the disciples on in their pilgrimage of faith that might be expected from the Bible Christian or United Methodist influence (though they used this same text). Neither is there a radical thrust leading towards the challenge to authority in Jerusalem that might have come from the Primitive Methodists. The text is very safe, conservative. It rocks no boats. While all Methodists traced their origins to evangelical and evangelistic roots, as denominations the uniting churches followed the sociological principle of being less fervent the more respectable and secure they became. The Wesleyans were, arguably, furthest down this route and this text spoke, perhaps, most suitably to them.

The way of the cross is vividly pictured. Philip Bliss, in a text that is dependent on Isaiah 53, sings of a saviour who is a 'Man of Sorrows!' (176) who bore 'shame and scoffing', who stood in the author's place condemned. This interpretation of the atonement was already being challenged by contemporary theologians.[331] This same man of sorrows would come as a 'glorious King' taking those he had ransomed home with him.

The cross is, for the most part, seen as something of glory and wonder, the enormity is avoided. A people who had seen the horror of the trenches of the First World War would have been appalled by a realistic description of crucifixion. At this point it is psychologically more comfortable to spiritualise the event and this is what happened. Jesus is not 'Tortured, beaten, scarred and tainted'[332] but one whose face is 'sunshine' (197). Texts like 'Bound upon the accursèd tree' (*Primitive Methodist Hymnal* No. 99), with its reference to flesh with scourges torn and 'baffled burning thirst', are omitted, though it is admitted that 'Salem's daughters weep' (195). This latter would have been all too apparent in cities, towns and villages across the land in the

331 E. G. Selwyn, ed., *Essays Catholic and Critical*, London, SPCK, 3rd edition, 1929.
332 A. E. Pratt, *Blinded by the Dazzle*, London, Stainer & Bell Ltd, 1997.

aftermath of the Great War. Jesus' blood fills a fountain (201). The language is metaphorical, and obviously so, rather than literal.

Having recognised the fact of the crucifixion and examined some of its theological consequences the next hymn begins to question what Jesus must have done to meet such an end. 'Ah, holy Jesus, how hast Thou offended' (177) continues in a scholarly manner.

Edward Caswall's translation of a Latin text, '*Stabat Mater dolorosa*', 'At the Cross, her station keeping' (185), demonstrates the influence of the Oxford Movement and its interest in themes more usually associated with Roman Catholicism. This should not surprise Methodists who understand the background of John and Charles Wesley, but at the time of the editing of this book such influences were less dominant in the uniting denominations, though championed by Ernest Rattenbury,[333] a member of the Hymn Book Committee. The hymn was adopted from the *Church Hymnary*. Telford is unapologetic in introducing the text[334] though its origins, history and imagery, focusing on the person of Mary and her grief at watching Jesus die, would have been singularly foreign to many Methodists.

The next text, 'O Love divine! What hast Thou done?' (186) brings the book back to more familiar ground. Faber's text 'O come and mourn with me awhile' (187), despite its origins in Roman Catholicism, had found its way into the books of three out of the four uniting denominations, only the Bible Christians not including it. The catholic appeal of Faber's hymnody perhaps owes itself to his Calvinist Anglican upbringing that often gave his texts an evangelical flavour.

'Behold the Saviour of mankind' (193) indicates Samuel Wesley Senior's grasp of both scripture and language:

> Behold the Saviour of mankind
> Nailed to the shameful tree!
> How vast the love that Him inclined
> To bleed and die for thee!
>
> Hark, how He groans! while nature shakes,
> And earth's strong pillars bend;
> The temple's veil in sunder breaks,
> The solid marbles rend.

---

333 Newton, *Heart Speaks to Heart*, p. 70–5.
334 Telford, *The Methodist Hymn-Book Illustrated*, p. 114.

'Tis done! the precious ransom's paid;
Receive My soul! He cries:
See where He bows His sacred head!
He bows His head, and dies!

But soon He'll break death's envious chain,
And in full glory shine:
O Lamb of God, was ever pain,
Was ever love, like Thine?

The ransom is 'precious', death's hold on us is 'envious'. The text was ripe for inclusion. The exploration of the nature of atonement continues with 'He dies! The Friend of Sinners dies!' (195). Isaac Watts had predated Charles Wesley's use of the appellation, 'Friend of Sinners'. The text moves from the depths of crucified agony to the 'Cherubic legions' who will welcome Jesus 'to the skies'. Here is reason indeed for the saints to cease crying and to 'Sing how He spoiled the hosts of hell, / And led the monster death in chains'. It might well be asked, 'Where's thy victory, boasting grave'. And so 'We sing the praise of Him who died' (196). The cross is the sign that 'God is love . . . it takes our guilt away'. This cross is the means by which the coward is made brave for it is 'The angel's theme in heaven above'.

The peroration is continued in the next text, 'Beneath the Cross of Jesus' (197). Elizabeth Cecilia Clephane takes the shadow of the cross for her 'abiding place'. She asks 'no other sunshine than / The sunshine of His face', words reminiscent of the sentimentality of Frederick Faber.[335] The tune is by Ira Sankey and indicates that the committee were willing to allow sparing inclusion of popular evangelistic hymnody. This view of the cross, and style of hymnody, is further explored in the next two hymns, 'Never further than thy Cross' (198) and 'Jesus keep me near the Cross' (199). These last three hymns signify, to some extent, the style of input that was being presented by the Methodist Free Churches, particularly the Bible Christian and the Primitive Methodist Church representatives.

William Cowper used the metaphor of a fountain (201) to speak of the cleansing from sin that was consequent on the crucifixion. 'O

---

335 '. . . our lives would be all sunshine/In the sweetness of our Lord' (318).

sacred head once wounded' (202) conveys a sense of awe that gives way to dedication. The text ends with the affirmation that one who is held in communion with Jesus, 'Dies safely through Thy love'. This is a powerful articulation of Christian faith in the grace of God facilitated by the cross of Christ.

In summary, the texts provided by the *Methodist Hymn Book* offer a description of the life, humanity and death of Jesus. Jesus' life is seen as being exemplary. As Janet Wootton has remarked,[336] little attempt was made to provide hymns that were descriptive of Jesus' teaching. To include hymns about this subject involves making choices in terms of interpretation. The theological mood of the committee was one that sought to avoid controversy. Hence, it must be concluded that it was safer to use hymns of a descriptive rather than a prescriptive nature. Only when the committee was dealing with issues that, for Methodists, were beyond likely contradiction is there any indication of forthrightness.[337]

The death of Jesus is described graphically but metaphorically rather than realistically. The language of the texts that the committee chose to include is more restrained than it might have been, given the plethora of hymns deriving from the evangelical revival of the turn of the century. In spite of this, for some, they were still too lurid.[338] The human responsibility for Jesus' death was emphasised. This underlines the view of the atonement to which the committee were, for the most part, seeking to give expression, that Christ died for sinners to enable their forgiveness.

The collection is catholic, giving evidence of the committee's willingness to incorporate texts that would demonstrate the widely differing influences that had played a part in forming the uniting denominations. They are drawn from many sources from within and beyond the bounds of Methodism. Nevertheless, the book is not radical. In spite of the breadth of choice exercised by the committee they worked judiciously to produce a collection which was not likely to offend or to be too *avant garde*. Contemporary fashions in theology were hardly allowed to influence the content to the end that no one would feel cut off from their heritage. The predominant theme is, understandably, that of the death of Jesus. Christian theology

---

336 Wootton, *Introducing a Practical Feminist Theology of Worship*, p. 10.
337 E.g., Arminianism versus Calvinism.
338 *Methodist Recorder*, 4 August 1932, p. 14.

demands this emphasis and the next section seeks to reflect theologically on the description that these texts have provided.

Soteriology

What theological expression of the nature of atonement is provided by
these hymns? Caswall provides a summary as he reflects that if he is
the cause of the injury of the cross,

> Ah, then let me strive,
> For the love Thou hast borne,
> To give Thee no longer
> Occasion to mourn! (174)

Underlying the text is a sense of personal responsibility for the death
of Jesus, an awareness of sin. Within Methodism the authority for
such an interpretation was deeply rooted. 'Died he for me, who caused
His pain? / For me who Him to death pursued?' (371) asked Charles
Wesley. This picture, which some regarded as demeaning human
worth, did not pass unchallenged.[339] From this point it is possible to
begin to examine the degree to which the *Methodist Hymn Book*
reflected the contemporary Methodist understanding of soteriology.

That Christ died in the place of the sinner would at one time have
been beyond question. For many this had already been challenged by
Lofthouse in his *Ethics and Atonement* (1906) and *Altar, Cross and
Community* (1921). In these works he broke away from traditional
substitutionary theories, approaching atonement from an ethical
standpoint. For him 'morality was determinative of religion'.[340]

John Scott Lidgett in a Fernley Lecture of 1897[341] had put forward
an exploration of atonement in which satisfaction was obtained by the
total identification of the Son with humanity and the perfection of
the filial. This was neither as individual, nor other-worldly, as other
current theories had been. Lidgett's arguments had been preceded by
those of Pope, the Wesleyan theologian, who sought to provide a

---

339 *Methodist Recorder*, 4 August 1932, p. 14.
340 Davies, George and Rupp, *A History of the Methodist Church in Great Britain*, Vol.
3, p. 215.
341 Davies, George and Rupp, *A History of the Methodist Church in Great Britain*, Vol.
3, p. 189f.

unifying theory, seeing something in all the chief doctrines, by placing the emphasis on love.[342] Lidgett had been threatened with a doctrinal charge for his work though he was by no means as radical as Lofthouse, who challenged the literal interpretations of sacrifice seeking an ethical assent and moral transformation in the believer.[343] Peake had, similarly, seen flaws in the substitutionary theory of the atonement.[344] Maldwyn Hughes continued this emphasis but was more sympathetic to the idea of sacrifice. What we are uncovering is a theological movement which was gradually spreading across the denominations.

To what extent did the editors of the *Methodist Hymn Book* follow these emphases? The answer to the question 'Who was the guilty?' for the death of Jesus is framed in the last two lines of verse 2 of 'Ah, holy Jesu, how hast Thou offended' (177). The question is answered: ''Twas I, Lord Jesus, I it was denied Thee / I crucified Thee'. Jesus' incarnation and death are portrayed as being 'For my salvation'. In 'O Jesus, my hope' (200) Charles Wesley pictures himself as the murderer *in whose stead* Jesus died. In the light of this revelation he pleads for his hardness of heart to be removed, to be 'vanquished . . . with the sense of Thy love'. The picture which is beginning to develop is one of a penal substitutionary theory of atonement. This is further underlined by Wesley's 'All ye that pass by' (188). The personal nature of this text is evident as the author directs the singer to the objective action that takes place on the cross, together with the image of Christ as intercessor, 'For you and me / He prayed on the tree'.

He goes on to ask, 'How shall a sinner find / The Saviour of mankind?' (203). Through the process of this agonising death Charles Wesley believes that there is salvation and so he pleads:

> What hast Thou done for me?
> O think on Calvary!
> By thy mortal groans and sighs,
> By Thy precious death I pray,
> Hear my dying spirit's cries,
> Take, O take my sins away!

---

342 Davies, George and Rupp, *A History of the Methodist Church in Great Britain*, Vol. 3, p. 188.

343 Davies, George and Rupp, *A History of the Methodist Church in Great Britain*, Vol. 3, p. 216.

344 Davies, George and Rupp, *A History of the Methodist Church in Great Britain*, Vol. 3, p. 202.

The need which this process meets is recognised as being universal. Isaac Watts's 'Plunged in a gulf of dark despair' (179) depicts the state of corporate humanity as hopeless and it is to such 'He flew to our relief'. Such grace demands praise from 'rocks and hills', angels should strike their 'harps of gold'. Even with all this assistance 'His love can ne'er be told'. What is demonstrated is a response to need that is just as all-encompassing. This is truly a 'God of unexampled grace' (191), the 'Redeemer of mankind'. Jesus is depicted by Charles Wesley as the 'Friend of Sinners' for, he marvels, 'Was never love like Thine!' Yet the love is equivalent to the sorrow that the saviour demonstrated, and both found their source in the divine nature of the sufferer, for 'Faith cries out: 'Tis He, 'tis He, / My God, that suffers there'.

What the hymns so far make clear is that, for the committee, Christ died in the place of the sinner. This seems to be beyond question, yet penal substitution is not as obviously spelled out as in the *Primitive Methodist Hymnal*, where 'O Christ what burdens bowed Thy head' included the line, 'Our load was laid on Thee'. For the most part triumphalism was avoided.

For Isaac Watts, what is taking place is exemplary. 'When I survey the wondrous cross' (182), he says, nothing is great enough in terms of my response, it 'Demands my soul, my life, my all'. 'In the cross of Christ I glory' (183) is a natural response, though John Bowring's text lacks the imagery and visual power of Watts' superlative hymn. Bowring was a Puritan and Methodism has always had within it an element of Puritanism that would find his words helpful. The sense of anticipation of suffering like that of Christ enables the author to see glory where others would be aware only of suffering. Again the atoning power of the cross is seen to have an exemplary component.

For Methodists salvation has always been a universal possibility.[345] Christ's work on the cross is available to all. This work is experienced at an individual level.[346] While the authority of God is maintained the justice of God is tempered with mercy. This emphasis had always been central to Methodism. Another facet was to be added to the gem. J. Alexander Findlay expounded a 'come to Jesus' religion.[347] The emphasis was on the human Jesus who would draw all people to

---

345 Berger, *Theology in Hymns?*, p. 109.
346 Berger, *Theology in Hymns?*, p. 115.
347 Davies, George and Rupp, *A History of the Methodist Church in Great Britain*, Vol. 3, p. 203.

himself over against the 'Christ' image. In today's terms we are picturing a charismatic human being:

> When he walked the fields, He drew
> From the flowers, and birds, and dew,
> Parables of God. (147)

The essential humanity of Jesus is underlined. This was a real man
walking in real places to whom humanity would respond. The sense of
God 'contracted to a span' (142) runs through Methodist theology and
hymnody. The whole life of Jesus was important. For Findlay Jesus
was 'hopeful and encouraging, not pessimistic and condemnatory'.[348]
The hymns carry the message: 'there is room in Thy heart for me'
(150). A similar emphasis on the centrality of the person and work of
Jesus was provided by Vincent Taylor.[349] It was this centrality of love
that, for John Wesley, could not be denied by the predestinarian stance
of Calvinistic theology. While a theology of predestination has
survived in certain branches of Methodism, that of Wesley was
Arminian. Charles wrote with passionate horror with regard to the
doctrine of Reprobation:

> Whoe'er admits; my soul disowns
> The image of a torturing God,
> Well-pleased with human shrieks and groans,
> A fiend, a Moloch gorged with blood.
>
> Good God! That any child of Thine
> So horribly should think of Thee!
> Lo! All my hopes I here resign,
> If all may not find grace with me.[350]

All can benefit from the work of God in Jesus. Calvinism was not
an acceptable option. While the early Methodists had disputed this,
those who followed the Wesley brothers were left in no doubt as to
which course they were expected to adopt. As far as the editors of the

---

348 Davies, George and Rupp, *A History of the Methodist Church in Great Britain*, Vol. 3, p. 204.
349 Davies, George and Rupp, *A History of the Methodist Church in Great Britain*, Vol. 3, p. 204.
350 Rattenbury, *The Evangelical Doctrines of Charles Wesley's Hymns*, p. 117.

Methodist Hymn Book were concerned there was no debate. The hymns are orthodox in this respect.

The soteriological work of Jesus begins with the incarnation. 'O love, how deep, how broad, how high!' (62) reflects the theology of Thomas à Kempis (and was once, doubtfully, attributed to him[351]). Healing and consequent salvation are rooted in the birth, life and death of Jesus. For the editors this was not narrowly the work of the cross. Nevertheless, John Wesley's translation of Paul Gerhardt's '*O Jesu Christ, mein schönstes Licht*', 'My Saviour, Thou Thy love to me / In shame, in want, in pain hast showed' (169) provides a characteristic theological examination of the soteriology of the cross. 'More hard than marble is my heart, / And foul with sins of deepest stain' is the description provided of the soul in need of salvation, but the author pleads, 'and may / Thy blood wash all these stains away'. The transforming action of sanctification follows: 'Till sweetly Thou hast breathed Thy mild / And lowly mind into my breast!' The author seeks guidance: 'Still let Thy love point out my way'. In every way he relies on his Saviour.

This theme of dependence on the crucified Jesus is seen in many texts. 'And can it be that I should gain / An interest in the Saviour's blood' (371) begins in a highly introspective manner, reflecting on what God has done for the author in the work of Christ. What has happened is impenetrable to rational, human understanding: ''Tis mystery all! The Immortal dies: / Who can explore His strange design?' Even the heavenly beings only manage to stumble on the verge of comprehension, for 'In vain the first-born seraph tries / To sound the depths of love divine', and ultimately the conclusion is reached that 'angel minds [should] enquire no more'. The next stanza is a straightforward exposition of the incarnation, the reason for this wonderment. Only then does the hymn begin to express something of what is happening, this realisation of the transformation of the slave of sin into the child of God. Only now can the vehicle for these words become a tune of triumphant, confident expectation and praise, and that is a part of the difficulty of the text. The first tune, 'Sagina', is fitting only for the last two verses, but neither 'Lansdown' (the second tune) nor 'Didsbury' (found in the later *Hymns & Psalms*), though more meditative, have gained acceptance.

---

351 Watson and Trickett, *Companion to Hymns & Psalms*, p. 158.

The theology that is presented by these words expresses a dependence on God and a response of faith. Yet anyone who makes such a response will find God to be accepting of them. There are no exclusion clauses. From a theological point of view it is clear that the editors believed in salvation by faith, through grace. Charles Wesley's 'O God of God, in whom combine' (65) relates the Godhead to personal salvation in which the author seeks to participate. The text recognises, using imagery of the sea, our need of grace from day to day. Heaven is referred to as 'our soul's abode' where our life can be 'Hid . . . with Christ in God'. Wesley looks forward to a time of perfect salvation, 'filled with Thee be all our thought, / Till in us Thy full likeness shine'.

It is clear that the editors were reflecting the theological stance broadly held across the denominations rather than trying to make any statement that might be regarded as either radical or divisive. Their task, at this point, seems to have been one of consolidating the Union by giving congregations words to sing with which they would have felt comfortable, regardless of their background.

Some texts move beyond the cross to anticipate the human response. A God of such salvation is approached with wonder and awe. John Mason's 'How shall I sing that majesty / Which angels do admire' (78) reflects on a vision of angels singing God's praise. In the light of this wondrous sight he asks, '. . . but who am I?' Few hymns have succeeded in better portraying the sense of the *mysterium et tremendum* spoken of by the prophets and mystics. The hymn 'Praise to the Lord, the Almighty, the King of creation' (64) sets redemption in the context of the span of salvation history. This is seen to elicit praise and adoration. There is an anticipation of salvation in the Old Testament and the committee did not wish to lose grasp of this thread. John Wesley's translation of Johann Scheffer's 'O God, of good the unfathomed sea!' (67) reflects on the majesty of God in words reminiscent of those used to describe the call of prophets:

> O God, of good the unfathomed sea!
> Who would not give his heart to Thee?
> Who would not love Thee with his might?
> O Jesu, Lover of mankind,
> Who would not his whole soul and mind,
> With all his strength, to Thee unite?

Thou shin'st with everlasting rays;
Before the insufferable blaze
Angels with both wings veil their eyes:
Yet free as air Thy bounty streams
On all Thy works; Thy mercy's beams
Diffusive as Thy sun's arise.

Astonished at Thy frowning brow,
Earth, hell, and heaven's strong pillars bow;
Terrible majesty is Thine.
Who then can that vast love express
Which bows Thee down to me, who less
Than nothing am, till Thou art mine?

High throned on heaven's eternal hill,
In number, weight, and measure still
Thou sweetly orderest all that is:
And yet Thou deign'st to come to me,
And guide my steps, that I, with Thee
Enthroned, may reign in endless bliss.

Fountain of good! All blessing flows
From Thee; no want Thy fullness knows:
What but Thyself canst Thou desire?
Yet, self-sufficient as Thou art,
Thou dost desire my worthless heart;
This, only this, dost Thou require.

Primeval Beauty! In Thy sight
The first-born, fairest sons of light
See all their brightest glories fade:
What then to me Thine eyes could turn –
In sin conceived, of woman born –
A worm, a leaf, a blast, a shade?

Hell's armies tremble at Thy nod,
And trembling own the Almighty God,
Sovereign of earth, hell, air, and sky:
But who is this that comes from far,

Whose garments rolled in blood appear?
'Tis God made Man, for man to die!

O God, of good the unfathomed sea!
Who would not give his heart to Thee?
Who would not love Thee with his might?
O Jesu, Lover of mankind,
Who would not his whole soul and mind,
With all his strength, to Thee unite?

The editors wished to affirm that salvation is a gracious act. The need
for God's initiative is underlined. John Henry Newman's analysis of
the process by which God seeks to address the fall is objective (74).
Adam, representative of humankind, brought sin into the world. A
second Adam is logically the means by which God seeks to alleviate
this burden.

From such a God 'All blessing flows' (943). The Arminianism of
Methodism, and that of the committee members, is clearly demonstrated by the texts that have been chosen: 'Love, like death hath all
destroyed, / Rendered all distinctions void' (720), 'He spreads his arms
to embrace you all' (361), 'The invitation is to all' (323). God's mercy
is 'Immense, unfathomed, unconfined' for Jesus is 'The general
Saviour of mankind' (75). Charles Wesley's majestic and scholarly
'Let earth and heaven agree' (114) concludes with a polemic which
would not have been lost on contemporary Calvinists: 'for all my Lord
was crucified, / For all, for all my Saviour died'. This is a constant
thread throughout the collection. Another text of Charles Wesley,
'Would Jesus have the sinner die?' (173) develops the theme in an
evangelistic manner. This is a God whose 'grace to all extends, /
Immense and unconfined . . . wide as infinity'. Such grace had 'never
passed by one, / Or it had passed by me' (77). The personal thrust of
this text is evident, and the more so when it is understood that Charles
recognised his need for continuing gracious forgiveness. Houghton[352]
notes that he had originally written 'My trespass *is* grown up to
heaven'. His brother John produced the more confident 'My trespass
was grown up to heaven' that is followed by the *Methodist Hymn
Book*.

---

352 H. Houghton, *The Handmaid of Piety*, York, The Wesley Fellowship, Quacks
Books, 1992, p. 5.

God has an irresistible attraction. God is a God of providence. 'We come unto our father's God' (71) provides a reminder that the challenges faced by each succeeding generation are similar and that God's providence is more than sufficient to meet their vicissitudes. The hymn concludes with a depiction of the Communion of Saints as an 'Unbroken . . . golden chain' leading into and beyond the present.

The hymns proceed from salvation and justification to sanctification. The right end of redemption for the Methodist theologian is perfect holiness. 'The mission of Methodism [is] to "spread Scriptural holiness through the land" ', asserted the Bible Christians in line with John and Charles Wesley and the tenets of historical Methodism. The editors would have undoubtedly defended this position from whichever perspective they had come. It is ironic then that the depiction of the holiness of God provided by Newman should be a source of heated debate at the time of the production of the *Methodist Hymn Book*. It was unthinkable, to some, that there should be a 'higher gift than grace' (74).[353] The place of grace in the process of salvation had been clearly underlined.

John Cennick, who had moved away from John Wesley's influence to espouse Calvinism, provided the text of 'Thou great Redeemer, dying Lamb' (104). A hint of the influence of a theology of election is found in the lines 'When we appear in yonder cloud, / With all that *favoured throng*',[354] though this had not prevented its inclusion in the collections of the Wesleyan and Bible Christian denominations. Prior to this the text had not appeared in *A Collection of Hymns for the Use of The People Called Methodists* of 1780, though it was included in the Supplement of 1889. This is evidence of John Wesley's attitude to the theology of the text[355] and, subsequently, the catholic capacity of the editors of the *Methodist Hymn Book* to include texts that would not be acceptable to all, that all might be acceptable to some. There is some indication that Methodism was evolving. Charles Wesley's 'Jesus, the First and Last' (105) offers a little balance in implying the place of human choice in the appropriation of the gifts of grace: 'On Thee my soul is cast'.

The redemptive work of God elicits both humility and evangelistic zeal. This redemption is brought about by the soteriological work of

---

353 *Methodist Recorder*, 30 June 1932, p. 16.
354 My italics.
355 Or perhaps his animosity to John Cennick.

Christ. God's work in Christ has been anticipated in the experience of
the people of the Old Testament. Isaiah 9.2 provides the starting point
for John Morison's 'The race that long in darkness pined' (139). The
text, which was first published in the *Scottish Paraphrases* of 1781, is
wrongly regarded by the editors of the *Companion to Hymns &
Psalms*[356] as having entered Methodism with the *Methodist Hymn
Book*, having been previously extant in *A Collection of Hymns for the
use of People called Bible Christians*.

From the outset it has been demonstrated that the theology that the
editors espoused was Arminian, but their inclusion of a text by John
Cennick demonstrated that they were going to seek to draw together
the disparate threads with which the cloth of Methodism had been
woven. By this time Findlay's 'come to Jesus' religion was clearly
beginning to have an effect and the humanity of Jesus is well displayed
in many texts. In spite of this the concentration on his teaching is
limited. Events are described and the work of the cross is expounded
but few texts enable the singer to interiorise Jesus' sayings.

It is clear that the main understanding of the atonement that is provided here is penal substitutionary, but it is not exclusively so. There
was a sense of ambiguity creeping in. The committee were not as sure
of their ground as they might have been 30 years before. Their view
was softening. The exemplary interpretation of the life and death of
Jesus was beginning to gain ground.

Penal substitution would, perhaps, have been most readily accepted
by the Bible Christians who had been using material from the
American gospel hymn tradition.[357] The hymns that they would have
espoused from these sources are sparsely represented in the *Methodist
Hymn Book*. Mankin notes that the Wesleyans had been slow to
adopt these hymns.[358] Wesleyans had been more readily influenced by
the Oxford Movement and the theological explorations of the atonement which were current in the previous 30 years. Nevertheless, the
work of Lofthouse, John Scott Lidgett and Peake seems not to have
been wholeheartedly adopted by the committee as they made their
choice of texts. As with other sections of the book we witness evolution rather than revolution, a gentle change of emphasis allowing a
more catholic collection of hymns with less aggressively vivid or

---

356 Watson and Trickett, *Companion to Hymns & Psalms*, p. 85.
357 Mankin, *How they sang on the way to Zion*, p. 201.
358 Mankin, *How they sang on the way to Zion*, p. 205.

realistic imagery. The sense that Christ 'died for all', a central tenet of Methodism, is retained.

Resurrection and Ascension

A. S. Peake, the Primitive Methodist scholar, had addressed both the virgin birth and the physical resurrection of Jesus from a critical point of view and come to the conclusion that both were warranted by the historical record.[359] Evidence of this level of scholarship indicates both the intellectual rigour and the orthodoxy represented within the uniting churches. If the hymn book was to be true to this context the texts chosen needed to be of similar quality. To this end we would expect the hymns to be theologically conservative yet imaginative in their structure while allowing for the questioning indicative of mystery. The idea of resurrection or ascension as myth had yet to be addressed by the denominations.

The fact of resurrection is asserted in many texts. The bodily resurrection of Jesus seems to have been beyond dispute for the people charged with compiling this book.

> On wings of living light,
> At earliest dawn of day,
> Came down the angels bright,
> And rolled the stone away (209)

provides an imaginative description of the resurrection. The keepers of the grave are pictured falling down 'with sudden fear' at which 'the Lord of earth and sky' rises 'Unseen by mortal eye'. The congregation is called on to rise with Christ, burying the old things of the past in the grave with him. The picture is entirely literal.

Death and resurrection are inevitably mixed together. 'The strife is o'er, the battle done' (215) states that Christ's death has made possible an objective change in the status of humanity. So it can be affirmed, 'Jesus lives! Thy terrors now / Can, O death no more appal us' (216). The grave can no longer 'enthral us'. Jesus has obtained the throne in heaven and 'We may go where He has gone'. 'Love's

---

359 Davies, George and Rupp, *A History of the Methodist Church in Great Britain*, Vol. 3, p. 201.

redeeming work is done' (204) and so we can 'Soar . . . where Christ hath led'. Through faith, it is implied, 'made like Him, like Him we rise'. There is no comfortable avoidance of the process through which we pass to achieve this exaltation, for 'Ours [is] the cross, the grave' as well as 'the skies'. Edmond Louis Budry's magnificent hymn, 'Thine be the glory, risen, conquering Son' (213), recognises that the process of salvation has not yet been concluded. The author understands the human need for sanctification and so the last stanza concludes, 'Make us more than conquerors, through Thy deathless love: / Bring us safe through Jordan to Thy home above'. 'Thine be the glory' indeed, for 'Endless is the victory Thou o'er death hast won'.

What is clear is the persistent assertion that such a hope is one that can be grasped by everyone. The Arminian theology of the editors of the *Methodist Hymn Book* continues to be woven as a thread through these texts that offer life and hope to all.

It is not surprising that such resurrection elicits praise. It is at this point that the possibility of doubt is addressed but in a rather emphatic and conclusive manner:

> all the doubting and dejection
> of our trembling hearts have ceased.
> 'Tis his day of resurrection;
> let us rise and keep the feast. (206)

This is hardly rigorous, or sensitive to the need for question for which critical scholarship and human credibility calls. The committee is seen to be more conservative than radical in its choice of texts. They were perhaps more strongly driven by an evangelical imperative, the penultimate verse of 'Christ the Lord is risen again' (207) moving in the direction of the Great Commission (Matthew 28.18–20), and concluding with an invocation that the Paschal Lamb might today feed his people and take away their sin and guilt.

All these affirmations rest on the belief that the tomb in which Jesus had been laid was empty and the next hymn, 'Ye humble souls that seek the Lord' (217), confirms that fact.

Ascension is, in one sense, the obverse of incarnation. This theological insight is not lost on the editors, as the inclusion of 'God is gone up on high' (219) illustrates with the statement: 'God in flesh below, / For us He reigns above'. This reign is one in which 'His foes and ours . . . Satan, the world, and sin' are subdued. Old Testament images of Kingship begin to pervade the texts at this point. Psalm 24 provides the inspiration for 'Our Lord is risen from the dead' (222), with its repeated references to the 'King of Glory' who will pass the 'everlasting doors' to the 'ethereal scene' which lies beyond the 'bars of massy light'.

The Kingship of the despised Jesus is recognised:

> Look ye saints! The sight is glorious,
> See the Man of Sorrows now,
> From the fight returned victorious;
> Every knee to Him shall bow.
> Crown Him! Crown Him!
> Crowns become the Victor's brow. (226)

Now Jesus is 'King of kings, and Lord of lords!' The hierarchy of heaven that mirrors, or is mirrored by, the hierarchy of society is reinforced by such texts and gives an insight to the ecclesiology of the committee. The uniting denomination was becoming a Church that was far more comfortable with an authoritarian form of government than something more democratic. The hymns reflect this. It is appropriate to suppose that such an influence came mainly from the Wesleyan contingent.

In spite of this there was still within the gestation of the denomination a belief in the priesthood of all believers. The death, resurrection and ascension of Jesus are seen as providing him with the credentials to be regarded as 'both priest and victim / in the eucharistic feast'.[360] But the cross is the point at which the transition, from temple worship and sacrifice, to the direct relationship of the worshipper with God, through Jesus, is marked. Priesthood is that role in which the people are represented to God and God to the people. No single individual can be, or needs to be, a priest. It is recognised that the sole priest is Christ. What is central is the relationship of each individual Christian through Christ with God with no other human intermediary. It is this understanding that would be expected to inform the *Methodist Hymn Book*. This is supported by the material in the section, 'His Priesthood and Sympathy', but it has been necessary for the editors to work

---

360 'Alleluia! Sing to Jesus', *Hymns & Psalms*, No. 592.

carefully to ensure that either the language of texts clearly supports
this position, or that they are sufficiently ambiguous to allow for
this interpretation. To that end the texts, without exception, speak of
the work of Christ on our behalf, as 'Entered the holy place above'
demonstrates:

> Entered the holy place above,
> Covered with meritorious scars,
> The tokens of His dying love
> Our great High-priest in glory bears;
> He pleads His passion on the tree,
> He shows Himself to God for me.
>
> Before the throne my Saviour stands,
> My friend and Advocate appears;
> My name is graven on His hands,
> And him the Father always hears;
> While low at Jesu's Cross I bow,
> He hears the blood of sprinkling now.
>
> This instant now I may receive
> The answer of His powerful prayer;
> This instant now by Him I live,
> His prevalence with God declare;
> And soon my spirit, in His hands,
> Shall stand where my forerunner stands. (232)

Jesus 'Entered the holy place above'. He is 'Our great High-priest in
glory'. The effect of Christ's mediation is immediate for 'This instant
now by Him I live' and it is the author's prayer that he might 'stand
where my Forerunner stands'. One aspect of the recognition of the
priesthood of Christ is the pre-eminent place that he must occupy in
the life of the Christian.

For Christians, and the Methodists who edited this book are no
exception, any theological assertion must result in a response from the
believer and so those who praise Jesus are addressed by Charles
Wesley, 'Ye faithful souls who Jesus know' (229), and reminded that
their faith must bear fruit. Horatius Bonar's text 'Rejoice and be glad!
The Redeemer hath come' (230) provides a fitting response to Wesley's

more restrained commentary. There is boldness in the acceptance of the stature of Christ and our relationship to him. Jesus is attentive to our needs in a variety of circumstances in this life and beyond.

Realised as well as future eschatology has a place in Methodist theology. Having explored the incarnation, life, death and resurrection of Jesus the hymn book now begins to offer an insight into contemporary eschatology as it considers the kingdom of God both present and future. 'Jesus, the conqueror, reigns' (243) offers an understanding of the present reign of Christ. There is no affirmation in the text of any triumphalist expectation, for those who follow Jesus are promised hardship.

The texts relating to the ascension are, for the most part, theological rather than descriptive in the sense that they address the significance of the ascension rather than the gospel narratives. For this reason they are dependent not on Lucan or Matthean material but on Old Testament apocalyptic and Psalms of kingship. This gives the section a sense of grandeur which owes itself to a transcendent theme rather than the other possibility, that of reflecting on the place of the disciples. Again we find that the material that has been chosen by the committee, with few exceptions,[361] distances the singer from the worldly consequences and challenges of an ascension that places responsibility for mission and service squarely with the followers of Christ. It is as though the opportunities to disturb the comfortable have been avoided. This again speaks of the influence of the Wesleyan members of the committee who seem to have been looking back to the solid, safe security of Edwardian England in which each class had and knew its place.

Jesus is 'King of kings and Lord of lords'. Rightly Christians should sing, 'Hail to the Lord's anointed' (245). James Montgomery's characteristic social concern is given expression in the second stanza of the hymn but, in this section, the flavour is rare.

Though the theme of Ascension is essentially rarified, the present imperative to evangelise, so characteristic of Methodism, is not lost. If this sense of God's reign is to have any present reality then mission is of the essence. The editors are aware of this. A missionary dimension is present. A social imperative is less strongly represented.

---

361 See James Montgomery's 'Hail to the Lord's anointed' (245), 'Jesu, the word bestow' (248) and 'In the Name of Jesus/Every knee shall bow' (249) discussed below.

'From north and south and east and west' (266) takes up the prophetic vision of the nations coming to God. The imagery is Victorian, for all are anticipated as finding their '*home* in Thee'.[362] It was difficult for the committee to detach themselves from texts that were popular even when they used sentiments that were becoming anachronistic.

An attempt to make the call to God contemporary is made by the inclusion of 'Saviour, we know Thou art / In every age the same' (269). Mission is done in the company of God who is bid in this time to 'exert / The virtue of Thy name'. 'God is with us, God is with us' (252) has a popular if militaristic format. It suggests an army moving with God's blessing across the earth, spreading the gospel message. There is no room for doubt as:

> Far across the field of battle
> Loud their holy war-cry rang;
> Never once they feared or faltered,
> Never once they ceased to sing.

Nowhere in hymnody is there a more explicit indication of the nature which Jeremy Paxman characterised as 'the Breed',[363] redolent of the personage of Richard Hannay in John Buchan's *Thirty-Nine Steps*.[364] Nowhere else in this book is there a more ready indication of the Edwardian confidence and public school influence that seems to have permeated many members of the committee.

More mystical, more expectant by far is Henry Burton's 'There's a light upon the mountains, and the day is at the spring' (256). The future reign of God is greeted with hope. The English texts on this theme have a naturalistic style while Catherine Winkworth's translation of Philip Nicolai's '*Wachet auf! ruft uns die Stimme*', 'Wake, awake, for night is flying' (255),[365] originates in biblical imagery of the bridegroom, watchmen and the heavenly city.

The one whose gospel is being proclaimed is 'The Lamb upon the throne', and so we 'Crown Him with many crowns' (271). Edward Denny's 'Light of the lonely pilgrim's heart' (268) broadens the

---

362 My italics.
363 J. Paxman, *The English*, London, Michael Joseph, 1998.
364 J. Buchan, *The Thirty-Nine Steps*, Ware, Wordsworth Editions, 1993.
365 Note that the translation here is not exact.

canvas by taking up the Pauline image of the whole creation groaning for the coming of Christ.[366] The committee had sufficient sense of scholarship to recognise the power of scriptural allusion within an affective text.

The Old Testament provides the source material for 'O come, O come, Immanuel' (257) which prays for God's reign to begin, while 'Thou art coming, O my Saviour' (258) anticipates that this is already happening.

Julia Ward Howe wrote

We women of our country will be too tender of those of another country to allow our sons to be trained to injure theirs. From the bosom of the devastated earth a voice goes up with our own: it says, 'Disarm, disarm!' Blood does not wipe out dishonour, nor violence indicate possession.[367]

Against this our interpretation of 'The Battle Hymn of the Republic' might be slightly different. 'Mine eyes have seen the glory of the coming of the Lord' (260) is not a call to war but a reminder of the final apocalyptic triumph of God at the eschaton and our part in working for justice and freedom in the present order. 'Light of those whose dreary dwelling' (261) is also eschatological in scope. The language prefigures the tendency in Victorian literature to view this life as dreary. Wesley's anti-Calvinist polemic is recognisable in the last lines of the second stanza, 'Come, Thou universal Saviour, / Come, and bring the gospel grace'. This grace offers forgiveness by 'mercy alone' acknowledging that salvation is by faith, as 'All thanks be to God' (262) illustrates. Reference in the fifth verse to 'the primitive days' refers to the days of the Early Church that the Primitive Methodist Church had sought to emulate.

The *Methodist Hymn Book* offers hymns on the ascension and resurrection that are essentially literal in their understanding of these events. The concepts of myth and metaphor are not explored or understood in relation to these narratives and 50 years on this would become a serious flaw for many people. This is less a criticism of the committee than of a Church that failed to respond to changes in

366 Romans 8.22.
367 Julia Ward Howe, quoted by H. Ward and J. Wild, *The Way of Peace*, Oxford, Lion, 1999, p. 104.

theology and understanding as the twentieth century unfolded. During this period metaphysical explanations of reality became less acceptable and so the texts presented here were increasingly inadequate to provide a vehicle for worship reflecting on the themes of resurrection and ascension.

The scholarship of the Editorial Committee is demonstrated in the range of material that they sought to include, with imagery derived from obvious texts in the New Testament through to more obscure passages in the Old. The temporal aspects, especially of the ascension, are downplayed, the emphasis being placed on mystical, eschatological and apocalyptic dimensions. There is, nevertheless, a missionary understanding derived most probably from the Bible Christians who were arguably the most evangelistic of the uniting denominations.

Ultimately what is depicted is a reign of God in which sin has been forgiven and peace obtained. This does not deny a social dimension that is clearly evident, though not dominant, within the texts. Again the committee presented this theme in a way which would seek to downplay any differences between the denominations while generally tending away from hymns which were overtly triumphalist.

The Holy Spirit

Pope, the Methodist theologian writing during the nineteenth century, stressed that belief in God is dependent on the direct witness of the Holy Spirit.[368] The Spirit 'is especially connected with mediating Christ to believers'.[369] George Osborn provided a more comprehensive account of the work of the Spirit in convicting sinners, recalling Christ to remembrance, enabling the adoption of people as children of God and building up believers in holiness.[370] Gregory comments that 'The Church is the organ of the Spirit [. . .] called into existence, created, shaped, animated, ensouled, actuated, by the Spirit'.[371]

368 Davies, George and Rupp, *A History of the Methodist Church in Great Britain*, Vol. 3, p. 185.

369 Davies, George and Rupp, *A History of the Methodist Church in Great Britain*, Vol. 3, p. 190.

370 Davies, George and Rupp, *A History of the Methodist Church in Great Britain*, Vol. 3, p. 190.

371 Quoted by Davies, George and Rupp, *A History of the Methodist Church in Great Britain*, Vol. 3, p. 191.

Tongue of Fire by William Arthur was the most influential exposition of the subject prior to the publication of the *Methodist Hymn Book*. Skilfully Arthur depicted the waiting and longing of the apostles for God's gift.[372] The hymn 'Come Holy ghost, all quickening fire' (299) fits this mode of thinking. It speaks of 'the lure of strong desire' with which the believer envisages the spirit being drawn. The eagerness of the believer mirrors that of the hart in Psalm 42, but by the end of the second stanza the metaphor is changed as the author is 'Plunged in the Godhead's deepest sea, / and lost in Thine immensity'. Frederick Hosmer's hymn also stresses human longing as he writes 'Go not, my soul, in search of Him' (281). The text is rather different, however, providing a picture of the Christian on a spiritual pilgrimage who is unsatisfied until he realises that God is to be found 'within'. This is in keeping with Arthur's further development of the doctrine.[373]

The Spirit is seen as being present in every believer. This lack of elitism is illustrated by the text 'To every one whom God shall call / The promise is securely made' (274). The sole condition to the receipt of this gift of grace is contrition, and the promise is reinforced by the inclusion of the next hymn, 'Jesus, we on the word depend' (275). This text goes on to affirm the sanctifying work of the Spirit. The presence of the Spirit is evidenced by moral power and the developing holiness of the recipient. The Spirit can inspire our present life. All of this is affirmed even though that life may, at times, seem to be lived in the context of a spiritual desert.

The Spirit's influence is not other-worldly and the believer is expected to apply Christian principles to social evils. It is very much a power for the life lived now.

'Gracious Spirit, dwell with me!' (291) has the intent that the singer should gain in grace, truth, tenderness, might and holiness, to the end of giving back to God what God has given. The path of such devotion is not easy and so Isaac Watts's text 'Come, Holy Spirit, heavenly Dove' (292) follows appropriately. Watts recognises that

---

372 Davies, George and Rupp, *A History of the Methodist Church in Great Britain*, Vol. 3, p. 190.

373 Davies, George and Rupp, *A History of the Methodist Church in Great Britain*, Vol. 3, p. 190.

> In vain we tune our formal songs,
> In vain we try to rise;
> Hosannas languish on our tongues
> And our devotion dies.

Only the Holy Spirit can 'Kindle a flame of sacred love / In these cold hearts of ours'.[374] 'Creator Spirit; by whose aid / The world's foundations first were laid' (293), considers the creativity of the Holy Spirit. This action is linked to God's purpose at Pentecost and the ability of the spirit to re-create humanity. The process of sanctification is addressed. Such sanctification provides anticipation. If God is 'My treasure and my all' it is possible to ask to be marked out as his heir and given a larger guarantee of heaven to which we are more sensitive so that 'all my powers Thine entrance feel, / And deeper stamp Thyself the seal' (299). The spirit is one which will overcome all opposition while, at the same time, providing 'lovely tempers, fruits of grace' (301).

As Arthur considered the role of the ordained ministry he stressed that the Spirit provided empowerment in a way that training could not. Ministers need training but without the Spirit ministry is lifeless. For Arthur the Spirit was to be accessed through prayer.[375] 'I want the Spirit of power within' (280) might have inspired Arthur's work. The text is sewn through with longing for the knowledge of the ownership of God. The gift is regarded as dependent on the request of the Christian and God's willingness to grant it. Once received, the work of this Spirit is one of cleansing and purifying, of breaking 'the power of cancelled sin', that of sanctification.

The texts on the Holy Spirit fit closely with the theological perspective in which the committee had been nurtured, yet the ordering of the texts is random. Arthur had underlined expectation.[376] 'Lord, we believe to us and ours / The apostolic promise given' (274) reflects this. The Spirit is to be claimed and so we are bid to sing 'Come down, O Love Divine' (273). The Spirit is a gift that must be claimed but first it is assumed, for 'Granted is the Saviour's prayer' (277). Charles Wesley

---

374 See 'O thou who camest from above' (386) – 'Kindle a flame of sacred love'.

375 Davies, George and Rupp, *A History of the Methodist Church in Great Britain*, Vol. 3, p. 191 f.

376 Davies, George and Rupp, *A History of the Methodist Church in Great Britain*, Vol. 3, p. 191.

speaks with confidence of the present reality of receipt of the Holy Spirit.

Amidst this orthodox collection Percy Dearmer's 'O Holy Spirit, God' (279) seems somewhat out of place. It begins with a pantheistic representation of the Spirit. The hymn then develops to indicate that this same Spirit which is found in the 'star-world' and 'sunshine' inspires 'The heroes and the saints' to become messengers so that light might be brought into the world, for 'All the lamps that guide the world / Were kindled at Thy flame'. The final gift which Dearmer seeks is that of fellowship so 'That we in counsel, knowledge might, / And wisdom, may increase'. This is an unusual text and an unexpected source for the missionary element in this section. One can only assume its inclusion resulted from a wish to find a text on the Holy Spirit that was at the same time evangelistic. Though Percy Dearmer's editing was too *avant-garde* for some, the quality of his writing could not be challenged by those of the committee who sought for literary excellence. Both needs were, thus, suitably met.

The Scriptures

The Methodist understanding of Scripture has never been fundamentalist but has always been evangelical. John Wesley put it like this: 'faith and salvation, include the substance of all the Bible, the marrow, as it were, of the whole Scripture'.[377] Humankind is the recipient of God's revelation confided in Scripture but that does not mean that God is perceived without a struggle.[378] By 1932 all the Methodist denominations had accepted that critical scholarship ought to be used in the interpretation of Scripture[379] though the extent to which that was applied within local churches varied considerably and still does.

The nature of God's word, though fundamental, only provides eight hymns in the section of the *Methodist Hymn Book* devoted to Scripture. The universal appeal of the Bible is underlined by John Keble's words: 'There is a book, who runs may read' (43). This text also indicates the scholarly base from which the editors were working, the term 'runs' being obscure even then. 'Runs' in this context means

---

377 A. C. Outler, *The Works of John Wesley*, Vol. 2, Sermons II, Nashville, Abingdon, 1985, Sermon 43, 'The Scripture Way of Salvation', p. 156.

378 Berger, *Theology in Hymns?*, p. 132f.

379 A number of the members of the Hymn Book Committee possessed such critical skills.

ordinary people. An alternative derivation from Daniel 12.4 seems less likely given the context of the whole stanza.

The theme of the hymns is, nevertheless, evangelical for within the Scriptures 'wretched sons of want / Exhaustless riches find'. 'Here the Redeemer's welcome voice / Spreads heavenly peace around'. Scripture is regarded as having been inspired by the Holy Spirit and the same Spirit is needed for right interpretation. 'The Spirit breathes upon the word, / and brings the truth to sight' (307).

If, as John Wesley had insisted, the Scriptures contain that which is necessary for salvation, an affirmation that is still part of the ordination service for Methodist presbyters,[380] then their character is ageless. The editorial choice of Henry Williams Baker's 'Lord, Thy word abideth' (308) clearly demonstrates that this was also the understanding of the Hymn Book Committee.

Methodism, across its denominations, had always followed John Wesley's maxim that the hymn book should be a source of 'experimental and practical divinity'.[381] The editors followed in this line of succession stating in the Preface that 'This hymn-book, like its predecessors, is intended for use in private devotion as well as public worship.'[382] Such individual use of hymns is illustrated by the inclusion of the text 'When quiet in my house I sit' (310), which asks 'Thy Book be my companion still'. The word is enduring enough to stay with Charles Wesley as he lays down to rest (rather as the image of daffodils was later to stay with Wordsworth) and it inspires him to sing his saviour's praise, 'Thee may I publish all day long', until he might join 'to the Church above'. Given this emphasis it is interesting to note that the editors decided against including a section dedicated solely to texts for private use. Minutes of the Editorial Committee [for texts] contains this note

the whole subject of Hymns 'chiefly for private devotion' seems to lie outside the work allotted to the Editorial Committee [. . .] This is largely a matter of index and will be dealt with at a later stage by the full Committee.[383]

---

380 *Methodist Worship Book*, London, Trustees for Methodist Church Purposes, 1999, p. 303.

381 *A Collection of Hymns for the Use of The People Called Methodists*, Preface, quoted in *Methodist Hymn Book*, p. vii.   382 *Methodist Hymn Book*, p. vi.

383 MARC 30/224.

The *Primitive Methodist Hymnal* had included such a section along-side hymns for family use. The *United Methodist Free Church Hymnal* had an independent section. In this light the editorial attitude seems to be somewhat contemptuous. The balance was perhaps, to some extent, redressed when J. C. Mantripp wrote on *The Devotional Use of the Methodist Hymn Book*, but this was separate from the hymn book itself and probably did not find its way into many singers' hands.

John Wesley stated that: 'The Scripture, therefore, of the Old and New Testament is a most solid and precious system of divine truth.' In one of the shortest sections of the *Methodist Hymn Book* this assertion is underlined. The choices of the committee indicate that they were, again, in the mainstream of Methodism with regard to the Bible and its interpretation. What is lacking is any recognition of the human role in the translation and interpretation of God's word.

Responding to God

Evangelical theology is predicated on the grace of God and the response of humanity. Victorian Methodists knew that there was a need for an apologetic to address the problems and doubts of those they sought to reach.[384] In the twentieth century this awareness and skill became diluted until Strawson was to comment that 'Methodist thought in this present century [the twentieth] can hardly be said to be adequate'.[385] All that was seen to be necessary was to 'preach a simple gospel'.[386]

In terms of hymnody the transition is also discernible. Strongly theological texts were replaced by those of a more strident, less scholarly nature. The *Methodist Hymn Book* offers a window into this process of transition and is, in some respects, the rearguard of this passing age.

Following the opening sections of the book the editors offered hymns relating the call of the gospel, and then others which described the Christian life and its goal in death, judgement and the future life.

---

384 Davies, George and Rupp, *A History of the Methodist Church in Great Britain*, Vol. 3, p. 187.

385 W. Strawson, in Davies, George and Rupp, *A History of the Methodist Church in Great Britain*, Vol. 3, p. 187.

386 Strawson, in Davies, George and Rupp, *A History of the Methodist Church in Great Britain*, Vol. 3, p. 187.

'Thy faithfulness, Lord, each moment we find' (311) begins by affirming God's faithfulness and kindness to which 'the vilest offender may turn and find grace'.[387] The next two verses describe the soteriological work of Christ in coming to save sinners. It is clear that the editors espouse a gospel of universal application. The assertion is firmly rooted in scripture. 'Behold the Lamb of God, who bears / The sins of all the world away!' (312) reflects on passages from Isaiah. The lamb is understood as God wearing a servant's form as 'He sojourns in a house of clay'. This incarnation hides his glory as 'God with God is man with men'. As such God 'calls His wandering creatures home'. In responding the aspiring Christian finds a place to 'hide within [God's] breast', a place of rest. The last stanza offers a suitably anti-Calvinist gospel call:

> Pardon ye all through Him may have,
> May now be saved, whoever will;
> This Man receiveth sinners still.

Charles Wesley's 'Come sinners to the gospel feast' (323) makes the same point. Here is the strongest indication, were it needed, of Wesley's, and the editors', Arminian theology:

> Let every soul be Jesu's guest;
> You need not one be left behind,
> For God hath bidden all mankind.

Clearly 'The invitation is to all'; that is, all can be saved.

Thus far we have witnessed orthodox theology posed in a restrained manner. 'To God be the glory' (313) is altogether more simple, more clamorous. The editors were trying to please a church of widely differing tastes.

Frederick Faber's confidence in God is given expression in the hymn 'Souls of men! why will ye scatter / Like a crowd of frightened sheep?' (318), for there is no need to flee from a '. . . shepherd / Half so gentle, half so sweet'. Faber seeks to underline his understanding of the inestimable love of God, but also the fickleness of human nature.

---

387 Cf., 'To God be the glory' (313) which contains the line 'The vilest offender who truly believes', which was softened in *Hymns & Psalms* to 'And every offender who truly believes', providing a more inclusive rendition.

What God offers is 'more than liberty'. Human failure cannot be judged in a more kindly way than it is by God. The evangelistic tone continues. The grace that is purveyed appears to be limitless for there is 'enough for thousands / Of new worlds as great as this'. The text is forward-looking,[388] giving weight to Strawson's assertion that Victorian Christians were aware of the world in which they were set and obliged to answer its questions.[389] For the editors this was, nevertheless, a safe text of established use and popularity, in spite of having been written by a Roman Catholic and making its first appearance in a Methodist hymnal.

At the turn of the century, with the American evangelical revival beginning to reverberate in this country through the work of Moody and Sankey, there was also fuel for those who wished to question Arminianism. The Methodist churches were not immune from this influence as, 'Hark! The gospel news is sounding' (315) demonstrates, but the selection of texts was careful to ensure that the assertion 'None need perish' continued to be made. The hymn illustrates well the tension between an understanding of universal grace, 'Grace is flowing like a river; / Millions there have been supplied', and the sense evangelistic urgency, 'Do not tarry, / come to Jesus while you may'. All of this can be summed up in the cliché, 'Jesus saves!' (316).

The hymns chosen by the editors suggest that this salvation was understood as saving not only from sin but also from the burdens of earthly life. Charles Wesley knew that peace could be found in Christ and he proclaims: 'Peace unspeakable, unknown' (319). An exploration of this sense of peace is, of necessity, complex. Such an exploration is enabled by scholarly texts such as 'Art Thou weary, art Thou languid' (320), a free translation by John Mason Neale of a Greek text.

Methodism has valued the concept of the 'open [communion] table' at which conversion can occur. By implication such communion is open to those outside the church and the scandal of this position is not avoided, as the inclusion of 'Sinners, obey the gospel word / Haste to the supper of my Lord!' (326) shows. In being addressed to the 'sinner', it lays to rest any suspicion that those who receive

---

388 The implication for Christianity of the possibility of life on other planets has been addressed as recently as 29 January 2004 in the *Methodist Recorder*.

389 Strawson, in Davies, George and Rupp, *A History of the Methodist Church in Great Britain*, Vol. 3, p. 186f.

communion have to be perfect. Acceptance of grace also results in obligation. Those who respond to the call must 'Justice pursue, and mercy love, / And humbly walk by faith with God' (343). The extent to which grace is dependent on the individual's response is debatable. Shades of Calvinism are seen to remain. There was certainly sufficient influence within the committee to suggest that turning from God had dire consequences. 'Sinners turn; why will ye die? (327) suggests that to resist is eternally fatal. This gives a sense of urgency to the task of evangelism. 'Rescue the perishing, care for the dying' (338) could be a call to offer simple human compassion. The second line makes it clear that the people referred to are to be snatched 'from sin and the grave'. Evangelists are being encouraged to 'Plead with them earnestly, plead with them gently' in order to waken 'by kindness' feelings lying buried 'that grace can restore'. Christian duty demands this act, and it is affirmed that 'Strength for thy labour the Lord will provide'.

Methodists believed that evangelism was a crucial task and no one needed to be excluded from its goal. The response to the gospel is, initially, one of repentance. The underlying theme is the need for God's grace. Eighteen hymns provide for this reaction. The Wesleyan theological statement that 'all can be saved' is underlined by the inclusion of texts such as 'There were ninety and nine that safely lay' (334). God is actively seeking those who are lost.

No sin need stand in the way of God. 'Depth of mercy! Can there be' (358) demonstrates that Jesus is persistent in calling even the most grievous sinner. 'Can God His wrath forbear? / Me the chief of sinners spare?' And we anticipate that the answer is in the affirmative. 'Ye neighbours and friends of Jesus draw near' (329) shows that a confident response can be made to God's grace for 'His love condescends' to invite the sinner. The word 'condescends' underlines not so much God's patronising manner towards the worshipper as the willingness to come down and be on a level with him/her. Nevertheless the archaism was to make the hymn less accessible as the years passed.

Methodist theologians of all denominations have underlined the importance of prevenient and justifying grace. Charles Homer Gabriel's classic revivalist hymn 'In loving kindness Jesus came' (336) acknowledges God's activity. There is no recognition of a process of sanctification. '*Now*[390] on a higher plane I dwell', writes Gabriel, as

---

390 My italics.

though this was an immediate consequence of justification. The hymn maintained its popularity as a result of simply expressed faith, 'And with my soul I know 'tis well', and a chorus with memorable imagery, allied to an effective tune.

In such a context we might expect conflict and doubt to be side-stepped. While some Methodists would have regarded the admission of these topics as admissions of failure of faith, the editors were worldly enough to understand the necessity for their inclusion. In spite of 'many a conflict, many a doubt' (353) Charlotte Elliott asserts 'O Lamb of God, I come'. The editors recognised that faith involves struggle and this is also given substance by the inclusion of Charles Wesley's 'Come, O thou Traveller unknown' (339), inspired by the account of Jacob's struggle with the stranger at Jabbok's well.

The question of whether or not the Christian can fall from grace is one which exercised John Wesley[391] and one which has continued to exercise Methodism. The editors recognised such a possibility by the inclusion of Charles Wesley's 'O Jesus, full of truth and grace' (346). Christ prays for us, and even if we fall through sin we never fall from grace, for we may pray, 'freely my backslidings heal':

> O Jesus, full of truth and grace,
> More full of grace than I of sin,
> Yet once again I seek Thy face;
> Open Thine arms, and take me in,
> And freely my backslidings heal,
> And love the faithless sinner still.
>
> Thou know'st the way to bring me back,
> My fallen spirit to restore:
> O for Thy truth and mercy's sake,
> Forgive, and bid me sin no more;
> The ruins of my soul repair,
> And make my heart a house of prayer.
>
> The stone to flesh again convert,
> The veil of sin again remove;

---

391 Outler, *The Works of John Wesley*, Vol. 3, Sermons III, Sermon 86, 'A Call to Backsliders', passim.

Sprinkle Thy blood upon my heart,
And melt it by Thy dying love;
This rebel heart by love subdue,
And make it soft, and make it new.

Ah! give me, Lord, the tender heart
That trembles at the approach of sin;
A godly fear of sin impart,
Implant, and root it deep within,
That I may dread Thy gracious power,
And never dare to offend Thee more.

The approach of the committee as evidenced by the hymns they have chosen to include is one in which repentance and forgiveness make sense because God is gracious and forgiving, accepts us as we are, and bears with our frailty. The texts on this theme are more varied in quality than in much of the book. 'Chorus' hymns are in evidence and underline the admission that 'the canons of literary merit used for the rest of the book' were suspended[392] for their inclusion. They are not always all that 'good'. Authors' names appear that would be unexpected elsewhere in the collection. Though many of the texts included here are theologically sound many are sentimental or romantic in their portrayal of the response of the believer to the call of God.

Growth of Faith

How does faith develop? For the young, arguably, through education. This has always been valued within Methodism. Education was implicit in John Wesley's evangelical technique and many of his publications sought to educate. Kingswood School in Bristol (it later moved to Bath) was opened in 1748 and was, effectively, Wesley's educational memorial.[393] In spite of this, the place of children within the Church has always been ambiguous and this is demonstrated by the contents of the *Methodist Hymn Book*. Hymns provided are written for children rather than echoing words or thoughts which children

---

392 *Methodist Recorder*, 1 December 1932, p. 14.
393 Davies, George and Rupp, *A History of the Methodist Church in Great Britain*, Vol. 3, p. 279.

might express. Rather than enabling a growth of faith consonant with the advances which were evident in theology during the nineteenth and the early part of the twentieth century, these hymns would have stultified any sense of exploration or growth. As an example, heaven is pictured 'Above the clear blue sky' (834). The text of this hymn is, in itself confused, placing both infants and youth as its subjects in consecutive verses making it inappropriate for either to sing.

Texts which speak of stories vary in quality. 'Tell me the stories of Jesus' (858) is simple and effective but has suffered from the elision of the verse relating to resurrection and therefore comes to an abrupt end. 'God has given us a book full of stories' (857) does not adequately describe the Bible, while the assessment of the story of Jesus being 'The most beautiful story of all' is bathetic. All of this is evidence that the editors were poorly prepared to assess what would be suitable for children and young people to sing. Most of them were of an older generation and distanced from everyday contact with children in day or Sunday schools.

The one person on the committee who might have been able to offer informed comment, Miss Lilian Cox, was marginalised, as is illustrated by her interchange with J. E. Rattenbury. In a letter to Edgar Barton she argues that a hymn of hers under consideration did not need alteration. In response to Dr Rattenbury's assertion [in Cox's words] 'that we ought all to be afraid of heresy', she asserted that 'our thinking ought not to be hampered by any fear, and that, moreover, all too often the label heresy was attached to new truth'. She felt that the point she was making was 'clear to many of the members'. She continued to remind Barton that the hymn was in use by the Girls' League and that any alteration ought to be sanctioned by their committee. She continued to explain that the criticised line contained 'nothing . . . to which Christian youth cannot subscribe. While not saying that I refuse to alter the hymn, I greatly hope that the Editorial Committee will be prepared to let the matter drop.' She also mentioned a possible introductory verse which would make the substance of the hymn clearer. If the hymn was not to have a heading allowing for clarification then she indicated her willingness to 'try to write an extra verse'.[394]

Far from containing matter to which 'Christian youth [might] subscribe', it would be difficult to think of the hymns that are collected

---

394 MARC 29/163.

here being sung readily by children or youths. As an example, 'Jesus, high in glory, / Lend a listening ear' (838) is an observation of children who are 'weak and apt to stray' rather than a picture with which children would readily identify. Intellectually able children and especially teenagers would soon find this fare wanting.

The hymns chosen that were written for children are, if anything, worse, as 'O Jesus, we are well and strong' (847) illustrates:

> O Jesus, we are well and strong,
> And we can run about and play;
> But there are children who are sick,
> And have to lie in bed all day.
>
> We thank Thee for our health and strength;
> And, loving Lord, we pray Thee bless
> The children who are weak and ill
> And suffer pain and weariness.
>
> Lord, give us thoughtful, loving hearts,
> Show us kind deeds which may be done
> By us, for Jesu's sake, to help
> Some sad or suffering little one.

Ultimately this hymn enables the child who is singing it to adopt a philanthropic if condescending tone. An image is conjured of a visitor to Tiny Tim in Dickens' *A Christmas Carol*, and perhaps this is what was imagined. Having grown up, at best, in the Edwardian shadows of the Victorian era this second-hand picture of childhood was a ready source to inform the minds of the committee.

Many of the texts are descriptive of children rather than to be sung specifically by them (835, 836, 837), and so 'Jesus loves the children' (843) and is described as 'a friend for little children' (839). The best of these hymns describes a biblical character. 'Hushed was the evening hymn' (848) tells the story of Samuel's call in a simple yet lucid manner. Many of the texts have a naive view of children, and even those of biblical provenance put unrealistic expectations on children and parents alike. Hence, 'little Lord Jesus no crying he makes' (860).

Clearly the section for little children is the weakest of the book, both theologically and in terms of application. Gillian Warson has provided a study of [Sunday School] Anniversary Services at Bicester Methodist Church from 1872 to 1968.[395] What is significant is the manner in which, over the years pertinent to her study, more texts from outside the *Methodist Hymn Book* appear to have been used in these services[396] and some of those from the hymn book were subject to extensive amendment. For example, the second verse of 'At the name of Jesus' allows that 'He, for selfless service, / Scorn received and shame'.[397] What had been seen as suitable to the editors of the *Methodist Hymn Book* clearly became outdated as time passed. Yet the book was not replaced. Increasingly Methodists began to look outside the corpus in order to meet their needs.

As the Christian grows and matures conflict can occur. Temptation is to be anticipated. Temptation and conflict are depicted as having two facets. Firstly, and predominantly, is the temptation to sin. Secondly, conflict can be brought about through human suffering. The emphasis on temptation to sin is greater than on the latter, though it is acknowledged that temptation may come from worldly sources but may also be embodied in pain or affliction. Hawks speaks of a need of God 'In joy or pain' and Charles Wesley acknowledges 'From trials unexempted / Thy dearest children are' (476). Eleven items in this section of the book come from the pen of Charles Wesley with only two items that might be characterised as 'popular' (475, 491).

The book mixes texts that recognise that maturing faith can doubt with those in which doubt would be regarded as culpable. The tension between those who would prepare a book for the new Christian and those editing one for those of mature faith is evident. Bible Christian and Wesleyan expectations meet head on.

Methodist theological perspectives continue to be underlined by the editors as they sought to bridge differences of intention. The range of perspectives for which the editors are having to provide expression is very wide.

Within the turmoil of growing faith the reassuring presence of God is presented from two angles. 'The Galilean fishers toil' (509) offers a sense of divine protection when the storms of life surround us. William Cowper's hymn, 'Sometimes a light surprises' (527), characteristically

---

395 G. R. Warson, *Jesus Wants Me for a Sunbeam, A musical history of Anniversary Services at Bicester Methodist Church, 1872–1968*, self publication, 2002.

396 Warson, *Jesus Wants Me for a Sunbeam*, p. 65–70.

397 Warson, *Jesus Wants Me for a Sunbeam*, p. 58.

explores the bleaker side of faith, 'when comforts are declining', but then sets this over against scriptural reflection that 'Who gives the lilies clothing / Will clothe His people too', and the context makes this no vain statement. The mind of the editor is clear in the next choice of text. The echoes are plain: 'safe is such confiding / For nothing changes here'; 'In heavenly love abiding' (528).

From this position of certainty it is possible to face conflict and still withstand. If this is accepted then the resignation illustrated by Catherine Winkworth's translation of George Christian Neumark's words 'Leave God to order all thy ways' becomes a reasonable option, though for the Methodist this is uncharacteristically fatalist rather than faithful:

> Leave God to order all thy ways,
> And hope in Him whate'er betide;
> Thou'lt find Him in the evil days
> Thy all-sufficient strength and guide:
> Who trusts in God's unchanging love
> Builds on the rock that nought can move.
>
> Only thy restless heart keep still,
> And wait in cheerful hope, content
> To take whate'er His gracious will,
> His all discerning love, hath sent;
> Nor doubt our inmost wants are known
> To him who chose us for His own.
>
> Sing, pray, and swerve not from His ways,
> But do thine own part faithfully;
> Trust His rich promises of grace,
> So shall they be fulfilled in thee:
> God never yet forsook at need
> The soul that trusted Him indeed. (504)

The pressure of a popularist constituency on the editors is evidenced here.

Such fatalism also appears elsewhere. Adelaide Anne Procter's 'My God, I thank Thee, who hast made / The earth so bright' (524) reaches a point of unhealthy masochism: 'I thank Thee more that all our joy /

Is touched with pain'. The best is yet to come. Perfect rest will only be found 'On Jesu's breast'. There is a clear recognition here that in spite of everything God is working out a purpose. More true to the denomination is John Wesley's translation of Nicolaus Ludwig von Zinzendorf's words, 'O Thou to whose all-searching light' (505), which suggest that it is sensible simply to follow Jesus.

This good sense is echoed by Henry Francis Lyte's 'My spirit on Thy care / Blest Saviour, I recline' (506). There is nothing that can come between God and his people, as 'Commit thou all thy griefs' (507) affirms. John Bunyan's experience in Bedford Gaol enabled him to view life and eternity in perspective. 'He that is down needs fear no fall' (514) states the obvious but is nonetheless powerful for that. From a degraded position Bunyan asserts that he is content with what he has and craves such contentment. While this is a true statement of his faith it leads to an acquiescent theology that can be used to oppress. His understanding is that to have little in this life is a guarantee of bliss hereafter. In such a choice New Historicism would recognise evidence of power vested in the most influential members of the body of the editorial committee, with their choice reflecting that which would reinforce rather than diminish such power.

Set against this is a less damaging, more affirming, expression of a similar strand of theological thought. John Greenleaf Whittier's meditation, 'who fathoms the eternal thought?' (513), arrives at the confident conclusion that,

> I know not where His islands lift
> Their fronded palms in air;
> I only know I cannot drift
> Beyond His love and care.

In struggling to provide texts which could give expression to the Christian's growth in faith the editors have made a number of errors. Generally speaking, when they have stayed with Charles Wesley's words they have remained true to the spirit of Methodism. Elsewhere what is presented can hardly be regarded as Methodist at all. It is difficult to strike a proper balance between the sovereignty of God, a right and proper submission of faith, and a sense of fatalistic acceptance of ill depending on the assurance that somehow, even if it is not immediately apparent, 'God is working his purpose out'. As the editors sought to address the needs of children their lack of experience of the present needs of the young made their choice even more precarious. Choices were made which suggest that there was strong influence to include what was popular, sometimes with scant regard to whether it was appropriate or whether its theology was sound.

Time took its toll on those items that were already dated when the book came to press and this was seen particularly in relation to hymns for children. It has been noted that, in spite of the influence of Lilian Cox, few contemporary texts for children were included and the omission made this section increasingly irrelevant as the years passed.

The editors had a difficult task and sometimes rose to it. Sometimes they did not. Most of what we have looked at so far would provide material for regular liturgical worship in Methodist preaching services. We have seen how theology and preference caused the committee to make choices. Having reached this point it is worth while asking why the editors arranged the material that they had chosen in the way that they did.

The editors of the *Methodist Hymn Book* seem to have had the structure of Methodist worship in mind when deciding on the ordering of the hymns in the book. There is a natural progression through invocation, adoration, confession, gospel and response that students of preaching would find familiar.

What is lacking here is material relating to sacramental services. Communion and Baptism come later in the organisation of the book. Two reasons for this may be discerned. Firstly, the majority of services in Methodist churches at the time of Methodist Union were non-sacramental. It is still true that the majority of acts of worship that take place in Methodist churches are led by lay preachers. Secondly, and related to this, is the fact that Communion services were not regarded as having the same importance as preaching services. For many congregations Communion was a second service which followed a preaching service and which was attended by a smaller group of people. Indeed, even following the process of liturgical renewal and the publication of *The Methodist Service Book* in 1975, printed services included the rubric 'Those who leave do so now, after this blessing.'[398] It was this perceived diminution of importance that the Methodist Sacramental Fellowship had been formed to address, but

---

398 *Methodist Service Book*, London, Methodist Publishing House, 1975, p. B9.

its effect on the organisation of the *Methodist Hymn Book* was considerable.

Looking at it another way, the *Methodist Hymn Book* began with an evangelistic imperative. Its purpose was to begin the process of seeking and saving those who were lost. Once incorporated into the body of Christ, the society of the Church, then other material would be needed. In contrast *Hymns & Psalms* provides a collection of hymns to fit in with the liturgical calendar of the Church year and to enhance the liturgical worship of the Church. It is less evangelistic in tone and using it to construct a liturgy from scratch is more difficult. In some ways it is apparently more secular, addressing issues of justice and the environment. In addition the manner in which sections are put together within the book do not allow for such easy devotional use however logical the progression of texts may be from other perspectives. The *Methodist Hymn Book* could hardly be more different. It was pre-eminently a preachers' hymn book.

5

The Hymn Book and Church Life

If the first two thirds of the *Methodist Hymn Book* related to preaching services the remainder of the book provided material for the life of the Church, of those committed to the membership of a Methodist Society. Such a society was founded on an understanding that holiness was the chief end for the Christian.

Holiness

A Plain Account of Christian Perfection[399] by John Wesley had been seminal for Methodists. Both John and Charles Wesley felt compelled to maintain that an element of Christian perfection was the attainable goal of every believer.[400] This doctrine was such an absorbing passion for John Wesley, and subsequently for Methodism, that Strawson stated that Christian Perfection or Scriptural Holiness was not only especially emphasised by Methodists but was 'sometimes regarded as their exclusive property'.[401]

Subsequently two strands can be discerned within Methodism. Firstly, there is an essentially scholarly line represented by Pope, Platt, Perkins and Flew. Secondly, there was a tradition that grew to see holiness as the central tenet of Methodist orthodoxy. This was proclaimed directly to the people rather than in scholarly discourse. Thomas Champness, Thomas Cook and Samuel Chadwick were its chief

---

399 *A Plain Account of Christian Perfection as believed and taught by the Reverend Mr John Wesley, from the year 1725, to the year 1777*, from *The Works of John Wesley* (1872 ed. Thomas Jackson), Vol. 11, p. 366–446, further editing by George Lyons for the Wesley Center for Applied Theology at Northwest Nazarene College (Nampa, ID).

400 Berger, *Theology in Hymns?* p. 143.

401 Strawson, in Davies, George and Rupp, *A History of the Methodist Church in Great Britain*, Vol. 3, p. 225.

proponents. Hugh Price Hughes can be regarded as a bridge between the two camps.[402]

A picture of the more popular strand is offered by reports of the Whitsuntide meeting at Cliff College in 1928 where it was stated that 'Souls are perishing; the nation is drifting back to paganism, bankruptcy and ruin.' The Church was criticised for having become intellectualised and respectable.[403] For some a 'second blessing', that of the gift of the Spirit manifest in enthusiasm, became a substitute for social action. Hugh Price Hughes was, however, not afraid of political comment while espousing holiness.[404] Contemporary with the Methodist Union, Robert Newton Flew noted the Wesleys' failure to relate holiness to human relations.[405]

At the time of Methodist Union the stance taken by the editors of the hymn book in relation to this theme was critical. Within the section devoted to this subject the texts they chose were primarily those of Charles Wesley. In a Moravian hymn by Ernst Lange, translated by John Wesley as 'O God, Thou bottomless abyss' (42), the theme is explored:

> O God, Thou bottomless abyss!
> Thee to perfection who can know?
> O height immense! What words suffice
> Thy countless attributes to show?
>
> Unfathomable depths Thou art;
> O plunge me in Thy mercy's sea!
> Void of true wisdom is my heart;
> With love embrace and cover me.
>
> Eternity Thy fountain was,
> Which, like Thee, no beginning knew;
> Thou wast ere time began his race,
> Ere glowed with stars the ethereal blue.

---

402 Davies, George and Rupp, *A History of the Methodist Church in Great Britain*, Vol. 3, p. 225.

403 Davies, George and Rupp, *A History of the Methodist Church in Great Britain*, Vol. 3, p. 228f.

404 Davies, George and Rupp, *A History of the Methodist Church in Great Britain*, Vol. 3, p. 229.

405 Davies, George and Rupp, *A History of the Methodist Church in Great Britain*, Vol. 3, p. 227.

Unchangeable, all-perfect Lord,
Essential life's unbounded sea,
What lives and moves, lives by Thy word;
It lives, and moves, and is from Thee.

Greatness unspeakable is Thine,
Greatness, whose undiminished ray,
When short-lived worlds are lost, shall shine
When earth and heaven are fled away.

Nuelsen described this as a prayer for perfect holiness and not at all subjective in its expression.[406] The path to holiness is a path to purity (544). The people who have been redeemed, who have committed their lives to God, who rest in trustfulness and peace, are being 'perfected in holiness' through the vicissitudes of their lives (87). This is the life towards which the early Methodists aspired. The picture painted by the choice of texts is firmly rooted in Wesleyan orthodoxy. The early Methodists sought for Christian perfection; they aspired to be perfect in love. To this end John Wesley wrote, 'Come, Saviour, Jesus, from above! / Assist me with Thy heavenly grace' (546). Such grace frees the believer from the ties of this world in order to obtain 'Thy pure love within [his] breast'. Charles Wesley understood that for this to happen a re-creation of the person was necessary and this is the theme of 'The thing my God doth hate' (547).

The content of these hymns makes a doctrinal statement that might be summed up as follows:

1. The place of people before God ought to be one of humility.
2. In spite of sin, through the redemptive action of Christ's work on the cross, perfection is an attainable goal.
3. This goal is universally available.
4. People may approach God in confidence.
5. The ultimate end of the Christian is in paradise in unity with God.
6. This end is reached through the transforming work of the Spirit.
7. It is an end that we can both anticipate, and for which we can pray.

---

406 J. L. Nuelsen, *John Wesley and the German Hymn*, trans. T. Parry, S. H. Moore and A. Holbrook, Keighley, Holbrook, 1972, p. 44.

What unfolded in the pages of the hymn book was a plain statement of Methodist orthodoxy that had more to do with John and Charles Wesley than the interpretive theology which came after them. The greater excesses of the more popular holiness movement were avoided, but neither is there any sign of the social application of Christian Perfection that Flew underlined, that Hugh Price Hughes was espousing.

Worship and Prayer

The styles of worship that were being yoked together at Methodist Union were diverse. The enthusiasm of the popular holiness movement, referred to above (see p. 140f.), was to be joined with a prayer book style not far distant from that of the Church of England. Indeed, in 1936 the Methodist Church adopted a *Book of Offices* that owed much to the *Book of Common Prayer*. In Wesleyan chapels Morning Prayer was read and Psalms were sung.

A less book-sourced, but no less structured, form of worship pertained elsewhere. The call to extempore prayer in the *Book of Offices* was included in response to Primitive Methodist promptings.[407] In all situations worship was centred on preaching, rather than Communion. When this sacrament was included it was often appended at the end of worship after a suitable blessing to allow those who did not wish to participate to leave.

The structure of the new Hymn Book reflected the domination of preaching. The sections were ordered to assist preachers preparing for worship. The Communion hymns were still relatively sparse when compared with the list of possible eucharistic hymns available from the pen of Charles Wesley, aside from anyone else.[408]

A Puritan element can be discerned for human worship is frail, 'Can it be that Thou regardest / Songs of sinful man' (668), our ways are 'foolish' (669), and yet such worship is not only possible but right. Therefore, moving from appropriate humility, the texts which follow recognise that we share in 'heavenly work' (670) and so we can participate 'With calmly reverential joy' in 'Setting forth Thy love'. Such action is an obligation, for we are bid to 'Sing alleluia forth in

---

407 Davies, George and Rupp, *A History of the Methodist Church in Great Britain*, Vol. 3, p. 332.

408 Rattenbury, *The Eucharistic Hymns of John and Charles Wesley*, p. 195–249.

duteous praise' (671). In such activity the worshipper draws near to heaven (672).

The editors sought to hold in tension earthly worship and the understanding of the transcendent. They did not always avoid over-sentimental expressions, as can be seen by the inclusion of hymns such as 'Summer suns are glowing / Over land and sea' (673). Such a hymn, however, continued to be popular long after the book came from the press.

Methodist worship of this period (and since) took place mainly on 'the Lord's Day', in fellowship rather than in solitude. This is in line with Methodist practice and theology.

The Sabbath was a day of rest, light a recurring theme. Isaac Watts used the adjective 'sweet' to designate the nature of this day (665). Morning and night were equally fitting times to offer worship. 'The day Thou gavest, Lord, is ended' (667) underlined the belief that the church, regarded as a world-wide body, never rests. 'The voice of prayer is never silent, / Nor dies the strain of praise away'.

Many of the texts imply that Sunday is a day of renewal and one in which things which are worthy are brought before God, but only Charles Wesley's 'Come let us with our Lord arise' (661) provides any overt connection of the Sabbath with the resurrection. Given the emphasis on this theme in the Gospels and in subsequent evangelical preaching this is strange.

While chapel worship was the norm the inclusion of words by William Cowper indicate that God can be found wherever people meet, that 'every place is hallowed ground' (675). There is a tension between the ubiquitous and the focused, for another hymn states 'Great is the Lord our God' who 'makes His churches His abode' (676), and the Methodists were going to sing with fervour 'We love the place O God, / Wherein Thine honour dwells' (677). If there had been any doubt before, Methodism was clearly now asserting its identity as a true Church within the Church catholic.

Prayer is individual as well as corporate. Devotional use of the hymn book has always been important for Methodists. The process of salvation is undergirded by prayer. 'Prayer is the soul's sincere desire' (533). It is 'the Christian's vital breath'.

Theologically there is nothing triumphalist or manipulative in the texts in the section on 'Prayer'. A breadth of styles of prayer was acknowledged for prayer can be 'uttered or unexpressed' (533). Prayer can come from 'infant lips' or the mouths of experienced Christians. God is seen as taking the initiative in providing the pattern for prayer and, through the Spirit, enabling such prayer. Participation in prayer is seen, chiefly, as a means of drawing close to God, 'Seeking fellowship divine' (537). The purpose of prayer is 'not to ask for gifts alone' (537), but it is a means of seeking and achieving God's will. It is pleasant, as implied by the rhetorical question 'My God, is any hour so sweet'? (536), though it also requires commitment. So the believer is bid to 'Pray, without ceasing pray' (541).[409] At all times and in all places the Christian should 'besiege [God's] throne'.

There is a separate section on 'The Church in Prayer'. This is suffused with an all-pervading sense of the unworthiness of the sinner pleading before God. Nothing is presumed and even those things that might be regarded as done well are pictured as flawed unless transformed by God's grace.

It is a cliché that Methodism was born in song. Hymns in themselves presume that worship will be corporate. The devotional use of hymns by Methodists, while important, has always been secondary to their congregational use. The book is not a choral resource but a depository for all worshippers. The editors' choice of texts demonstrates that, in their view, worship was to be entered into in a state of humility (725). A close relationship with God was assumed and, in line with the understanding that all can be saved, there was a sense of expectation.

Salvation is to be found within worship. Jesus is the 'Lord of life and glory' (724) who 'died our souls to save, / To sanctify us by His blood' (724). In this light the initial prayer of the expectant Christian is one for mercy and forgiveness offering a 'solemn litany' (726). But God is a 'Father of everlasting grace' (730), and so that is not the end. The theme of a growth towards holiness carries the worshipper forward. This is in keeping with the theology of Methodism in which salvation precedes sanctification and sanctification can take place 'to the uttermost'.

What the *Methodist Hymn Book* provided was a source of material to allow for hymn singing in corporate worship together with devotional material that could be read in fellowship meetings or in private prayer. Some Methodist ministers still read the hymn book

---

409 1 Thessalonians 5.17.

daily, one hymn at a time, as part of their private devotions. Many older Methodist lay-folk continued to use the hymn book in this way to the end of the twentieth century. In addition the editors made some attempt to understand the varying needs of the liturgical and non-liturgical streams of Methodism in the material that they selected. Psalms and Canticles were retained.

The Church

In addressing the Church, reference should also be made to 'Fellowship and Communion' (p. 152). As preparations were being made for the production of the *Methodist Hymn Book* the *Methodist Recorder* asked, 'What Doctrine of the Catholic Church will it set forth?'[410] John Wesley defined the catholic (universal) Church as:

> all the persons in the universe whom God hath so called out of the world as to entitle them to the preceding character; as to be 'one body,' united by 'one spirit;' having 'one faith, one hope, one baptism; one God and Father of all, who is above all, and through all, and in them all.'[411]

By the second half of the nineteenth century Methodism, and Wesleyan Methodism particularly, felt itself to be a 'real Church', claiming its place in the 'One Holy Catholic Church'. This self-assurance was expressed in the face of 'the persistent Anglican assumption that the Church of England represented the true and only Church of this land'.[412] The disparate denominations that were to make up the new Methodist Church underlined the identity of the body that they were to form simply by the act of union with each other. This should have resulted in a renewed sense of confidence.

The unique contribution of Methodism to the understanding of ecclesiology was that of Connexionalism which mirrored the New Testament concept of the relatedness of the members of the body of Christ but extended this to apply to the association of groups of Christians with each other. The concept became the foundation not

---

410 *Methodist Recorder*, 14 November 1929.
411 Outler, *The Works of John Wesley*, Vol. 3, Sermons III, 'Of the Church', p. 50.
412 Davies, George and Rupp, *A History of the Methodist Church in Great Britain*, Vol. 3, p. 192.

only of a theological understanding of interrelatedness but also the basis for the administrative and organisational structure of the body politic of the Methodist Church. Though distinctive, the Methodists still regarded themselves as part of the Church universal.

Methodists of all denominations understood that to gain access to the universal Church each person must first respond to the call of God. As a consequence the hymns in the *Methodist Hymn Book* that relate to the Church begin with the individual. The response of faith to the grace of God results in salvation, and it is those who are saved who subsequently make up the Church. Through repentance and God's gracious forgiveness the sinner becomes part of the body of Christ. Stress is laid on salvation by faith. There is a guard against the heresy that this might suggest human initiative in the process. Faith itself comes from God: 'Faith to be healed thou know'st I have, / for *Thou*[413] that faith hast given' (366). Wesley underlines that faith is a gift, that deliverance is found in the person of Jesus and that it is through the power of the Spirit that sin is conquered.

The editors' understanding of the response to God's call is illustrated by Charles Wesley's 'Where shall my wondering soul begin?' (361). This starts, appropriately, at the point of conversion. The scriptural allusions within the text are diverse but they are also personal. For instance, 'A brand plucked from eternal fire' refers to Zechariah 3.2. The text relates to Joshua and Charles Wesley adopts it as his own in two ways. Firstly, this hymn and the text associated with it marks his own conversion. As Joshua was chosen by God so was the author. Secondly, Charles and John had both been rescued from a fire at Epworth Rectory in their childhood. The experience left a vivid impression on them and they allied it to this text. The second stanza then provides a classical exposition of evangelical salvation. Understanding what God has done for him, Wesley reflects that it would be to 'slight my Father's love' if this gem were hidden 'within my heart' and so the evangelical imperative is born and given expression in the fourth verse. Without the preceding stanzas this would be patronising indeed, but Wesley has indicated his own need for redemption and can call effectively to others in similar circumstances. The text is an anthem of Methodist evangelicalism that could be sung by any member of the uniting denominations.

---

413 My italics.

Dedication is regarded by the editors as something which is evangelical in its motivation, yet soundly rational. In this light it makes sense to sing, 'Let Him to whom we now belong / His sovereign right assert' (383). The editors place themselves firmly in line with Wesleyan theological understanding. As Christ has 'bought us with a price', 'He justly claims us as His own'. Christians owe everything in life and death to Christ. To this end they should expire in God's cause recognising that they are God's 'to all eternity'.[414] This is not a sacrifice but a condition for which the believer longs. 'Being of beings, God of love' (383) proceeds to a conclusion in which we sing, 'So shall we ever live, and move, / And be with Christ in God'. The sense of self-giving is total. While the Arminian strand within Methodism was not denied the editors also chose those texts that firmly linked faith and works in a manner that was expressive of the Protestant work ethic.

It is this that made the imposition of ethical principles by the church possible. Dedication to God is ultimately understood as dedication through the Church. The Church in its interpretation of Scripture then begins to mould the mind of the latent disciple. Methodist theology understands that, following conversion, the Holy Spirit works in the life of the individual to enable his/her regeneration. The response to the teaching of the Church is indicative of the reality of this process. Again the editors are in the mainstream, choosing at least six hymns of Charles Wesley to underline the centrality of this transformation.

Commitment is shown as a willingness to accept what God has graciously offered: 'I'll take the gifts He hath bestowed', but then 'humbly ask for more'. Frances Ridley Havergal's hymn which follows next, 'Take my life, and let it be' (400), is simple yet not simplistic. Everything is to be offered to God.

This dedication leads towards an imitation of Christ depicted by the text 'Jesus, I fain would find' (385). The use of the image of the flame of love and the purifying fire of God continues with 'O Thou who camest from above' (386), and looks to an end where the trembling flame of the author's faith might burn with 'inextinguishable blaze' until, returning to its source, the sacrificial dedication is absolute, ending only in death which 'make[s] the sacrifice complete'.

The editors thus move from the point of conversion to the

---

414 This text is evidence of Charles Wesley's emphasis on the Christian exertion which is evident in his sermons. K. G. C. Newport, *The Sermons of Charles Wesley*, Oxford University Press, 2001.

expectation of perfection in holiness and love. The hymns they have chosen are pervaded by a sense of wonder at the gracious mercy of God. There is no distinction between the Church temporal and the Church eternal. Charles Wesley points people beyond the converting experience to the hope of heaven. The process of sanctification must follow conversion and justification. God's initiative in the process of salvation is acknowledged, lest it be thought that appropriating salvation by faith puts power into the hands of the penitent sinner. The gift is such that Wesley calls for its universal application: 'O that the world might know / The all-atoning Lamb'. Salvation is never an end in itself. In the light of conversion a question is raised: 'My Saviour! How shall I proclaim, / How pay the debt I owe?' (388). There is also a sense of joy and thanksgiving. The editors explore the gifts and nature of God and the human response to this exploration. A thread uniting the texts is the sense of joy derived from dedication to God. On occasion this expression is ecstatic (for example, 422), at other times it is more restrained (for example, 412).

Reflecting St Augustine's maxim that 'My heart is pained, nor can it be / At rest till it finds rest in Thee', 'Thou hidden love of God' (433) explores the observed distance between the perceived love of God and the Christian appropriation of that love, the necessary humility in the heart of the believer:

> Thou hidden love of God, whose height,
> Whose depth unfathomed, no man knows,
> I see from far Thy beauteous light,
> Inly I sigh for Thy repose;
> My heart is pained, nor can it be
> At rest, till it finds rest in Thee.
>
> Thy secret voice invites me still
> The sweetness of Thy yoke to prove;
> And fain I would but though my will
> Seems fixed, yet wide my passions rove;
> Yet hindrances strew all the way;
> I aim at Thee, yet from Thee stray.
>
> 'Tis mercy all, that Thou hast brought
> My mind to seek her peace in Thee;

Yet, while I seek but find Thee not,
No peace my wandering soul shall see;
O when shall all my wanderings end,
And all my steps to Thee-ward tend?

Is there a thing beneath the sun
That strives with Thee my heart to share?
Ah, tear it thence, and reign alone,
The Lord of every motion there!
Then shall my heart from earth be free,
When it hath found repose in Thee.

O hide this self from me, that I
No more, but Christ in me, may live!
My vile affections crucify,
Nor let one darling lust survive!
In all things nothing may I see,
Nothing desire or seek, but Thee!

Each moment draw from earth away
My heart, that lowly waits thy call;
Speak to my inmost soul, and say,
'I am thy Love, thy God, thy All!'
To feel Thy power, to hear Thy voice,
To know Thy love, be all my choice.

In the choices that they made the Hymn Book Committee indicate that they were still wedded to the tradition of the catholic Church and the influence of the Church Fathers valued by John Wesley.

The committee understood that, within a mature faith, there is room for doubt. William Cowper is, characteristically, introspective, uncertain as he writes, 'Hark, my soul! It is the Lord' (432) for, although he provides a text which is threaded through with certainty, he finds it difficult to apprehend this for himself. Balanced with this is the evangelical certainty of 'My God I am Thine' (406) which speaks of intense happiness in the knowledge of the possession of Jesus as a saviour such that 'my heart it doth dance at the sound of His name'. The tension of alloying evangelical fervour to restrained theological reflection has clearly influenced these choices.

The committee provide evidence of their understanding of the soteriological supremacy of Christ. 'Worship, and thanks, and blessing' (412) are offered to Jesus. He is 'Head of thy Church triumphant' (411). This is 'The God of our salvation' who has brought us safely to the present in the same way that he protected his people who 'Passed through the deep, / By crystal walls protected'. Ultimately by the grace of this saviour the author anticipates eternal deliverance.

A definite sense of direction begins to be discernible as the editors ask, through the texts, what is the end, in human terms, of worship? What is the purpose of this Church of which they are a part? The answer which is provided, through the authors they have chosen, is that there is no end to such praise. What has begun on earth is continued and, it is anticipated, will never end in heaven as long 'as a deathless soul shall live' (429). The Church, as God's people, is taken up into heaven.

Alongside such joy is an expectation of reciprocated love and consequent communion. This is expressed in three distinct ways in the hymns included in this book. The classic evangelical form, in which the individual is aware of sin, accepts the saving gift of grace and, in commitment to God, enters into loving communion, is used freely. 'My Jesus, I love Thee, I know Thou art mine' (437) offers a clear affirmation of the author's commitment to Jesus deriving from God's love for the author.

Secondly, there is a distinct thread of mysticism in which authors speak of a particular and intimate intercourse with God within their lives which seems independent of their state of grace, and is mediated by a natural experience of God, through hearing God's word or in prayer. 'Loved with an everlasting love' (443) provides a theological exposition of love, its mediation by grace and the witness of the Spirit to its veracity. The consequence of this love is 'full and perfect peace'. Such love 'cannot cease'. The author is aware of the mystic's affirmation that within divine love there is a heightened sensibility, something known also to the writer of secular love songs: 'Heaven above is softer blue, / Earth around is sweeter green', but here this awareness is linked to a relationship with Christ. In 'That mystic Word of Thine, O sovereign Lord' (469), the word 'mystic' provides the expectation that the author anticipates close communion with God in this life and this assumption is substantiated by the hymn. Three out of six of the stanzas begin with the words 'Abide with me'. It is a present relationship that is sought.

Thirdly, if less prominent, there is a strand which implies that close communion with God is only attainable after death. A sense of evolving pilgrimage inspires: 'O Jesus Christ, grow Thou in me' (463). The end point of this development is such that the believer is totally taken over by God. To attain this height of intimacy it may well be necessary to die, as Sarah Flower Adams states: 'Nearer, my God, to thee . . . / E'en though it be a cross / That raiseth me' (468). The movement is inexorably towards heaven.

All three cords are drawn together in 'Love divine, all loves excelling' (431) which ends with an exultant peroration: 'Till we cast our crowns before Thee, / Lost in wonder love and praise'. This, then, is the perceived end of the Church.

The sense of a universal Church of which believers are a part is a constant theme running through these hymns. The Church is not bounded by time or space. The Church has one foundation. It is focused in and through the person of Jesus. It comprises those saved by grace through faith.

What is absent from the collection is any sense of the uniqueness of Connexionalism. It is true that fellowship is prominent but the inter-connectedness of Methodist Societies and the integrity of a Connexion are absent from the vocabulary of the hymns. Were this not such a distinctive feature of Methodism this would not be surprising. It could be argued that Connexionalism was purely organisational but it was expressive of a deep theological understanding that is more significant than a matter of simple practicality. Perhaps no hymns existed to fill this space. But new hymns can be commissioned and written. Perhaps the committee assumed Connexionalism as a fact or, which is more likely, in order to assert the place of Methodism in the universal Church, they sought to give expression to those things that would include, rather than make the denomination distinctive.

Fellowship and Communion

Close fellowship was one of the formative features of Methodism. Class Meetings and Bands allowed for organisational structure but also brought people together with the expectation that they would support one another. Fellowship was to involve study and prayer. Confidence in the group was such that the Band Meeting became the place for personal confession and reconciliation. Members were expected to look out for one another's spiritual well-being. If prayer binds people to God then the fellowship are bound to each other in equally powerful ways. Here was a pilgrim band:

> The little fellowship of Christian people was, as it were, the micro-cosm through which [Charles Wesley] understood and interpreted the deepest principles of the Church of God [. . .] like his brother, he believed that Christianity was in its essence a social religion.[415]

While Charles Wesley's main emphasis was directed to another world for which God was the 'Captain of Israel's host, and Guide' (608) his sense that it also involved a fellowship in which we 'build each other up' (745) was inescapable.

Within the *Methodist Hymn Book* both views can be discerned. The Communion of Saints is seen to mix the human and divine. It is the right goal of fellowship and this is given a tangible expression in the Lovefeast, something more than a meal yet less than communion. There is a sense of camaraderie of the faithful who reflect 'And are we yet alive, / And see each other's face?' (709). On gathering together there is a celebration of the continuity of existence. There is an acknowledgement that such survival is by no means presupposed.

In another denomination the part played by the Lovefeast might, in part, be displaced by the Eucharist or Lord's Supper. Methodism's origin as a movement within the Church of England meant that the evolving Methodist Societies depended on the parent Church for this sacramental provision. The link with Anglicanism enabled the Wesleyan J. E. Rattenbury to state that 'the Anglican Communion Office very slightly altered, has always been that of the parent [Methodist] Church in England'.[416] Those associated with others of the uniting denominations shunned this heritage and cherished a dissenting position that saw much associated with a formal Com-munion liturgy as questionable. As a consequence of these historical factors, although Charles Wesley had written many Communion hymns[417] few of these found their way into mainstream use within any of the uniting denominations. The inclusion of only 18 Communion

415 Rattenbury, *The Evangelical Doctrines of Charles Wesley's Hymns*, p. 320.
416 Rattenbury, *The Eucharistic Hymns of John and Charles Wesley*, p. 150.
417 Rattenbury, *The Eucharistic Hymns of John and Charles Wesley*, passim.

hymns in the *Methodist Hymn Book* reflects this heritage. The editors again had to enable a compromise between disparate parties.

Those hymns that were chosen do not represent the high sacramental position of the Wesleys, or they are expurgated. For instance, 'Jesus we thus obey / Thy last and kindest word' (761) omits any allusion that could be interpreted as referring to transubstantiation:

> He bids us drink and eat
> Imperishable food;
> He gives his flesh to be our meat,
> And bids us drink his blood.

Methodism had moved from the position of the Wesleys and the editors reflected this in their choice of texts. Rattenbury was later to remind Methodism of its Eucharistic heritage, the value of the eucharistic hymns of Charles Wesley, and to provide evidence that in certain quarters Holy Communion was still highly valued.[418] Eventually he became an outstanding leader of the Methodist Sacramental Fellowship.[419] Later British Methodist hymnals were, to some extent, to hear his call and rectify the omissions of the past.

Generally speaking, the texts included in the *Methodist Hymn Book*, in line with Methodist theology, see the elements of communion as tokens, as signs (756, 767). Against this the Congregationalist Ray Palmer's translation of Thomas Aquinas' words (768) seems strangely out of place.

> O Bread to pilgrims given,
> O food that angels eat,
> O Manna sent from heaven,
> For heaven-born natures meet,
> Give us, for Thee long pining,
> To eat till richly filled;
> Till, earth's delights resigning,
> Our every wish is stilled.

418 Rattenbury, *The Eucharistic Hymns of John and Charles Wesley*, p. 150.
419 Newton, *Heart Speaks to Heart*, p. 70.

O Water, life bestowing,
Forth from the Saviour's heart,
A fountain purely flowing,
A fount of love Thou art:
O let us, freely tasting,
Our burning, thirst assuage;
Thy sweetness, never wasting,
Avails from age to age.

Jesus, this feast receiving,
We Thee unseen adore;
Thy faithful word believing,
We take, and doubt no more:
Give us, Thou true and loving,
On earth to live in Thee;
Then, death the veil removing,
Thy glorious face to see.

Its reference to water implies an understanding of mixed Communion, which is so foreign to Methodism, and there is no mention anywhere in the hymn of wine.

The meaning of Communion is explored. Here is a means of accessing the 'feast divine' (757), of keeping alive the 'memory of Thy love' (757, 762, 763, 773). The words of Henry Williams Baker are to be those of the congregation: 'I am not worthy, holy Lord / That Thou shouldst come to me' (758). This is appropriate for we are 'Mindful of the love / That bought us, once for all, on Calvary's tree' (759). The sense of wonder is an underlying thread through this corpus as the next hymn, 'Saviour, and can it be' (760) demonstrates.

The Lord's Supper is seen as the place of spiritual sustenance for the believer. Here are 'fresh supplies of love' (764) which is 'our immortal food' (766), 'The true and living bread' (770) and 'Thy flesh is meat indeed' (769), the nearest the singer is allowed to come to transubstantiation. Christ is the 'Victim divine' (771) but lest it should be thought that this is the language of the Mass the text reminds us that he was '*Once*[420] offered up' for the atonement of 'all

---

420 My italics.

mankind'.[421] The allusion to 'real presence' in this hymn is sufficiently ambiguous to pass. The next text clarifies this understanding, for it is not a case of tasting but seeing: 'Here, O my Lord, I see thee face to face' (772). Communion is mystical. The association of the Eucharist with the cross is confirmed in the final text, 'By Christ redeemed, in Christ restored' (773).

Communion within the context of the *Methodist Hymn Book* is presented almost as an interlude. This reflects Methodist practice of the time. Fellowship had a greater emphasis. Rattenbury pointed the Church back to the doctrinal authority of the hymns on the Last Supper and his belief that they should be sung.[422]

Fellowship is presented as companionship on earth. This is recognised as a precursor to 'heaven's unutterable bliss' for here believers offer each other 'the right hand / Of fellowship' indicative of worldly trust and a spiritual bond. These are 'Brethren in Christ, and well beloved' (710) who know that God's uniting love 'will not let us part' (712), who 'join hearts and hands' in order to 'gain our calling's hope' (713). There is an expected mutuality of support (713, 717). In spite of this the fellowship that is experienced finds its source in God. 'Jesus we look to Thee' (718) affirms Charles Wesley's expectation that not only are the believers in fellowship one with another, but 'Thou in the midst of us shalt be'. Believers are 'Brethren in Christ' (710) and as such need no friends, having the love of God (714). It is the might of God which cements fellowship and for this God is blessed (715). What is provided is a fine hymnic expression of the atmosphere of the Class Meeting.

The activity of God, in what might otherwise have been seen as a simply human occupation, is never far away. Unity is found through grace (721), a unity which renders 'all distinctions void' (720), words of Charles Wesley which echo those of John Wesley on 'The Catholic Spirit'. There is a recognition that such fellowship is enabled by God but also consequent on the believer's response: 'O happy day that fixed my choice / On Thee, my Saviour and my God' (744).

---

421 'O God of our forefathers, hear' (723), found in the section on 'The Church in Prayer', follows a similar theme with the lines:

> With solemn faith we offer up,
> And spread before Thy glorious eyes,
> That only ground of all our hope,
> That precious bleeding sacrifice.

422 Rattenbury, *The Eucharistic Hymns of John and Charles Wesley*, p. 151f.

Through growth in fellowship it is appropriate to look 'to things above' (722), beyond this temporal realm. The appropriate context for this journey to begin is God's dwelling (711). Believers will 'hand in hand go on' to their 'high calling's glorious hope' (745). There is an eschatological feel as Wesley ponders, 'What heights of rapture shall we know / When round His throne we meet'. The signs of the Kingdom are anticipated.

The section entitled 'The Church Militant and Triumphant' takes us to the Kingdom anticipated in this contemporary fellowship and communion. Here we find hymns of triumph (821) and those which seek to encourage the believer in spiritual (822) and temporal (816) warfare. Alongside are devotional texts which remind the singer of those who have died, their place in heaven and an anticipated time of reconciliation. If this situation is to pertain for others they must also be drawn beneath 'the banner' and so hymns of an evangelistic nature are also included (817, 820).

The language of some of the items in this section is vivid. 'The Son of God goes forth to war' (816) speaks of 'The martyr first, whose eagle eye / Could pierce beyond the grave', of 'valiant saints' meeting 'brandished steel':

> The Son of God goes forth to war
> A kingly crown to gain;
> His blood-red banner streams afar:
> Who follows in His train?
> Who best can drink his cup of woe,
> Triumphant over pain,
> Who patient bears his cross below,
> He follows in His train.
>
> The martyr first, whose eagle eye
> Could pierce beyond the grave;
> Who saw his Master in the sky
> And called on Him to save.
> Like him, with pardon on his tongue
> In midst of mortal pain,
> He prayed for them that did the wrong:
> Who follows in his train?

A glorious band, the chosen few
On whom the Spirit came,
Twelve valiant saints, their hope they knew,
And mocked the cross and flame.
They met the tyrant's brandished steel,
The lion's gory mane;
They bowed their necks, the death to feel:
Who follows in their train?

A noble army, men and boys,
The matron and the maid
Around the Saviour's throne rejoice
In robes of light arrayed.
They climbed the steep ascent of heaven
Through peril, toil and pain:
O God, to us may grace be given
To follow in their train.

The hope which is contained within these texts is best expressed by Isaac Watts and Charles Wesley. Watts prays 'Give me the wings of faith to rise / Within the veil' (831). Wesley grasps the vision and sings 'Come, let us join our friends above' (824). The oneness of the Church and the communion of saints is acknowledged and, in words that have never been surpassed, the dynamic unity and continuity of this communion is pictured. The strength of the text is witnessed to by its continued use as a memorial hymn at each year's Methodist Conference and its more occasional use as a funeral hymn.

Death is inevitable, as is judgement. Images of the sea, ebbing (641), drifting (642), the 'ocean's wave beat shore' (651), provide a dominant source of metaphors to enable reflection on these themes. Alfred Tennyson's 'Sunset and evening star' (640) provides the fullest exposition of death from this perspective.

One text which might have been expected, with its line 'Swift to its close ebbs out life's little day', 'Abide with me' (948) is found not here but in the section devoted to Morning and Evening. This remembrance leads to another image which is present in the current section, that of the closing of the day.

The Victorian image of heaven as home is represented here as is the sense of reunion with loved ones who have died. Those who anticipate death are moving inexorably on called by angels (651) to a better land. This is 'Jerusalem the golden' (652), 'a land of pure delight' (649). How effective these texts would have been in giving expression to the emotions of those left with the uncertainty that pervaded Europe after the First World War is doubtful. They are, perhaps, witness to the editors' longing for a time past when all did indeed seem more secure.

Vivid images of judgement are few and this does reflect the new mood of the age. The image of life passing through the darkness of death that opens into light is explored in a number of hymns.[423] There is little sense of impending doom. What there is is depicted by texts from Charles Wesley, Walter Scott and a translation of Thomas of Celano's '*Dies irae, dies illa*'. Wesley suggests that the faithful are 'To pray, and wait the hour' (644), but the hymn is tempered by the remembrance of the need to rely on God's grace. This is not a message of fire and brimstone but, rather, a sensible warning of the anticipated judgement of a merciful God. The final verse therefore hopes for 'A lot among the blest'. Scott is altogether more graphic in his use of judgemental allusions. 'That day of wrath, that dreadful day' (645) is one on which the 'flaming heavens' will shrivel 'like a parched scroll':

> That day of wrath, that dreadful day
> When heaven and earth shall pass away:
> What power shall be the sinner's stay?
> How shall he meet that dreadful day?
>
> When, shrivelling like a parchèd scroll,
> The flaming heavens together roll,
> When louder yet, and yet more dread,
> Swells the high trump that wakes the dead.
>
> O! on that day, that wrathful day,
> When man to judgement wakes from clay,
> Be Thou, O Christ the sinner's stay,
> Though heaven and earth shall pass away!

The trumpet that wakes the dead is 'louder yet, and yet more dread'. Thomas of Celano's 'Day of wrath! O day of mourning' (646) has that

---

423 See for example 629, 630 and 631.

same trumpet making a 'wondrous sound' ringing through 'earth's sepulchres' for 'All before the throne it bringeth'. The words are more hopeful as 'Death is struck' and 'all creation is awaking'. Nothing is hidden from the judge who has all things accurately recorded in his book but can grant a 'gift of absolution' which opens the way to 'eternal rest'. There is a sense of the 'happy retribution' spoken of elsewhere.[424] This tempering of language gave rise to resistance from the floor of Conference.

The editors regarded 'Funerals and Memorial Services' as times of rejoicing. While it is true that Christian faith can provide a sure ground for 'hope, confidence and even for joy' in the face of death; grief is also one of the components of the human response. Only one text here, 'When our heads are bowed with woe' (978), takes this aspect of mourning seriously, though the texts that offer praise are not triumphalist as much as relieved.

Not until the publication of *Hymns & Psalms* in 1983 did the Methodist Church finally demonstrate in a hymn book that it had broken away from the pastoral structures which had been formative during the lifetime of John Wesley. The *Methodist Hymn Book* still clearly focuses on a fellowship that is closely bound, in which people seek to build each other up in faith. This fellowship is seen as a precursor to the Communion of Saints and the hymns relating to this communion and the subject of death are derived from an internalised understanding of the pre-eminence of a fellowship which is God-given, initiated and sustained by grace.

Within this fellowship meals are shared but the place of the Eucharist is almost incidental. 'There were a few survivals of Wesleyans taking communion at the Parish Church in the late nineteenth century.'[425] The paucity of eucharistic hymns used within Methodism following Union was commented on in 1948 by J. E. Rattenbury who sought to account for the decline in sacramentalism that he observed within the Methodist Church.[426] The lack of hymns in this section of the *Methodist Hymn Book* reflected partly the historic development of the Methodist Church as a movement within the Church of England and the reaction against formal communion

---

424 'Brief life is here our portion' (652).
425 Davies, George and Rupp, *A History of the Methodist Church in Great Britain*, Vol. 3, footnote, p. 153.
426 Rattenbury, *The Eucharistic Hymns of John and Charles Wesley*, p. 148–50.

that was seen by some as reflecting too close an association with the Anglican Church from which separation was fundamental. Still others associated communion with 'Popery'.[427]

Only as Methodists shared in liturgical renewal with other denominations in the latter half of the twentieth century did communion begin to regain the place that it once, arguably, had for John and Charles Wesley. The loss of this focus, as the denominations that had begun as movements within the Church of England became separated, is clearly reflected in the choice and organisation of hymns within the *Methodist Hymn Book*.

The Ministry of the Church

Ministry in Methodist understanding is inclusive, deriving its authority from the Methodist Conference, which Bunting, not long after the death of John Wesley, saw as 'a kind of corporate Wesley'.[428] This emphasis acted as a defence against both individualism and the claims of Anglo-Catholics that authority had to come through apostolic succession. Rattenbury made the point that the Church was constituted not by hierarchies but by the 'presence of Christ amongst his people' and that 'the whole Church of Christ is continuous with the Apostolic Church.[429] This is important in understanding at least one view of the nature of the Church and its ministry pertaining at the time of the publication of the *Methodist Hymn Book*. The independent nature of Methodism and the tenacity with which Methodists hold to this key feature of their structural organisation owes itself, however, as much to an association with John Wesley's example in ordaining superintendents as to any carefully elaborated theological reasoning. For Wesleyans ministers came to have authority and divine commission that was confirmed by ordination. Strawson stresses that this did not prevent real partnership with the laity in church government.[430] Rattenbury, commenting on Luther, understood his emphasis to be 'on the priesthood of *each* believer rather than on the corporate priesthood of the whole church'. He goes on to state that 'The hymns

427 Rattenbury, *The Eucharistic Hymns of John and Charles Wesley*, p. 149.

428 Davies, George and Rupp, *A History of the Methodist Church in Great Britain*, Vol. 3, p. 195.

429 Rattenbury, *The Eucharistic Hymns of John and Charles Wesley*, p. 167f.

430 Davies, George and Rupp, *A History of the Methodist Church in Great Britain*, Vol. 3, p. 196.

of Wesley enlarge, develop, and enrich the Lutheran conception of the priesthood of each believer.'[431]

Some of the non-Wesleyans understood the priesthood of all believers to mean that the sacraments could be administered by lay people. At no point was this seen to be outside the authority of the Church though in practice local rules almost certainly applied.[432]

The pre-eminence of preaching has always meant that the preaching function has preceded the sacramental role. 'Methodists accept "men who are, when they have tested and proved the claim, convinced that God called them to *preach*, and these men become the Ministry." '[433] Indeed, preaching itself has been seen to be sacramental. This has further strengthened the links between ordained ministers, Local Preachers and teachers. All of these factors can be seen to have had an effect on the editors of the *Methodist Hymn Book*.

The role of ministers and teachers is that of enabling the people of God. The editors provided a section of 16 texts addressing these roles. Both ministers and teachers are depicted as having the care of souls as their task, and the enlightenment of those souls by the Scriptures. Those who preach are welcomed by the words 'How beauteous are their feet / Who stand on Zion's hill' (778), which derive from Isaiah 52.7. The sacramental nature of preaching is already underlined in the words of this first hymn. The inspiration for such preaching comes from God through the Holy Spirit (779). The spoken word is to be a 'living echo' of God (781).

The source of the word that is to be spoken is not simply determined by the spirit but is to be found pre-eminently in Scripture (782). This ideal is for children as much as adults. The Spiritual inspiration of this word must not be constrained (783) for what is being offered is given in response to God's 'boundless grace' (784). Allusions to harvest are presented as the 'sower's seed' is multiplied (784) and sown (792), and the harvest of the Lord is gathered (787, 793). Eschatological images indicate the imperative nature of the task (786, 788) that is both spiritual and pastoral (785).

Access to the Church is by means of baptism. The numerical

---

431 Rattenbury, *The Eucharistic Hymns of John and Charles Wesley*, p. 153.

432 A. Gleave, a Local Preacher in the Northwich Circuit, recounted to me how, in pre-Union days as a preacher on note, he had been expected to officiate at communion and this was not regarded by him as unusual. Circa 1982.

433 Rattenbury, *The Eucharistic Hymns of John and Charles Wesley*, p. 168. My italics.

poverty of texts on this subject is sharply accentuated. Four out of five texts in this section are for infants, as might be expected in a denomination in which infant baptism was, and remains, the norm. The small number of texts provides a very limited choice. Two are translations from German by Catherine Winkworth, 'Blessed Jesus, here we stand' (752) and 'Lord Jesus Christ, our Lord most dear' (755). These hymns indicate the belief that children are brought at God's command. Interesting in this respect is the fact that both avoid any direct reference to baptism and are, in fact, hymns of infant dedication. This is also true of 'See Israel's gentle Shepherd stand' (751). Each of these texts owes its inspiration to Mark 9.37 and 10.13ff. Of the remaining items, 'Friend of the home, as when in Galilee' (753) speaks overtly of infant baptism:

> Friend of the home, as when in Galilee
> The mothers brought their little ones to Thee,
> So we, dear Lord, would now the children bring,
> And seek for them the shelter of Thy wing.
>
> Thine are they, by Thy love's eternal claim,
> Thine we baptize them in the threefold Name:
> Yet not the sign we trust, Lord, but the grace
> That in Thy fold prepared the lambs a place.
>
> Lord, may Thy Church, as with a mother's care,
> For Thee the lambs within her bosom bear;
> And grant, as morning fades to noon, that they
> Still in her love and holy service stay.
>
> Draw through the child the parents nearer Thee,
> Endue their home with growing sanctity;
> And gather all, by earthly homes made one,
> In heaven, O Christ, when earthly days are done.

'Stand, soldier of the cross' (754) is clearly in both language and intent an adult hymn.

Marriage is not regarded as a sacrament within Methodism and of the four texts presented in this section only one, 'O perfect love' (777), has remained in popular usage. Similar if more sentimental in its approach, 'The voice that breathed o'er Eden' (775) speaks of a 'mysterious union' and is the only text to speak of children. John Ellerton's 'O Father all creating' (776) is written in the hope that bad things will be avoided or guarded against and concludes with a paraphrase of the opening verse of Psalm 127: 'Except thou build it, Father, / The house is built in vain', in the understanding that in the construction of Christian marriage God has a place. If not a sacrament marriage is certainly presented as being open to God's grace and influence.

The Church is regarded as a place of privilege and security. It is envisaged here as the rock, the dwelling place beloved of the Psalmist. This sense of security has been proclaimed and experienced by each succeeding generation (694). The Church is likened to Zion, the 'City of God'. The foundation, the cornerstone, of this city, and by implication the Church, is Jesus Christ:

> Christ is our corner-stone,
> On Him alone we build;
> With His true saints alone
> The courts of heaven are filled:
> On his great love our hopes we place
> Of present grace and joys above. (702)

The hymns relating to the ministry and the functions of ministers reflect very much the actual expectation being placed on ministers in this period. The editors have provided a window on this expectation. Ministry is theologically functional. Ordination recognises gifts and confers grace but, as Strawson records J. H. Rigg as having remarked in 1879, 'the sign of such grace having been given is more likely to be a sense of need of further grace than a sense of adequacy and authority'.[434] The minister is preacher first and presbyter second. The shared nature of ministry is underlined by the parallel texts for ministers and teachers and their arrangement in the same section of the book. The Church is presented as the place of the people rather than the domain of the minister. An egalitarian air is apparent. This underlines further the part played by fellowship in the Methodist

---

434 Davies, George and Rupp, *A History of the Methodist Church in Great Britain*, Vol. 3, p. 195.

understanding of the nature of the Church. The editors of the hymn book reflect all that might be expected at this period of Methodist history with the exception, again, of any explicit working out of the concept of connexionality.

Mission and the World

Individuals bound together into the Church moved out into the world as well as deepening their relationship in fellowship with each other. Methodism prior to the Union of 1932 was awake to the world. F. W. Dillistone was to say of the Report of the Conference on Christian Politics, Economics and Citizenship, which took place in 1924, that it 'could well be regarded as blue-print for the Welfare State'.[435] Education was a prominent and continuing concern for Methodists in the context of both schools and universities. If this was true of the hierarchy of the denominations, at the grass roots a different story pertained. Drink and gambling were the two social concerns that exercised the majority of Methodists of all three denominations. These concerns were exaggerated out of all proportion and the more significant evils of unemployment, war, unbridled nationalism, racial discrimination and oppression, homelessness and world poverty were, to a great extent, overlooked.[436] As the united Methodist Church developed these issues began to be addressed.

The *Methodist Hymn Book* was produced at a time of transition. Mission was still operating largely in the manner it had acquired during the nineteenth century, as a polite adjunct to imperialism. The First World War had begun to open people's minds to issues beyond those of drink and gambling. Mission and evangelism had two strands. Firstly, there was the argument that the world would only be changed as individuals came under the Lordship of Christ. This ran hand in hand with the popular holiness movement prevalent in Methodism. Secondly, there was a perceived need to attack social evils through politics and to move towards a more egalitarian society. This *modus operandi* was championed most obviously by Donald (later Lord) Soper.

---

435 F. W. Dillistone, quoted in Davies, George and Rupp, *A History of the Methodist Church in Great Britain*, Vol. 3, p. 361.

436 Davies, George and Rupp, *A History of the Methodist Church in Great Britain*, Vol. 3, p. 369f.

How were the editors to respond to this dynamic situation? The social conscience of Methodism is demonstrated by the inclusion of 34 items in the section concerning 'Service and Influence'. As might be expected, with the heightened awareness consequent on the experience of the Great War, these look beyond individualism to a greater awareness of, and fellowship with, those around us. This compares with 28 texts in the section related to 'Resurrection and Ascension', suggesting that the application of religion was of equal if not greater importance to the editors than its basis. From this starting point it might be assumed that the collection was radical.

Closer examination reveals that the section relies heavily on texts that speak of the service of God, rather than the service of society, and many are written in tones that encourage oppression, with the acceptance of task and class as foreordained by God. The section has not moved much beyond the 'Rich man in his castle, / The poor man at his gate' (though this verse is expurgated from 'All things bright and beautiful' in the *Methodist Hymn Book*). The opening hymns underline this theme. Only when we reach the fourth hymn, 'Servant of all, to toil for men' (575), do we receive a hint that the work of humanity might have some importance as the text compares the author with the 'Son of the carpenter' who is asked to receive 'this humble work of mine':

> Servant of all, to toil for man
> Thou didst not, Lord, refuse;
> Thy majesty did not disdain
> To be employed for us.
>
> Son of the carpenter, receive
> This humble work of mine;
> Worth to my meanest labour give,
> By joining it to Thine.
>
> End of my every action thou,
> In all things Thee I see;
> Accept my hallowed labour now,
> I do it unto Thee.
>
> Thy bright example I pursue,
> To Thee on all things rise;

And all I think, or speak, or do
Is one great sacrifice.

Careless through outward care I go,
From all distraction free;
My hands are but engaged below,
My heart is still with Thee.

This is an isolated text.

William Vaughan Jenkins' 'O loving Lord, who art forever seeking' (577) takes a more worldly perspective, seeking to be 'True to ourselves, our brethren and our Lord'. The third stanza states: 'In duties small be Thou our inspiration, / In large affairs endue us with Thy might'. Later in this same verse the theology is defective, offering as it does a presentation of salvation by works: 'Through faithful service cometh full salvation'. Charles Wesley's text, 'A charge to keep I have' (578), is more circumspect allowing the interpretation that sanctification takes place while we are working out our time in faithfulness. Failure to be faithful to the charge leads to eternal death, something which later editors have found unpalatable.[437]

Thomas Toke Lynch's 'Dismiss me not Thy service Lord' (580) has a militaristic air speaking of 'Thy young men at the war / Thy little ones at home'. It is not clear whether the war is a literal one or an allusion to spiritual warfare, though the latter seems most likely.

Many of the texts see work as being equated with evangelism.[438] James Montgomery's hymn 'Sow in the morn Thy seed' (599) offers an image of harvest. Other hymns seek to inculcate a sprit of subservience. 'Forth in Thy name, O Lord, I go' (590) is satisfied to accept whatever is done as assigned by God's wisdom. George Herbert's text, 'Teach me my God and King' (597), views daily work with a sense of resignation that could be seen to justify oppression. 'They who tread the path of labour' (601) reinforces the view that working without discrimination is praiseworthy, hence 'They who work without complaining do the holy will of God' and 'Every task, however simple, sets the soul that does it free'. 'Father, I know that all my life / Is portioned out for me' (602) goes further in adopting a fatalistic position, though

---

437 See *Hymns & Psalms*, No. 785.
438 See, for example, 'Go, labour on; spend and be spent' (589).

this is veiled by the understanding that this apportionment is initiated by God. Such sentiments, backed by the authority of the Church, gave fuel for the growth of Marxism. There is a tacit acceptance of God's authority that, by implication, is mediated by the Church. Those who have power and influence within the Church are placed beyond contradiction if these texts are taken at face value. It is less likely that this expressed any conscious application by those in authority but was, rather, a reflection of the status quo that went unquestioned. The contents are reactionary rather than radical. Whatever our judgement, Anne Brontë's text 'Believe not those who say / The upward path is smooth' (591) expresses a truism.

The work of caring is sufficiently important to warrant its own section. 'Hospitals and Philanthropy' provides six texts logically progressing from an incarnational understanding that God shares in the act of care, through participation in the active work of caring, to an affirmation that this, itself, derives from God. Texts on Temperance are noticeable by their absence.

Following this focus on Christian service the editors turn to the image of life as a pilgrimage. Most of the Christian life is spent 'in the world' rather than 'in church'. Many texts use vivid, almost literal, language after the style of Bunyan's *Pilgrim's Progress*. Other hymns speak of a metaphysical transformation in which the believer is enabled by God to reach a higher plane. In these latter texts it is often recognised that such a change involves an ethical dimension in the present life. An awareness of sin and an antidote for it is paramount. It is interesting to note that these texts are the ones that most clearly anticipate a realistic rather than romantic end to the life of pilgrimage.

As life proceeds it is affirmed that God both sustains and also guides and protects the believer. Nowhere is this more clearly expressed than in the next text, 'Captain of Israel's host, and Guide' (608):

> Captain of Israel's host, and Guide
> Of all who seek the land above,
> Beneath Thy shadow we abide,
> The cloud of Thy protecting love;
> Our strength, Thy grace; our rule, Thy word;
> Our end, the glory of the Lord.

By Thine unerring Spirit led,
We shall not in the desert stray;
We shall not full direction need,
Nor miss our providential way;
As far from danger as from fear,
While love, almighty love, is near.

The image of a shepherd predominates and the texts have a distinctly Victorian feel, the world being depicted as a grim vale through which humanity must pass towards heaven. We need forgiveness, the world is a 'tempestuous sea', 'The night is dark and [we] are far from home', 'Doubts appal and sorrows still increase'. In spite of all it is affirmed that 'Heavenly Father, Thou hast brought us / Safely to the present day' (614).

Psalm 121 taken from the *Scottish Psalter*, 'I to the hills will lift mine eyes' (625), succinctly summarises what has gone before in that help is derived from a God who has ultimate care for the believer. Charles Wesley's 'I want a principle within / Of jealous, godly fear' (626) builds on the understanding of the perceived tenuous nature of the believer's hold on grace.

The pilgrimage is not exclusive. The Christian is ever willing to proselytise. Methodism has always been an evangelistic movement. Mission is a sign of influence which is enabled by those whose hearts are inflamed with perfect love.[439] It looks beyond this life to the time 'when created nature dies', when 'Thy never ceasing glories shine'. This purpose is carried forward by the church which goes out into a world of shame, proclaiming the universal truth of the love of God.

The Arminianism is clear, the doctrine of the priesthood of all believers emphasised. The Church is, nevertheless, dependent on God, having been ransomed,[440] and its task is urgent. Images of the returning bridegroom underline this premise. The call is to 'Speed Thy servants, Saviour speed them' (808). Such servants go into a world that is dark with nothing but 'toils and dangers'. This imagery gives way in some texts to a sense of sentimentality which to modern ears is patronising: 'Once again, dear Lord, we pray / For the children far away' (797). Such texts disparage the religious beliefs of other faiths

---

439 'Eternal Son, eternal love' (794).
440 'Lord, Thy ransomed Church is waking' (796).

and see no value in any expression of worship other than that of evangelical Christianity. An adult expression of this perspective is found in 'Let the song go round the world' (806) which speaks of 'Lands where Islam's sway / Darkly broods o'er home and hearth'. The juxtaposition of these cosy images and the supposed plight of those of other faiths is particularly characteristic not only of a particular view of mission but also of Victorian spirituality.

The context is clarified by reference to the hymns on 'King and Country'. Many of the texts in this section speak with an air of chauvinism, if not jingoism. Here is the National Anthem (omitted from *Hymns & Psalms* to the consternation of some). The ethos is occasionally tempered:

> Lord, while for all mankind we pray
> Of every clime and coast,
> O hear us for our native land,
> The land we love the most.
>
> Our fathers' sepulchres are here,
> And here our kindred dwell,
> Our children too: how should we love
> Another land so well?
>
> O guard our shores from every foe,
> With peace our borders bless;
> With prosperous times our cities crown,
> Our fields with plenteousness.
>
> Unite us in the sacred love
> Of knowledge, truth, and Thee;
> And let our hills and valleys shout
> The songs of liberty.
>
> Lord of the nations, thus to Thee
> Our country we commend;
> Be thou her refuge and her trust,
> Her everlasting Friend. (881)

Some of the texts are general in application but could be readily used in a nationalistic context. 'Judge eternal, throned in splendour' (883), which in later revisions has become a helpful hymn placing all under God's judgement, here speaks with Christian, if not racial, superiority.

An awareness of the need for forgiveness is growing, nevertheless, and this is brought to fruition in 'Before Thy throne, O God we kneel' (884). While born of empire the words are aware of 'lust of gold' and the 'crafty trade and subtle snare' which can be used commercially 'To catch the simple unaware'. If used nationally the hymn is one of penance, recognising the flaws of nationalism and empire. Rudyard Kipling provides the greatest foil for pride in nationhood. His text 'God of our fathers, known of old' (889) begins patriotically. But he has not finished: 'The tumult and the shouting dies, / The captains and the kings depart'. When all this is over the historic sacrifice, 'a humble and a contrite heart', remains. Over against this, asserts Kipling, 'all our pomp of yesterday / Is one with Nineveh and Tyre!' Both judged and wasted. This must not be forgotten and the author pleads, 'spare us yet'. Kipling depicts his nation as people who are 'drunk with power', boasting like gentiles. The 'heathen heart' of which he speaks is the heart of his fellows who have put their trust 'In reeking tube and iron shard', in guns, instead of in God. Thus he concludes 'for frantic boast and foolish word – / Thy mercy on Thy people Lord!' This gives an indication that texts in this section need not necessarily have been aggressively patriotic. Similarly, 'Far round the world Thy children sing their song' (798) indicates that not all missionary texts needed to take a negative approach to other nations. There was an opportunity of choice for the editors.

There is a sense of anticipation, that the nations are waiting. The scope of this mission is unlimited. The message is not just proclaimed by word of mouth for 'The heavens declare Thy glory, Lord' (802). It is as though the whole of creation participates in promulgating the gospel. The presence and activity of God throughout salvation history is affirmed by the inclusion of 'Thou whose almighty word' (803). This word is that for which 'the nations long'. The union of all in Christ throughout the world is asserted by Charles Wesley's 'And let our bodies part, / To different climes repair' (807). This overview is allowed by the characteristic understanding that all this work on earth provides a foretaste of eternity.

The impetus for mission finds its roots in the Passion, a theme which is explored in the hymn 'I cannot tell why He, whom angels worship' (809). The mission ends with the anticipated Kingdom of God. The imagery is often pictured as the militaristic domination of other faiths: 'Tyrant thrones and idol shrines, / Let them from their place be hurled' (810). If this view is Victorian there is evidence of some movement by the editors in their choice of texts. Arthur Campbell Ainger's 'God is working his purpose out' (812) is in some ways a foil to this mentality as it speaks of 'The brotherhood of all mankind'. It is also consonant with the evolutionary spirit that characterised the latter half of the nineteenth century and which anticipated a persistent and perpetual sense of progress in all things.

Hymns, and their choice, are conditioned by context. Experience can be called on to support contemporary faith. The God who has been 'our help in ages past' (878) gives reason to adore and 'trust Him for all that's to come' (69). Arthur Campbell Ainger's 'God of our fathers, unto Thee' (887) looks towards a universal fatherland, 'One fatherland throughout the earth', but the sense is inextricably bound up with a fatherland of empire, under God, with authority delegated to those for whom the text was written. The sense is Calvinist.

Throughout this world friends roam and so it is pertinent to think of 'Travellers and Absent Friends'. Hymns on this theme catch the spirit of a belief in the all-encompassing care of God, such that as we leave and reunite again we come and go enfolded in divine providence. Such care cannot be thwarted by the 'mighty ocean', the 'foaming deep', 'the angry tumult'. Indeed this treasuring of humanity transcends even life itself (915). Seasons come and go and are marked. Those texts which are provided range from the traditional hymns for harvest thanksgiving, including one for the harvest of the sea (964), together with hymns offering thanks for the wider created world. Stewardship of creation is not addressed except in the sense of humanity being a partner with God in planting, sowing and reaping: 'But it is fed and watered / By God's almighty hand' (963). 'Hymns for Anniversaries and Dedications' have infrequent use but those provided are of sufficient quality to be serviceable.

As the year ends it would be expected that people would wish to look back, to reflect and then to move forwards. Hymns here are collected together in the reverse of this order but their intention is plain.

The last third of the book has been structured to reflect on and to enable committed fellowship. It is assumed that those who have responded to the gospel call will meet together with others for prayer and worship. The needs of such meetings are provided for. The greatest depth of fellowship, in spite of the Methodist tendency to suggest that this was less important, was envisaged as being experienced at the Lord's Table. There was an ambiguity here which sacramentalists were beginning to underline. While communion was central it had been subjugated in favour of preaching, yet for the Wesleys the two had gone hand in hand.

The Church had been built on mission, its children grew up within its influence, adults married according to its rites, and these were provided for. All ends in death and a triumphant, militant church overcoming even this sting was envisaged. Around the Church there was necessary reflection on the nation and the world.

The *Methodist Hymn Book* provides an understanding of the Church that might be viewed as a series of concentric circles. At the centre is a core of committed believers in close fellowship with each other, moving inexorably towards a goal of personal holiness. From this fellowship, which is as close in death as in life, welcoming arms reach into the world. Holiness always has a social perspective in Methodism. But for the *Methodist Hymn Book* the predominant view of this outreach is that it draws others into the fold rather than seeking to influence the political and cultural activity outside its bounds. The more the umbrella of fellowship can be spread, the better the world will be. There is little evidence of the Christian acting as leaven outside the Church except in very specific situations such as those of hospitals and philanthropy, to borrow two sectional titles from the book.

The editors have struggled with their own experience and prejudice. The *Methodist Hymn Book* represents the culture of which they are a part, rather than challenging it. The past has generally held them in thrall. Evidence of the enlightened awareness of a world beyond the imperialism of Victorian Britain is not absent but it is sparse. Mission is all-conquering and the expression of social care limited. The emphasis is towards evangelical outreach rather than social care or radical political change. Methodism of this period has been characterised as politically liberal, seeking conservative rather than revolutionary solutions to social ills. Whatever was happening in the world this picture is reinforced by an examination of the manner in which the *Methodist Hymn Book* approaches the issues of mission and the world.

In summary it can be said that the *Methodist Hymn Book* has provided a resource that supports a Trinitarian, evangelical theology, within an Arminian framework. God is defined, worship is enabled, the concept of fellowship is affirmed. The whole collection accompanies the believer from the earthly understanding of the need for, and the possibility of, salvation to the heavenly realisation that the heirs of Christ may cast their 'crowns before Thee / Lost in wonder, love and praise' (431).

6

The Hymn Book –
What People Thought

In order to assess the contemporary responses to the *Methodist Hymn Book* (1933) it is necessary to investigate a variety of sources. The most abundant are those provided by the letters columns of contemporary Methodist newspapers. Copies of the *Methodist Recorder* (a Wesleyan paper) and the *Methodist Times and Leader* (which had been formed from the merger of the evangelical *Methodist Times* and the Primitive Methodist *Methodist Leader*) from April of 1932 through to August 1934 chronicle the popular and establishment responses to the preparation and publication of the book. People who had a personal recollection of this period also provide an interesting reflection.

Unfortunately the reporting of Methodist Union was biased by the changes that resulted in the *Methodist Times* and the *Methodist Leader* amalgamating and then being edited by John Scott Lidgett, a Wesleyan. At the time of Union there was no Methodist paper not under the editorial influence of the Wesleyan Methodist Church.

Currie notes that reports in the *Methodist Recorder* were given a positive Wesleyan perspective by the appointment of J. B. Watson as editor. He had been appointed to succeed the high Wesleyan, Nehemiah Curnock. Under Watson, he states, the paper was to surpass the *Methodist Times* in its ecumenism and it became not only a platform for those seeking Union but a vocal source of encouragement for those involved.[441] Ecumenism is generally regarded as the working together of Christian denominations within an atmosphere of mutual acceptance. In Wesleyan understanding what was taking place was that a junior partner was being allowed to join in relation-

---

441 Currie, *Methodism Divided*, p. 249.

ship by a senior partner.[442] That is to say, this ecumenism was not evenly balanced and reports have to be assessed in this light. There are messages in this for all who seek to work ecumenically in any period, not least our own!

People began to correspond with newspapers prior to publication. Most letters are to be found in the *Methodist Recorder*. It seems that the readership of this paper were better informed, and more vocal than readers of the *Methodist Times and Leader*. The comments are illuminating in that they offer criticisms of the draft contents lists. The committee responded to some of these comments during the editorial process while others were disregarded.

In an era that looks for transparency the workings of the Hymn Book Committee seem cloaked in secrecy. The correspondence under review begins on 7 April 1932. Albert Walker[443] asked that the preparation of the new book should not be undertaken hastily and that the Uniting Conference should be presented with the first lines of texts to enable consultation. It was affirmed that this would indeed happen and on 23 June the *Methodist Recorder* reported that a review of contents had been submitted to Conference.[444] The work had already been in progress for two years, suggesting that consultation to this point had been limited. The committee worked in private and only made their work public when pressed to do so.

An editorial in the *Methodist Recorder* on 28 July[445] referred to the proposed contents as presenting 'a book sufficiently Methodist to satisfy the conservatives and sufficiently comprehensive to satisfy the progressives' yet 'the book leans to the conservative side'. Given the Wesleyan leanings of the *Methodist Recorder*, this point is telling: '. . . every section reveals the mind of the twentieth century', an era which was beginning to espouse a sense of universality in respect of salvation. 'The book does not altogether escape the pensiveness and wistfulness characteristic of the last 50 years, nor a touch of the long heavy lines which many young thinkers seem to prefer.' 'The whole collection bears the characteristic stamp of sincerity, clearness, vigour and cheerfulness.' Significantly, in this context, Sydney B.

442 Currie, *Methodism Divided*, p. 250f.
443 *Methodist Recorder*, 7 April 1932, p. 17.
444 *Methodist Recorder*, 23 June 1932, p. 4.
445 *Methodist Recorder*, 28 July 1932, p. 1.

Gregory[446] had written bemoaning the omission of 'Praise to the holiest in the height', which had been excluded because it was 'offensive to evangelicalism', that there could not be a 'higher gift than grace'. The debate ran on in subsequent issues and the hymn was ultimately included. A further review of contents appeared on 14 July with 'M. B.' commenting: 'It is a good book – isn't it?'[447] 'M. B.' was not identified.[448]

The correspondence continued. On 4 August A. J. Norman[449] noted the disproportion of hymns for public worship, 90 items, over against those for the 'Person and Praise of Jesus Christ', 194 items. He asked that God the Father might not be depicted as full of wrath, such wrath being deflected by the sacrifice of Jesus. He noted that there was little included relating to the teaching of Jesus on the worth of personal character. Clearly Norman had been influenced by the theology that had been propounded by Findlay.[450] What was observed was the unnecessary depreciation of human worth, for example the texts 'We cannot think a gracious thought', 'False and full of sin I am', 'I have spilt his precious blood', 'Me, who him to death pursued', 'We from out our graves must spring' – 'weird apocalyptic!' he concludes, and then asks that expressions that might estrange people from the gospel be excluded from the book. This elicited a less liberal response from Y. M. Crookes, F. M. Moore, and W. Palmer Morris.[451]

An examination of the *Methodist Hymn Book* suggests that Norman was not heard. Had he been, another voice, that of Dr Kirtlan, might have been even more strident. Kirtlan objected to the reduction in the number of hymns on 'Death and Judgement'. F. L. Wiseman questioned the quality of material that was presently available on these subjects. Lysons has recognised that this reduction was part of a trend that had a sociological significance and which was not simply to do with the quality of texts that were available.[452] In addition Dr Kirtlan regretted the omission of some Passion hymns. Wiseman also disposed of this criticism. His authoritarian manner seems to have been one of the most formative influences during the

---

446 *Methodist Recorder*, 30 June 1932, p. 16.
447 *Methodist Recorder*, 14 July 1932, p. 7.
448 Research so far has not uncovered the identity of this contributor.
449 *Methodist Recorder*, 4 August 1932, p. 14.
450 Davies, George and Rupp, *A History of the Methodist Church in Great Britain*, Vol. 3, p. 203.   451 *Methodist Recorder*, 11 August 1932, p. 15.
452 Lysons, *A Little Primitive*, p. 202.

compilation of the book. What is apparent is the tension which can be read into such exchanges, and the tightrope that the editors were having to walk in order to accommodate different points of theological perspective. Clearly the Hymn Book Committee was seeking to meet the requirements of a disparate constituency and the question of the judgement of God was one that continued to exercise them during the last year of work on the volume.

The committee was not without its supporters. Henry Elderkin wrote an appreciation of the new book. He pleaded for tolerance and understanding of the difficult task facing the committee. He believed that the book would 'introduce an element of freshness to our public worship and lead to a more thought-inspiring devotion'. With regard to present hymns he recognised a sense of 'indifference' if not contempt.[453] What is not clear is whether the 'present hymns' to which he refers were ones currently in use by one of the uniting denominations or other hymns currently in use outside Methodism.

Week after week letters pointed out matters of detail particularly in relation to the omission of popular hymns and debate took place as to the precise numbers of hymns included or omitted. Regret was expressed that 'Cradled in a manger meanly' was absent.[454] In correspondence to the *Methodist Recorder* this was the most frequently noted omission. On 1 December an editorial note confirmed that the hymn was to be included.[455] The committee was not entirely unresponsive to public opinion. The following week an article by 'M. B.' on Christmas in the new Hymn Book stated that the new selection added a note of 'jolliness'. No mention was made of 'Cradled in a manger meanly'.[456] From April to November 1932 not a week went by without the Hymn Book being mentioned.

Clearly the book was raising a great deal of interest. Some of this was informed from a literary or theological point of view. Much of it was not and came simply from the feeling of having one's favourite text omitted. There is no single thread of coherence through this correspondence save the sense that much of it had been generated by a lack of consultation. A book that was so near to the heart of a singing people was bound to raise passions.

---

453 *Methodist Recorder*, 20 October 1932, p. 1.
454 *Methodist Recorder*, 24 November 1932, p. 19.
455 *Methodist Recorder*, 1 December 1932, p. 1.
456 *Methodist Recorder*, 8 December 1932, p. 2.

Strangely, the *Methodist Times and Leader*, at this time, had little comment on the book. On 13 October Arthur Hancock admitted to having repeated 'My chains fell off [my heart was free, / I rose] went forth and followed Thee' in the singing of 'And can it be', at 'the displeasure . . . of the conductor' in the Royal Albert Hall. He offered no apology for this saying that he wanted a 'bit of old-time Methodist Emphasis'.[457] It is as though a whole swathe of Methodists were unaware of what was happening and their press was doing nothing to counter their ignorance. It would be interesting to know whether the silence of the *Methodist Times and Leader*, and its correspondence column, at this time was due to editorial control of the paper. The Wesleyans certainly knew what was going on. The smaller denominations seem to have been less well informed. The correspondence that would come at a later date suggests that this was not a matter of a lack of interest. One possible reason for this ignorance could stem from an understanding that, within a democratic fellowship, friends will share things of importance. This was the culture in which Primitive and United Methodists operated. They saw no reason to delve. They trusted the process.

The Wesleyans had an altogether different way of working and they were in control. Those of their number who heard nothing asked, as the next correspondent demonstrates. On 4 August W. H. Jackson Picken wrote to the *Methodist Recorder* asking that the contents of the book be made available to those beyond the Conferences so that others might pass a critical eye over it. It was suggested that all new texts be printed in full and others provided with references so that they could be examined.[458] The request was not heard. Harold Spencer regretted certain omissions but also asked that hymns on the resurrection and ascension be distinguished from each other.[459] A suggestion was also recorded that an order for the sacraments and other forms of worship be included in the book.[460] The committee did not accede to either request. Some of the critique was quite detailed and specific, as in the request that 'Abide with me' should read 'in life, in death' not 'in life and death',[461] and that 'Who would true valour see' be amended

---

457 *Methodist Times and Leader*, 13 October 1932, p. 24.
458 *Methodist Recorder*, 4 August 1932, p. 1.
459 *Methodist Recorder*, 11 August 1932, p. 1.
460 *Methodist Recorder*, 29 September 1932, p. 1.
461 *Methodist Recorder*, 18 August 1932, p. 15. MARC 29/15 is a letter from the Revd

with the removal of 'Hobgoblin nor foul fiend' according to the version found in the *Rydal School Hymn Book*.[462] The first of these suggestions led to a conversation within the committee to the effect that the suggested reading was that which had been accepted.[463]

A plea came from Mr B. B. Hardy that 'Lead kindly light' not be included because of its allusions to Romanism. He read it thus: 'the encircling gloom' represented Anglicanism and Protestantism, while 'night is dark' and 'I am far from home' meant outside Romanism.[464] A suggestion was offered that 'Britain' be substituted for 'England' in Blake's 'Jerusalem' and other places and this was followed by correspondence in opposition and support.[465] 'When wilt thou save the people' was seen, by one correspondent, to 'sneer at royalty' and thus be offensive.[466] There was another objection to 'When wilt thou save the people' on grounds of theology. A call was made to provide hymns for evangelism, while Arthur Trusswell could not 'imagine any true Methodist wanting to exchange 'O joyful sound of gospel grace' for 'I am not skilled to understand'. 'Better', he says, 'pure spiritual doggerel than mere poetical fascination'.[467] The committee did not agree.

On 1 September H. R. Hindley produced an article entitled 'The New Hymn Book, A Friendly Criticism'.[468] He noted that the selection of hymns was wider and more catholic than before. The book had, in his estimation, escaped from the grasp of the Wesleys while retaining their best material. Judicious inclusion of chorus hymns was applauded. The book was deemed both 'catholic' and 'popular'. He criticised the title for the children's section stating that 'For Young Children' would be preferred to 'little children' which was deemed patronising. He felt that hymns that dwelt literally on physical aspects of the passion should be omitted. The sections on 'The Gospel Call' and 'Repentance and Forgiveness' were 'over-

---

R. Lee Cole of the Methodist Church in Ireland to Dr Wiseman. It is inscribed with a note relating to 'Abide with me' initialled 'F.L.W.'

462 *Methodist Recorder*, 25 August 1932, p. 1. Requests to Rydal School and other sources have not identified this version of the text.

463 MARC 29/15.

464 *Methodist Recorder*, 13 October 1932, p. 2.

465 *Methodist Recorder*, 8 December 1932, p. 37.

466 *Methodist Recorder*, 25 August 1932, p. 1.

467 *Methodist Recorder*, 1 September 1932, p. 1.

468 *Methodist Recorder*, 1 September 1932, p. 7.

weighted theologically, and deficient in human feeling and interest, especially for young people'. The latter, he said, 'needs much revision'. Hindley sought for the exclusion of hymns which were of 'peculiar metre and archaic phraseology' that he assumed had been included for devotional use. He asked that 'Thou shepherd of Israel and mine' be excluded as it carried 'the love metaphor to an unreal and enervating extreme'. There is evidence in the criticisms here that the author of the article was more in touch with public opinion and taste than the editors of the book. It was not an overt modernising that was sought but rather the abandoning of that which was seen to be anachronistic.

The following week a number of correspondents responded to H. R. Hindley seeking the inclusion of hymns containing sensuous language that he had wished to be omitted.[469] To this Hindley replied asserting his position with still greater force.[470] His comments on the section for children, however, echoed some earlier correspondence. On 7 July J. T. Watson had written stating that many Sunday School attenders were aged over 15 and would resent being called 'little children'. He felt that the children's section would be better re-titled 'For Young Worshippers' or 'For Young People'.[471] The compromise 'For Children' was adopted. F. W. L. Darby was disappointed that the children's section contained only 30 hymns, and mostly from the *Methodist School Hymnal*, when 'so many fine new hymns are available'.[472]

During 1932 there was an extended correspondence on Darwinism and Democracy[473] in the *Methodist Recorder* and on 26 May Colonel S. D. Ingram indicated that many hymns suggested for the *Methodist Hymn Book* would need revision in order for them to be acceptable in a contemporary context.[474] Meanwhile Mr L. Vivian Rogers expressed the fear that 'the cult of the Modernist [. . .] may be so allowed to influence the revisers that many of our old evangelical hymns may be Expunged' [sic]. [475] Opinions were, again, at odds, yet the committee could not claim to be ignorant of the fact that what they were assembling seemed dated to many critics.

---

469 *Methodist Recorder*, 8 September 1932, p. 1.
470 *Methodist Recorder*, 15 September 1932, p. 2.
471 *Methodist Recorder*, 7 July 1932, p. 16.
472 *Methodist Recorder*, 30 June 1932, p. 1.
473 See *Methodist Recorder*, 5 May 1932, p. 21, for example.
474 *Methodist Recorder*, 26 May 1932, p. 1.
475 *Methodist Recorder*, 29 September 1932, p. 2.

At the beginning of December an editorial comment was printed in the *Methodist Recorder* relating to the meeting of the Hymn Book Committee. It noted that 'To make the book more generally useful the Committee has included a number of hymns with chorus for evangelistic services.' It was observed that 'The canons of literary merit used for the rest of the book must be suspended here',[476] a comment which clearly reflected the position of the committee in relation to what they regarded as less literate material. There is an implicit assumption that the readership would know what those canons were. The attitude of the committee to hymns that would have been beloved of Bible Christians and many Primitive Methodists was clearly unhelpful.

During the early months of 1933 the *Methodist Recorder* letters column was mainly exercised with correspondence relating to the Tune Book and to Psalm singing, as far as anything pertaining to the Hymn Book was concerned.[477] Geo. Wootton Reynolds, writing in the *Methodist Times and Leader*, suggested that, at a time of Union, there would be many calls on Connexional funds and that therefore the publication of the New Book should be put off.[478] Spinney notes that at the Conference in 1935, which saw the formation of the Methodist Church Music Society, the subject of the cost of the book was still exercising members. 'There were complaints at this Conference about the price of the new book – 7/6 (38p) being the cheapest edition with music.' The effects of inflation on publication costs were blamed for this.[479]

On 18 May 1933, in the *Methodist Recorder*, there was reference to 'Nearer my God to Thee' as it appeared in the *Primitive Methodist Hymnal*.[480] A letter was published looking forward to the publication of the Hymn Book,[481] but others sought a year's delay to enable the restoration of several of Charles Wesley's hymns to the collection.

It was also suggested that a pamphlet be published containing a list of texts and tunes.[482] This call for transparency continued to thread its

476 *Methodist Recorder*, 1 December 1932, p. 14.
477 *Methodist Recorder*, 5 January 1933, p. 17; 12 January 1933, p. 17; 19 January 1933, p. 18; 9 March 1933, p. 21; 16 March 1933, p. 19; 23 March 1933, p. 1.
478 *Methodist Times and Leader*, 5 January 1933, p. 1.
479 Spinney, *Tuned for Praise*, p. 19.
480 *Methodist Recorder*, 18 May 1933, p. 1.
481 *Methodist Recorder*, 25 May 1933, p. 1.
482 *Methodist Recorder*, 1 June, 1933, p. 21; 8 June 1933, p. 1.

way through the correspondence. The committee could, perhaps, have avoided some criticisms by acceding to this request. Confidential lists had been made available to Conferences, though by now this was very late in the day. From the outset the secrecy of the work of the committee could only be justified in terms of the culture of Wesleyan Methodism in which those appointed by Conference were given authority to make decisions without any extensive consultation. The other denominations had a more democratic approach. Consequently much criticism was directed at the committee via the letters pages to the Methodist newspapers, and the *Methodist Recorder* in particular.

Through June and July little correspondence of direct relevance to the book was seen in the *Methodist Recorder*. On 22 June a correspondent noted two instances when the Holy Spirit was referred to as 'it'.[483] A letter relating to the use of an appropriate typeface followed.[484]

Meanwhile the *Methodist Times and Leader* was exercised with articles and correspondence addressing the question of the quality of worship. None of these referred specifically to the hymn book.[485] In an article on the Tune Book H. R. Hindley made reference to the 'book used by the ex-Wesleyan Methodist Church which [. . .] lacks the essential Methodist qualities of ringing confidence and jubilant faith'. A decline in attendance was observed between 1906 and 1914 while in a Central Mission where other hymns and tunes were used the congregation grew and prospered. Widespread use of the *Crusaders' Hymnal* and *Gypsy Smith's Choruses* was also noted in this context. The writer believed that 'musical and poetical perfection in hymns and tunes must be subservient to sincere and enthusiastic worship'. The current book (presumably the Wesleyan book of 1904) was seen as being fit for a parish church. Yet he asserted that if the Tune Book Committee did as well as the Hymn Book Committee it would produce a good book.[486] Hindley was clearly being diplomatic, and continuing to point up the disjunction between the choices of the committee and the appreciation of the people to whom he believed the Church should minister. This article generated a number of letters in response. One suggested that 'tunes that go' must also be

483 *Methodist Recorder*, 22 June 1933, p. 1.
484 *Methodist Recorder*, 29 June 1933, p. 17; 6 July 1933, p. 2.
485 *Methodist Times and Leader*, 16 March 1933, p. 10.
486 *Methodist Times and Leader*, 8 June 1934, p. 14f.

appropriate to the words.[487] On 29 June a letter appeared relating to
the Tune Book and disagreeing with Hindley's article. It was signed:
'only a choirmaster'.[488] On the same date Norman Sargent bemoaned
the lack of temperance hymns in the new book.[489] This drew a
response from Edgar C. Barton indicating that four temperance hymns
had been submitted by Henry Carter but it had been difficult to find
such hymns of suitable quality.[490] The day of the temperance hymn
had all but passed. In some respects the editors had moved on.

Some time later (in September) the *Methodist Times and Leader*
carried a letter from T. H. Ashelford expressing sadness at the inclusion of Wesley hymns to the exclusion of more modern material but
also stating that 'The number of chorus hymns is great; some are
crude; and ought not to have been inserted.'[491]

The *Methodist Recorder* of 20 July carried a Report on the [now
united] Methodist Conference. The Hymn Book Committee was dis-
charged by the Conference and a Continuation Committee was
appointed to deal with any further matters. Sir Walter Essex put a
motion to Conference that the foreign introductions, which were
printed at the head of translated texts, should be omitted. This was
lost. It was complained by W. H. Heap that attempts to obtain a list of
possible Passion hymns from Dr Kirtlan, who had sought changes to
the book, had elicited only an unmarked copy of *Hymns Ancient and
Modern*.[492] The members of the committee were clearly willing to
justify themselves in the face of the most vituperative criticism.

Correspondence continued with reference to the supply of books
'For the use of visitors' to be at cost and better bound; together with a
note indicating that 'Amen' should be included, when sung, in both
words and music editions.[493] The following week correspondence on
the 'Amen' continued with the comment that it should not be used
half-heartedly. It was also suggested that the practice witnessed in
Songs of Praise of starring verses that might be omitted be adopted for
the hymn book, so that when hymns were shortened it could be done

487 *Methodist Times and Leader*, 15 June 1933, p. 20.
488 *Methodist Times and Leader*, 29 June 1933, p. 20.
489 *Methodist Times and Leader*, 29 June 1933, p. 20.
490 *Methodist Times and Leader*, 6 July 1933, p. 24.
491 *Methodist Times and Leader*, 21 September 1933, p. 18.
492 *Methodist Recorder*, 20 July 1933, p. 1.
493 *Methodist Recorder*, 17 August 1933, p. 19.

properly without having an effect on the sense of the hymn.[494] The committee had considered this on 21 May 1931[495] but clearly the correspondent did not know this, another indication of poor communication. The idea was dropped.

Throughout October letters appeared in the *Methodist Recorder* referring to the Tune Book. These were surely too late to have any effect, as on 16 November the *Methodist Recorder* carried the headline 'The New Hymn Book at the Printers' – an interview with Edgar C. Barton by Arthur Page. The article began: 'It is more than 29 years since the present Hymn and Tune Book was issued by the Methodist Publishing House.' The new book was seen to differ from its predecessor [singular!] in that 'very great attention has been given to hymns for young people'. These had been placed throughout the book and indicated by an asterisk in the index. 'The Social Service section has been distinctly strengthened.' There was an increased number of Psalms and Canticles. 'Another addition is a section of verses suitable for special occasions such as after meetings on a Sunday night, community-singing and devotional meetings.' The 'Amen' had been retained with discrimination. In relation to Wesley hymns it was stated that 'if some have disappeared others have been restored that will be new to all branches of the United Church'. The book was anticipated for Christmas with an announcement as to the exact date of publication within a week or two. Prices were to be announced but there would be a shilling edition in limp cloth. It was reported that:

> The members [of the committee] have vied with one another in their desire to produce a Hymn Book that is not an anthology, but a collection of hymns and tunes consonant with the robust, sincere, and kindly spirit of Methodist [sic], suitable in form and feeling for congregational worship, and regardful of the sentiments and traditions of the several branches of the Methodist Church.[496]

The lack of ecumenical sensitivity in a paper regarded for its ecumenism is astounding. Clearly the author wrote from his own, Wesleyan, perspective. Even as the book began to be promoted there

---

494 *Methodist Recorder*, 24 August 1933, p. 17.
495 MARC 30/224.
496 *Methodist Recorder*, 16 November 1933, p. 7.

was a lack of understanding that there was a need to carry forward all three denominations if it was to be a truly successful publication.

An interview in the *Methodist Times and Leader* with Edgar C. Barton entitled 'The Methodist Tune Book in the Making' indicated that there were to be no 'expression marks' (though these had previously been sought[497]) or 'split leaves' (to enable words and tunes to be matched). 'The spirit of the hymn should be learned and then the correct expression will come spontaneously,' it was stated, somewhat pompously. The date of publication was not known, a surprising admission given that the book was then being printed. The comment was made that 'modern music [. . .] is not pleasing to the average person'. The author of the article felt that in future more hymns on the Holy Spirit would be needed. This was not promised but the section on the Sacraments had been extended.[498] Once more the tone of the article is discriminatory, coming from the position of a scholar who 'knows best' and, again, a Wesleyan.

From this point forward articles appeared in the *Methodist Recorder*, usually penned by members of the Hymn Book Committee, seeking to provide reviews of its contents.

On 30 November it was announced that the new book was to be published on 14 December. It was described as 'truly and characteristically Methodist. It is in true succession, and bears the strongly-marked family features.' Fewer Wesley hymns were noted. Bryan Spinney records the contemporary comment, 'it is a sad thing that Wesley should be wounded in the house of his friends'.[499] The Christmas hymns provided one of the 'most complete and varied sections of the Book'. 'All the great epochs of our Lord's life among men are well provided for.'[500] The inclusion of missionary hymns was cited as evidence that 'Cultured speech and good literary form [are not things] to be clung to', there was a willingness to 'make itself more vile' to commend the gospel and save some. The inclusion of 'O love that wilt not let me go' was applauded, as it was to have been omitted. The committee was regarded to have been 'rather hard on Anne Steele, and possibly a little more than kind to the American

497 *Methodist Times and Leader*, 27 July 1933, p. 24.
498 *Methodist Times and Leader*, 16 November 1933, p. 2.
499 Spinney, *Tuned for Praise*, p. 15.
500 Janet Wootton has commented on the lack of hymns on Jesus' teaching in the MHB. Wootton, *Introducing a Practical Feminist Theology of Worship*, p. 10.

Unitarian, F. L. Hosmer, whose hymns are usually in long and rather grandiloquent phrases'.[501] This prompts the question as to whether this was really a veiled theological criticism.

On 7 December various articles were published. J. E. Rattenbury regarded the book as 'rich in literary charm'. Given his opposition to Methodist Union one can only assume that this was either further evidence of the Wesleyan tenor of the publication, or an indication of Rattenbury's political skill.[502] Comparison was made only with the Wesleyan predecessor. Changes to hymns were regarded as being made to save good texts from disuse.[503] It is worth remarking at this point that critical correspondence had passed between Rattenbury and Lilian Cox during the production of the book regarding the exclusion of one of her texts.[504] None of Cox's texts was ultimately included. The words of a woman carried little weight, or perhaps they were genuinely of poor quality. None survive, so it is hard to judge.

Rattenbury regretted the loss of hymns for back-sliders but this point was answered by F. L. Wiseman with the assertion that such texts were included under 'Faith and Regeneration'.[505] Rattenbury was a sufficiently astute critic to have known whether or not this was so and is unlikely to have made the statement if he had felt satisfied.

W. R. Maltby made comparison with former hymnals but mentions none by name except the *Sunday School Hymnal*. Maltby indicated that since 1903 73 books had been published, all of which had been examined. The figure does not equate with those listed within the archive. 'In its general arrangement the new book does not greatly differ from the old',[506] he wrote. Here was an admission from a Wesleyan of the truth that close comparison of the *Methodist Hymn Book* with the *Wesleyan Methodist Hymn Book* would demonstrate.

A. L. Humphries (ex-Primitive Methodist) offered general assent to the book. Humphries observed that translations of older hymns, sometimes ancient, with 'peculiar' metres, were over-done. The

---

501 *Methodist Recorder*, 30 November 1933, p. 1.

502 In 1938 Rattenbury, making a defence of the Methodist Sacramental Fellowship, was able to counter a report that suggested it carried a 'Romanizing' influence. Newton describes his speech as 'masterly', indicating Rattenbury's persuasive skill to further his own position. Newton, *Heart Speaks to Heart*, p. 72.

503 *Methodist Recorder*, 7 December 1933, p. 3.

504 MARC 30/238.

505 *Methodist Recorder*, 14 December 1933, p. 3.

506 *Methodist Recorder*, 7 December 1933, p. 3.

arrangement of the book followed 'time-honoured usage'. This euphemism would not have blinded an astute reader. Passing reference was made to the section on ancient hymns, canticles and psalms.[507]

S. G. Dimond (ex-United Methodist) provided a very positive response to the book: 'it is not easy to write without extravagance . . . whatever omissions or exclusions may prove mistaken, it is the fruit of the most scrupulous regard for a sacred trust'.[508] The comment is uncritical.

Henry Bett, a member of the Hymn Book Committee and a Wesleyan, sought to assess the literary quality of the book. Bett stated that 'it includes much that is below the level of our characteristic Methodist hymns . . . there is no element of permanence, religious or literary, in such hymns; they have merely some quality of novelty or quaintness or sentimentality that happens to make them acceptable to some people at the moment.' Bett felt that such hymns would be 'cast out remorselessly at the next revision, unless the general level of taste is greatly debased in the interval'. The book would have been better for the omission of at least 50 hymns that 'are only pious doggerel like "Sing we the King who is coming to reign" and "Will your anchor hold in the storms of life?" and "I am so glad that my Father is in heaven"[509] and "The Galilean fishers toil", to give a few examples at random'.[510] Like Humphries he questioned the usefulness of translations of medieval texts. Jean Ingelow's text 'And did Thou love the race that loved not Thee?' and Caswall's 'See! amid the winter's snow' were welcomed.[511] In spite of the literary criteria that the committee had applied they had suspended these too often for Bett's taste! But there is another possible reason for his criticism. Those hymns that he wished to exclude were not in the *Wesleyan Methodist Hymn Book*. Of those of which he praised the inclusion, one came from the Primitive Methodist hymnal and the other from the *Church Hymnary*. Bett was a literary scholar and understood the quality of English, but an examination of his book suggests a subjective preference for hymns that had stood the test of time.[512]

---

507 *Methodist Recorder*, 7 December 1933, p. 3f.
508 *Methodist Recorder*, 7 December 1933, p. 4.
509 Presumably Bett was referring to 'I am so glad that our Father in heaven' (421).
510 Wiseman dissented from this view: the Church is one 'of composite feeling. We cannot all be "high-brows" '. *Methodist Recorder*, 14 December 1933, p. 3.
511 *Methodist Recorder*, 7 December 1933, p. 4.
512 Bett, *The Hymns of Methodism*, 1945.

Bett's response can be compared with an article in the *Methodist Times and Leader* by Robert Strong entitled 'A Literary Estimate', in which florid language was criticised (for example, No. 27) and the influence of Robert Bridges was noted. It was commented that 'The amount of new material is slight – a sign perhaps of the comparative sterility of the period in first-rate religious poetry.' It was seen as a pity to have to sing about 'lesser breeds without the law'[513] and the author felt that few would want to vow 'the love that asks no question'.[514] Not everyone received the book with joy and for some there was a critical awareness of what had happened in the editorial process, that is, the conservation of much that was familiar to Wesleyans in the *Wesleyan Methodist Hymn Book*, with little injection of anything that was contemporary or fresh.

The *Methodist Recorder*, noting that one of the most modern characteristics of the book was the preponderance of comparatively ancient tunes, reflecting the fashion being best promoted by *Songs of Praise*, also provided similar articles.[515]

Turning to the *Methodist Times and Leader*, a similar series of reviews can be found. In a generally appreciative article Isaac Foot MP referred to Wiseman as an outstanding influence.[516] Again we are presented with an implication of the power of the Editor within the editorial process.

A Hymn Book reflection was provided in a series called 'A Preacher's Watch Tower'. Many new hymns were observed. The book was praised and welcomed. The view was expressed that fewer hymns would have been better. The question was posed: should the book be good poetry or contain useful material of lesser worth? The lifetime of a hymn book was assessed at 25 years with the view that 'some of the hymns now included will have worn out their welcome before the quarter century has passed'. History has demonstrated this to have been the case. The catholic nature of the collection was acknowledged though it was felt that there were too many Wesley hymns.[517]

513 A reference to 'God of our fathers, known of old'.
514 A reference to 'I vow to Thee my country'; *Methodist Times and Leader*, 4 January 1934, p. 2. For an assessment of this text which puts the verse in question in the context intended by the author see E. James, 'I vow to Thee, my country', *Bulletin of the Hymn Society of Great Britain and Ireland*, Vol. 10, No. 1, 1982, p. 1.
515 *Methodist Recorder*, 7 December 1933, p. 5.
516 *Methodist Times and Leader*, 11 January 1934, p. 1.
517 *Methodist Times and Leader*, 11 January 1934, p. 10.

In an article announcing the publication of the book the general order of contents was regarded as 'fairly familiar'.[518] What follows suggests that this article was seeking to make the book palatable for Primitive Methodists. It was a way of saying, in effect, 'you'll recognise this, though it is not your book'. A comparison of the numbers of hymns with those contained in preceding books was made. The contents were regarded as 'truly catholic'. The Primitive Methodist denominational anthem 'Hark! the Gospel news is sounding' had not been lost. The contribution of the Primitive Methodist books was regarded as considerable, not least because the Supplement was the latest in date of the pre-Union books. This assertion cannot be backed up by a statistical analysis of the contents and must thus be regarded as political. There are signs here that the *Methodist Times and Leader* was seeking to heal wounds (it was, as we have seen, edited by a Wesleyan) and bring the Primitive Methodists on board. An indication of items from the different contributory books was given. Hymns by contemporary Methodists R. Wilfrid Callin, James R. Batey and George Osborn Gregory were noted. It was stated that the book contained 'as judicious a selection of revival and "chorus" hymns as could be made'. Style and prices were indicated and the Tune Book was similarly reviewed.[519]

According to an article entitled 'An Appreciation and Some Criticisms', Archibald Lauder stated that this was 'A Noble Volume'. It had been awaited with 'lively anticipation or a pardonable anxiety'. The book was seen as splendid but 'too long'. Some verses included were described as 'mediocre' and some 'worse than mediocre'. 'Sentimentality should not be confused with spirituality, and doggerel is no aid to devotion', the author asserted. Here was an ally for Henry Bett. Nevertheless, 'Let all the world in every corner sing' and 'Love came down at Christmas' were welcomed, as were other specific hymns. Medieval hymns in translation were noticed.[520] The contribution of the Wesleys was regarded as unduly generous.[521]

An article by R. H. B. Shapland compared the old United Methodist books with the new book. The author recognised his prejudice of

518 *Methodist Times and Leader*, 14 December 1933, p. 1f.
519 *Methodist Times and Leader*, 14 December 1933, p. 1f.
520 It might be asked whether this was a legacy of the Pre-Raphaelite movement – popular accession to artistic fashion usually follows some time behind.
521 *Methodist Times and Leader*, 14 December 1933, p. 2f.

unfamiliarity overlaid with the inertia of age, yet the book made him 'very glad'. The book was more alike than different. Similar processes of selection seemed to have been involved. There was evidence of 'the same catholicity, although with larger opportunity'. The conservatism of the committee was thus underlined. Yet the new book appeared 'more ecclesiastical than the old'. This reflected Methodism's move towards the 'institutional churches' and again the influence of Wesleyanism. In the author's opinion the increase in the number of hymns about the Church ought to be welcomed. The re-instatement of original texts, which had been altered, was also regarded positively. There had been 'a sweeping out of sentimental hymns'. The writer felt that 'In this greater emphasis on enterprise and venture the Humanism of our age, with its belief in the resident forces of the soul of man, finds at least an echo'. The book was not regarded as being as evangelical in tone as the last. 'This book has been made to bring men to God. It recognises that we do not all come by the same path to Calvary.' There is a charitable tone, and one of resignation, in this article, suggesting that the author felt let down but was intending to make the best of it.[522]

An article by A. W. Harrison offered the accolade that this was 'the best hymn book [. . .] that Methodists of any kind have ever used'. Nevertheless, he expressed the opinion that if Wesley's arrangement could not have been re-adopted an order based on the Christian year would have been better,[523] though the new book was an improvement on that of 1904. This is a veiled way of acknowledging the link with the *Wesleyan Methodist Hymn Book*. Changes in the Wesley hymns included were noted. Sections on Christmas, Easter and the Sacraments were regarded as having been enriched. Hymns for National and Social Life were deemed better. Items by Sankey were welcomed: 'Some of these chorus hymns have been criticised as doggerel, but it is not merely mission halls that will use them.' Old tunes that had found their way back into the book were regarded as good. Plainsongs were thought to be of doubtful use, while very early tunes were nearly always good.[524]

An article entitled 'Youth and the New Hymn Book' by Clifford W. Towlson (a headmaster) noted that the book contained 300 hymns

522 *Methodist Times and Leader*, 21 December 1934, p. 3 and 5.
523 This eventually came with *Hymns & Psalms* in 1983.
524 *Methodist Times and Leader*, 28 December 1933, p. 2f.

suitable for young people.[525] It was observed that their nature was more likely to have been applauded by adults than by the youth destined to sing them. This has been recently underlined again by Warson.[526] N. F. Hutchcroft noted the usefulness of the new book in a mission context,[527] while Stanley Sowton welcomed missionary hymns included in the new book.[528] J. Alec Findlay was grateful that 'most of the best of characteristically Methodist hymnology' had been left.[529]

The *Methodist Times and Leader* sought to promote the book through a free gift offer to readers. Anyone getting a friend to subscribe to the paper would receive a gift of the book. On 7 December it was indicated that the book was to be published in a few days.[530]

Subsequent to publication a 'Retreat' for organists was promised with gatherings in principal towns to discuss and illustrate the book. An outline of the proceedings of this 'conference' was published under the title *A Mightier Music*.[531] A book by Albert H. Walker entitled *How to Receive and Use the New Methodist Hymn Book*[532] was commended. A reading of these books gives an indication of the way in which those seeking to promote the book perceived it. The latter outlined how the hymn book might be used in the home, in literary associations, as an influence on Sunday Schools and in public worship. The new book was presented to ministers and choirs as 'Our Text-Book'. It is worthy of mention that Walker's booklet assumes that the 1904 (Wesleyan) book was the most recent predecessor to the new book.[533] The suggestion was made that on New Year's Day all churches should sing 'O for a thousand tongues'.

Each of these comments underlines, again, the Wesleyan influence that had informed the production of the *Methodist Hymn Book* and was now continuing to influence the process of its adoption. 'Hark! the Gospel news is sounding' would have been a more appropriate opening hymn for Primitive Methodists.

---

525 *Methodist Recorder*, 21 December 1933, p. 11.
526 Warson, *Jesus Wants Me for a Sunbeam*, p. 65–70.
527 *Methodist Recorder*, 14 December 1933, p. 6.
528 *Methodist Recorder*, 28 December 1933, p. 5.
529 *Methodist Recorder*, 14 December 1933, p. 6.
530 *Methodist Times and Leader*, 7 December 1933, p. 6.
531 C. W. Towlson (ed.), *A Mightier Music*, London, Epworth Press, 1934.
532 A. H. Walker, *How to Receive and Use the New Methodist Hymn Book*, London, Epworth Press, 1933.
533 Walker, *How to Receive and Use the New Methodist Hymn Book*, p. 16.

Over the Christmas period 70,000 books were despatched.[534] The book was in use on 24 December 1933.[535] Thomas W. Cowap wrote indicating that the book had been dedicated at Comberbach (a village in Cheshire, the church having been Wesleyan) on the first Sunday after Epiphany. For two years before they had been practising tunes anticipated as being in it.[536] Wilfred Callin (Primitive Methodist and a member of the Hymn Book Committee), then Superintendent of the Chester Circuit, invited members to donate two books each, while choir members bought their own copies.[537] Not all Circuits moved as quickly. Over a year later (July 1935) the Orrell (ex-Primitive Methodist) Circuit was advertising 'Get YOUR New Methodist Mymnal [sic] from your Minister, T. Bonney'.[538] By 18 January 1934 impatience was being expressed at the difficulty of obtaining copies.[539] Nevertheless, an editorial in the *Methodist Recorder* commented that the book 'may suffer neglect by its very excellence'.[540] It is interesting to conjecture what might have lain behind such a comment. The only area in which lack of excellence had been pointed to from within the committee had been at the inclusion of chorus hymns. Was it their small number that would prevent the take-up of the book? And if so, by whom? Thomas Cowap did not much like such material,[541] following Rattenbury and Bett. The people who would miss this material and be put off by the 'excellence' of the book would mostly have been those outside Wesleyan circles.

The lack of material by contemporary composers such as Geoffrey Shaw (who was un-represented) and Martin Shaw (who had only six tunes included) was lamented,[542] while concern was expressed about chanting and about the 'futurist' tune by T. C. Gregory to 'Nearer, my God, to Thee'.[543] One correspondent wrote, 'It is most crude and I notice the composer is still alive. Why?'[544] An article in the *Methodist*

---

534 *Methodist Recorder*, 4 January 1934, p. 4. This amounted to an uptake by 7.6 per cent of the membership of the united church.

535 *Methodist Recorder*, 18 January 1934, p. 17.

536 *Methodist Recorder*, 25 January 1934, p. 19.

537 A. A. Taberer, personal correspondence, 6 March 2000

538 *Orrell Circuit Plan of Public Services*, 21 July to 13 October 1935.

539 *Methodist Recorder*, 18 January 1934, p. 3.

540 *Methodist Recorder*, 4 January 1934, p. 6.

541 Verbal recollections by members of Comberbach Methodist Church, 2002.

542 *Methodist Recorder*, 4 January 1934, p. 17.

543 *Methodist Recorder*, 22 February 1934, p. 6.

544 Spinney, *Tuned for Praise*, p. 22.

Times and Leader during March 1933 had made the point that not only Victorian composers should be used but also pre-Victorian, while the lack of S. S. Wesley tunes in preceding Wesleyan books was deplored.[545] The Hymn Book Committee had, of the most part, chosen material that such critics would find acceptable. To be more *avant-garde* would have been difficult, yet in doing so they would, arguably, have served better the future of the Church.

The Revd Frank Fairfax asked 'where are the latter day hymn writers? Are there no great hymns of this post-war time or did the Committee lack vision at this point?'[546] In an article on 'Youth and the New Hymn Book' by Lilian Cox there was the admission that the book contained 'but a few hymns previously unpublished',[547] while H. Merlyn Rees felt that only hymns which had not been used previously had been omitted.[548] It has been noted that Lilian Cox was a member of the committee and that none of her texts had been used, while Rees's comment assumes that nothing original should be included at all.

Even at this stage the disjunction between what the *Methodist Hymn Book* had provided and the contemporary needs of the Church was being recognised. C. Phillips Cape complained about 'the mutilated condition' of 'Bishop Heber's famous missionary hymn'.[549] The misattribution of 'Jesu, the very thought of Thee' to Bernard of Clairvaux was noted.[550]

On 25 January correspondence began relating to the number of tunes omitted from the *Wesleyan Methodist Hymn Book* that had been present in the 1876 Wesleyan book that had now been restored. This indicated that, even if following fashion, the editors were backward rather than forward looking. Not only that, but that the influence of Wesleyan choice was reaching back before 1904.

The discussion on the provenance of 'Jesu, the very thought of Thee' continued.[551] R. H. Wray stated that the new book would be welcomed in the villages, a generalisation which would be difficult to substantiate. Hymns with choruses were regarded as particularly

545 *Methodist Times and Leader*, 30 March 1933, p. 10.
546 *Methodist Recorder*, 18 January 1934, p. 17.
547 *Methodist Recorder*, 8 February 1934, p. 9.
548 *Methodist Recorder*, 11 January 1934, p. 17.
549 *Methodist Recorder*, 8 March 1934, p. 19.
550 *Methodist Recorder*, 18 January 1934, p. 17.
551 *Methodist Recorder*, 25 January 1934, p. 19.

pertinent for use in evening services.[552] By 1 February comment had been made that preachers were only using a limited range of hymns.[553]

A letter from C. Oscar Hammond was published in the *Methodist Recorder* suggesting that the Continuation Committee ought 'to keep in touch with new work, both poetry and music, or with fresh discovery, and recommend it to our people'. Ironically the letter went on to assert that what was traditional within Methodism was best.[554] The suggestion was made that when Methodist hymns were broadcast tunes from the new book should be used.[555]

Throughout the late winter and spring reports of hymn festivals were carried regularly in the *Methodist Recorder*. After 8 March 1934 letters and articles relating to the Hymn Book seem to have dried up until 26 April when a letter greeting the arrival of the book in Australia was published.[556]

On 5 July a report on Telford's Commentary on the new book was published in the *Methodist Recorder*. Telford was now 83 and about to retire![557]

A concluding word is left to F. W. Drew. The book was, he intimated, 'an interesting mixture of ancient and modern'. 'If the committee aimed, as it obviously did, at giving something to everyone's taste, they have succeeded. Whether such a policy makes for progress is another matter.'[558]

What can be derived from these responses is a sense that, at the outset, there had been very little consultation outside the confines of those who had been appointed to serve on the Hymn Book Committee. The response to this is demonstrated in two ways. Those who had been brought up with an understanding of the authoritarian Wesleyan style of church government questioned again and again what the committee was doing in order to find out what hymns were being considered, and how the book was taking shape. Those who had been familiar with a more democratic form of church government, who had worked in a less hierarchical, more congregational, style of church, enquired less,

---

552 *Methodist Recorder*, 25 January 1934, p. 19.
553 *Methodist Recorder*, 1 February 1934, p. 17.
554 *Methodist Recorder*, 22 February 1934, p. 17.
555 *Methodist Recorder*, 7 June 1934, p. 20.
556 *Methodist Recorder*, 26 April 1934, p. 19.
557 *Methodist Recorder*, 5 July 1934, p. 9.
558 *Methodist Times and Leader*, 18 January 1934, p. 18.

initially. Their response at being presented with what appeared to be a *fait accompli* was one of shock, expressed in requests that a list of contents be published and the time of publication be delayed. The dominance of the Wesleyans, aided by their style of clerical domination, meant that the book could more easily be formed on the pattern of their expectations.

A second conclusion that can be drawn from this material is the growing awareness, provided by negative and positive evidence, that the *Methodist Hymn Book* was being recognised as reactionary rather than radical. Some correspondents praised the way in which old material had been reinstated and familiar texts had been retained, while others deplored the lack of anything contemporary, particularly in certain sections of the book.

A picture is provided of many people with different points of view seeking to influence, albeit retrospectively, the work of the committee. Even those matters that were raised before the *Methodist Hymn Book* began to arrive at its final form were only adopted if expressed by a sufficient number of people. While there were no stated criteria for the Hymn Book Committee to follow in the work of compilation and editing they were set in their minds as to what they found to be acceptable. Two particular strands stand out in the critique. Firstly, that of the place of material for children and young people. The quality of such material as was extant at the time of production of the *Methodist Hymn Book* was not of a uniformly high standard and the committee were aware of this. Correspondents to the religious press were knowledgeable enough to recognise that youth can be fickle and that what was being presented was not sufficiently contemporary in nature. Secondly, the critique of the section on 'Death and Judgement' demonstrated the rearguard action of those who were fighting against what Lysons has recognised as a tide of sociological and cultural significance.[559] He points out that the Victorian obsession with eschatology declined throughout the twentieth century and the evidence for this could be traced in the number of hymns dedicated to the theme as the century progressed. The committee were more than usually astute in moving with this cultural imperative.

It is now necessary to look beyond the bounds of denominational newspapers. Here the material is, understandably, more sparse and difficult to obtain.

---

559 Lysons, *A Little Primitive*, p. 202.

The Hymn Society of Great Britain and Ireland was not established until 1935 and so no contemporary account can be found in its Bulletin. The Methodist Church Music Society was also formed after Methodist Union.

In addition to the contemporary journalistic record, an assessment of the reception accorded to the book can be gleaned from later retrospective sources. Bryan Spinney, writing in 1999, judged that 'the success of the new book owed much to Luke Wiseman', who through 'his enthusiasm overcame many of the prejudices which naturally arise at times of changes in hymnody'.[560] He goes on to state that 'readers of the *Methodist Recorder* wrote to the editor just as frequently and feelingly after [publication] as before'.[561] Given the record provided above that is, perhaps, an overstatement. What is clear is that as publication neared, and following publication, readers of the *Methodist Times and Leader* began to write in a way that had not been seen previously. Spinney judges that the process of consultation and selection of material was responsible for the book having a life of 50 years. This is, again, an oversimplification. Consultation was not as wide ranging as it could have been, as has been shown above, and the response to the book was not fulsome in all quarters as even he records. A correspondent wrote

> Some of us have struggled to provide Hymn Books in the past for our churches, now with our factories closed and many un-employed or on short-time, we are expected to buy new hymn-books. An appendix could have been produced for the few extra hymns and bought by those desiring them. Also the great majority would not be required to buy what they did not require.[562]

What is inferred here is that what was on offer was, in effect, a supplement to the previous (Wesleyan) hymn book. Spinney acknowledges that the exigencies of a tight budget might not be all that lay behind the comment. His assessment, nevertheless, must be tempered by two observations. Firstly, his booklet traces Methodist hymnody almost entirely through Wesleyan sources. Secondly, he is of the opinion that 'In Methodism all material used in public worship should

---

560 Spinney, *Tuned for Praise*, p. 18f.
561 Spinney, *Tuned for Praise*, p. 21.
562 Spinney, *Tuned for Praise*, p. 21.

be approved by the Conference through the Faith and Order Committee.'[563] This standpoint, while extant in the British Methodist Church of today, has its origins in Wesleyanism and takes no account of Primitive or Free Church Methodist tradition that had emphasised a less structured form of worship, extempore prayer and greater congregational freedom.

What is clear is the observation that the domination of Wesleyanism, that was seen to be in the ascendant at the time of Union, continued at least to the end of the twentieth century, evidenced in the increased use of written liturgies and the production of a hymn book (*Hymns & Psalms*) to service such a style of worship.

Individual correspondence and conversations have elicited interesting recollections from the time of publication of the *Methodist Hymn Book* that are not available elsewhere. Wilfrid Little recollected that the Hymn Book Committee had its moments of fun. Arthur Gregory expressed a dislike for the tune 'Beatitudo' and received the riposte from Wiseman, 'Well, if that's your attitudo!' Little, on going to a new Circuit after Union, remembered being greeted with 'Are you one of those musical ministers? – if so we don't want you', which was interpreted as a resistance to the change which was taking place finding its focus in the new book. On his first Sunday the question of tackling the 'problem of the new book' was raised and 'it all went up in smoke'. There was tension between ex-Wesleyan and ex-Primitive ministers that led to somewhat caustic, if good-hearted, exchanges. A Wesleyan church had succeeded in getting a new organ and the neighbouring ex-Primitive minister greeted his colleague with 'All you need now is the monkey!' This received the retort 'And all you need is the organ!'[564] Humour can often overlay a deeper animosity.

Alfred Taberer recorded that J. Swinden, the Primitive Methodist Book Steward in the 1920s who was known personally to his family, 'expressed the opinion that the Primitives were well satisfied with the book they were using'. Swinden did, however, agree that the production of the new book made sense. Taberer also recalled that James Bradburn was consulted by F. Luke Wiseman as to which hymns he would suggest for the section entitled 'The Gospel Call'.

---

563 Spinney, *Tuned for Praise*, p. 24.
564 W. Little, personal telephone conversation, 28 February 2000.

'Old "Jimmy", who was a man of humble origins and well known as a plain-spoken home mission advocate, drew up a list of 28 hymns, which duly appeared at Nos 311 to 338.'[565]

'Praise to the holiest in the height' caused some discussion, 'the PMs and UMs objecting to the inclusion of the verse "And that a higher gift than grace", which their own books omitted'. 'Tennyson's "Strong Son of God" came in for criticism, one member exclaiming "I will not sing anything expressing doubt!" It was cut down to four verses.'[566]

In later correspondence Taberer reflected on 'the book's reception in the Connexion as a whole'. 'As far as the ex-Wesleyans and other users of the 1904 book were concerned, I should say that the new book was readily accepted.' This constituency found the layout to be familiar and they benefited from 'the inclusion of some hymns and tunes from the PM Hymnal which they hadn't had previously [. . .] they had the advantage of being able to use a book in which the majority of the hymns were set to tunes they could readily sing instead of having to look for alternatives to make them acceptable to some of their congregations.' In addition 'some "high" Wesleyans' had a much wider selection of Psalms and Canticles to use'.[567] Taberer, a Primitive Methodist, recognised the clear family resemblance of the *Methodist Hymn Book* to the *Wesleyan Methodist Hymn Book*, yet he underlined the advantage that the Wesleyans were gaining by the inclusion of some Primitive Methodist material.

'With the ex-PMs the reaction to the new book could perhaps, in some cases, be said to have lacked ready enthusiasm.' Kenneth Lysons agreed with this assessment.[568] The reason, Taberer asserts, was sometimes dependent on the attitude of the ministers and sometimes for financial reasons. Taberer's father anticipated that George Street Chapel in Chester would be slow to adopt the book. 'He reckoned without R. W. Callin who was then [. . .] Circuit Superintendent.' Here the book was in use from August 1934. Taberer noted the diplomacy that was necessary in the choice of tunes so that even if the set tune was not one expected by the congregation, one which they knew and liked could be found. As generations passed 'these

---

565 A. A. Taberer, personal correspondence.
566 A. A. Taberer, personal correspondence.
567 A. A. Taberer, personal correspondence.
568 K. Lysons, personal telephone conversation, 3 November 2000.

prejudices gradually disappeared – but not before there were a few skirmishes!'[569]

In the Leicester Claremont Street Chapel the Superintendent, who was ex-Wesleyan, chose 'I would commune with Thee, my God' and was astonished to hear the tune 'Rochester' being played over. This had been the Primitive Methodist tune and 'was sung most heartily – leaving him as the only one who could not sing it!' Claremont Street had been head of the ex-Primitive Methodist North Circuit where they would only invite a Superintendent of Primitive Methodist background.[570]

The social element in the new book was welcomed by those of ex-Primitive Methodist background though this had, it was felt, been diluted. The translations of hymn texts from overseas were regarded as excellent.[571]

The conversations and correspondence outlined above give a flavour of what was happening in actual situations. There is a reiteration of the Wesleyan tone of the book and an indication that its adoption, symptomatic of the birth pangs of Union, was not always easy or immediate.

One further source is of use in assessing the reception of the *Methodist Hymn Book*. C. P. Hancock, writing since 1983, reflected on his initial impressions of the book when it was first published. Repeating the words of those who sought to promote the book, and thereby giving his recollections a sense of authenticity, Hancock described it as 'the visible symbol of Methodist Union'.[572] It then becomes clear that there is not a little bias in his text as he refers to 'The two major streams of the three groups who came together in 1932' each having their own hymnals. This is followed by the admission that 'We belonged to the Wesleyan stream, and the Primitive Methodists were not strong in our area.'[573] There is no indication here of the input of the United Methodist Free Churches. He then proceeds to describe the Methodist [Wesleyan] Hymn Book of 1904 as a 'little stuffy musically', and, as it contained 'about 45% by the Wesley brothers', a bit one-sided in terms of the words.[574] Wilfrid Callin is

569 A. A. Taberer, personal correspondence.
570 A. A. Taberer, personal correspondence.
571 K. Lysons, personal telephone conversation.
572 C. P. Hancock, *A Hymn Lover's Diary*, Leominster, Orphans Press, nd, p. 47.
573 Hancock, *A Hymn Lover's Diary*, p. 47f.
574 Hancock, *A Hymn Lover's Diary*, p.48.

recorded as being 'sometimes sensitive and justifiably so about the apparent ignorance of the Primitive Methodist contribution displayed by some Methodist speakers and writers who spoke of "our former hymn book" as if there had been only one'.[575]

Hancock clearly admired some of the material that had been gained in the Union, giving veracity to Taberer's assessment of this benefit. He writes favourably of the tune, taken from the *Primitive Methodist Hymnal* of 1886, to 'Saviour, blessed Saviour'.[576] The addition of 'a judicious selection of Sankey type hymns' he describes as 'distinctive'.[577] It is interesting to reflect that Jaspar, recalling a Bible Christian heritage persistent after Union, felt that many hymns deriving from the 'Moody and Sankey corpus' were included in the *Methodist Hymn Book* and that these were much used.[578] Hancock recognised that some people regard these as anathema while others 'seem to think that unless a hymn has a long, repetitive chorus after every verse, it is not a true gospel hymn'. He confessed to being somewhere in the middle: 'Some of the hymns have sentimental words that make me curl up; some tunes are so banal and the harmonies so bare that they are tedious; and some have choruses that seem to disobey our Lord's injunction to use "no vain repetitions".'[579] Yet there are some that clearly moved him. He affirmed the inclusion of 'Beneath the cross of Jesus', 'To God be the glory', 'Blessed assurance, Jesus is mine' and 'What a friend we have in Jesus', among others.[580]

Hancock was critical of those hymns which he ascribed to Unitarian Americans, and which were written in the nineteenth century. These he regarded as accepting Jesus as an ethical revolutionary while denying his divinity. The texts puzzled him.[581] Hancock attributed the longevity of the book to its 'all-embracing outlook and style'.[582]

Clearly the responses to a book such as this are going to be many and varied. From the outset consultation was limited and the book might have been both more representative and more contemporary

575 C. Towlson, quoted in K. Lysons, *Robert Wilfrid Callin, Parson, Padre, Poet*, Buxton, Church in the Market Place Publications, 1996, p. 28.
576 Hancock, *A Hymn Lover's Diary*, p. 48.
577 Hancock, *A Hymn Lover's Diary*, p. 55–62.
578 A. Jaspar, personal conversation, 13 January, 2003.
579 Hancock, *A Hymn Lover's Diary*, p. 55.
580 Hancock, *A Hymn Lover's Diary*, p.55–62.
581 Hancock, *A Hymn Lover's Diary*, p.62.
582 Hancock, *A Hymn Lover's Diary*, p.64.

had the committee risked such interchange. This omission seems to have been quite a conscious one on the part of the committee, as on many occasions they were called upon to make their decisions more public but they failed to respond. Responses in the denominational press, and from individual authors and correspondents, demonstrate that the book was recognised as being more akin to its Wesleyan predecessors than to the books of the other contributing denominations. Consequently the Wesleyans found the book easier to adopt. In other denominations selective use of material within the book has been evident.[583] While this would have been unfortunate for the book, it was symptomatic of what was happening through the process of church union that had taken place. The book was becoming not so much 'the outward and visible sign of Union' as the symbol of a church that was struggling to unite and looking back to a past that would never be regained.

The intrinsic conservatism of the editors was underlined by the reception that the book received. While many people appreciated the sense of nostalgia, though they might not use that term, that the book engendered, others recognised that contemporary composers had been omitted and living authors had not been encouraged.

The book represented, in the estimation of those who received it, the best of Methodist hymnody from the past, with the addition of some popular material of lesser quality. The change from the book that had served Wesleyan Methodists for nearly 30 years was not great enough. An opportunity had been missed.

---

583 A. Jaspar, personal conversation, 13 January 2003.

7

The Hymn Book and
Methodist Union

The process of Methodist Union brought together three disparate strands of Methodism. The uniting denominations shared a mutual heritage but the way in which that heritage had developed and had been given expression varied. As the denominations came together, with a formal declaration of unity, there was anything but uniformity. The genesis of the *Methodist Hymn Book* gives an insight into some of the ways the denominations tried to work together within these tensions and differences on one particular project. In any other denomination the editing of a hymn book might be considered peripheral but for Methodists hymns were integral to religious expression, theology and church life.

So far this book has examined the origin of the *Methodist Hymn Book* in some detail. In the light of this, questions are raised which are pertinent not only to the book but also to Methodist Union and the ongoing development of the denomination.

1. To what degree was the book really a new hymn book?
2. Why did the book last so long? Was this because of its inherent excellence?
3. Did Methodist Union in some way paralyse the new Church in such a way that the replacement of the book became a very low priority?
4. Was there simply no new material to warrant the production of a new book?

Edmund S. Lamplough, speaking in 1932 on the occasion of the Uniting Conference in the Royal Albert Hall, said of the proposed new *Methodist Hymn Book*:

Both hymns and tunes are being compiled for Methodists . . . We trust we shall not be guilty of the parochialism and smug self-satisfaction which refuses the new book the enrichment of the best hymns and tunes of Churches other than our own. But we prize too much our share in the priceless inheritance of the Evangelical Revival, to allow what is distinctive of Methodism to be obscured by anything else in our new Hymn Book. Rest assured that the new book will be Methodist, the best that can be compiled by the best Methodist Committee which the three uniting Methodist Churches could choose to compile it.[584]

The degree to which the committee was successful reflects, in part, the ability of these disparate parties to work together in harmony and to find a way forward which was acceptable to each party. The future health of the Church was also dependent on its capacity to serve the age in which it was set and, given the longevity of the hymn book, those which lay ahead.

The World at the Time of Methodist Union

This was a time of response to immense political and cultural change. The First World War punctuated the period in which the Methodist Union talks had taken place. This war marked the end of the nineteenth century and its belief in the potential and possibilities of human progress. It was also the first modern war which saw the first extensive use of what are now known as 'weapons of mass destruction'. It was the end of the world as people had known it. By comparison, the cultural and religious effects of scientific and technological progress and, in particular, Darwinism on ordinary people in the previous century were far less significant. True, these had intellectual ramifications that were unimaginable at the time, but the Great War changed the lives of a generation in a way that was immutable. All art responded to this and was affected by it. Siegfried Sassoon was able to date, to the day, the writing of his first 'outspoken' war poem.[585] Poetry was beginning, illustrated by the work of Gerard Manley

---

584 *Methodist Recorder*, 29 September 1932, p. 14.
585 S. Sassoon, *War Poems*, London, Faber & Faber, 1983, p. 10.

Hopkins in particular, to evolve in a new and radical way. It was now opened to the intellectual expression of T. S. Eliot and the influence of the ordinary exhibited in the work of W. H. Auden. Even Robert Bridges, whose influence on hymnody and the *Methodist Hymn Book* in particular has been noted (see p. 69), witnessed to the effect of the Great War in his poem 'The Widow', first printed privately in 1929.[586]

It must, however, be admitted that these examples illustrate only one possible response, and the work of John Betjeman seems reactionary by comparison. Social norms had been disrupted by the experience of men in the trenches. Everything had been thrown into the melting pot. Humanity was presented with a choice, to begin again with something radically different or to try to reconstitute the mould, to re-forge that which had been destroyed. Cecil Lewis writing in 1936 put it like this:

> The fixity with which men pursued immediate trivialities alarmed and disgusted me. The magnitude of the effort spent on daily futilities was too awful to be faced; it was a sort of St Vitus dance, bound to end in exhaustion. The mentality of the post-war years was no different from that of the war itself – an obsession to take the next objective, [. . .] whether you had any idea of where to go next or not . . .
>
> We needed effort, not greater in quantity, but other in quality; a different point of view, a new perspective.[587]

Men who could provide this existed but the task before them 'demanded heavy sacrifice and drastic change – both utterly abhorrent to those who could not see the danger they were in'. The choice was to be radical or reactionary. Studies of American revivalist religion have identified similar cultural contexts from which can be drawn criteria to examine the response with which we are presented.[588] Revivals have been shown to follow times of awakening. Such awakenings may be occasions of secular discovery or political upheaval. Presented with these situations religious groups invariably pursue one of two options. Either there is a reaction to the new and re-entrenchment, an increased

---

586 R. Bridges, *Poetical Works of Robert Bridges*, London, Oxford University Press, reprinted 1959, p. 564.

587 C. Lewis, *Sagittarius Rising*, Harmondsworth, Penguin, 1977, p. 82f.

588 W. McLoughlin, *Revivals, Awakenings, and Reform*, University of Chicago Press, 1978, passim.

emphasis on the values of the past and their supposed immutability, or the opportunity for growth and renewal is grasped with a repositioning in relation to theological understanding.

It would be expected that a comparison of the Methodist hymn books prior to and following the Great War would demonstrate a significant change in response to this event, or a reaction against the changes that it had forced on society at large. The extent to which the Hymn Book Committee responded to this imperative for change, and the degree to which they resisted it, offers a barometer of the attitudes held within the embryonic denomination. A reading of the *Methodist Hymn Book* gives an indication, therefore, not only of the status of the book, but also an insight into the relations between the Methodist denominations at the time of Union.

Numerically the dominance of Wesleyan Methodism is clear. The consequence of this dominance is demonstrated in the manner in which its representatives related to those of the other denominations and the way in which they perceived themselves. Part of this attitude found its origin in the culture of clerical domination and the low level of democratic representation within the denomination. Most of the members of the Hymn Book Committee were older men acknowledged to be past their intellectual best.

In the period between 1907 and 1932, when the process of ecumenical conversation was taking place, the blindness of certain key figures to the process that was gathering pace, to its necessity, and the action needed for its progression, is lamentable. This is particularly noticeable in the response to requests for data relating to the geographical distribution of Methodist Societies. F. L. Wiseman's response to a request for statistics, 'The work of compilation would be enormous', and 'the utility of the whole is not obvious to me',[589] is indicative of the negativity that greeted those who were working towards the Union. Though it is fair to say that other parties to the discussions were equally obstructive, it seems incredible that this was the person chosen to chair the ecumenical Hymn Book Committee. The language of participants also indicates their attitude, the Primitive Methodists and the United Free Church Methodists being styled 'junior Methodist churches'.[590] Wesleyan questions drafted for

---

589 Currie, *Methodism Divided*, p. 250.
590 Currie, *Methodism Divided*, p. 250f.

presentation to the other denominations speak not of dialogue but of the determination as to whether or not the other denominations would be willing to adhere to Wesleyan Methodist principles.[591] Only when Union was inevitable did Rattenbury and the 'Other Side' accede.

Once the Hymn Book Committee had been established the arguments were not over.[592] The debate which took place between Gerrard and Sharp (see p. 37f.) relating to the composition of sub-committees has been recorded.

All of this is indicative of the exclusivity of a denomination (the Wesleyans) characterised by what Don Cupitt describes as 'a sub-culture of like-minded people . . . [with] a strong and distinctive atmosphere that works to exclude sceptical outsiders and their uncomfortable questions'. In this context 'the more we are able to assume that our truth is *the* truth and our world *the* world, the less we shall be aware of any world outside our own world'.[593] Holloway has also drawn attention to the way in which institutions work for their own survival by excluding those things that would work for change.[594]

In this context the likelihood of the committee producing a book that could be rightly seen to be representative of the uniting denominations seems slim. We should not be surprised, therefore, by what we find. The *Methodist Hymn Book* of 1933 has little to distinguish it from the *Wesleyan Methodist Hymn Book*, a book that had also been used by the Methodist New Connexion. Little here is radical. Most of what we encounter is 'safe'. There are fewer hymns that can be attributed to Charles or John Wesley but, equally, little twentieth-century hymnody has been included.

A casual glance at the contents of the *Methodist Hymn Book* and the hymn books of the uniting denominations indicates that large blocks of hymns have been taken from the *Wesleyan Methodist Hymn Book*. This hymnal provided the basic content listing for the new book. The list was then amended. This view is substantiated by a rigorous examination that demonstrates that 604 texts out of 984 in the *Methodist Hymn Book*, over 61 per cent, are to be found in the *Wesleyan Methodist Hymn Book*. This compares with 56 per cent

---

591 Currie, *Methodism Divided*, p. 252.
592 MARC 29/130.
593 D. Cupitt, *The Sea of Faith*, 2nd edition, London, SCM Press, 1994, p. 166.
594 R. Holloway, *Doubts and Loves*, Edinburgh, Canongate, 2001, p. 232.

from the two Primitive Methodist books, and 44 per cent in respect of the *Methodist Free Church Hymnal* and *A Collection of Hymns for the use of People called Bible Christians*. What these figures indicate is a degree of influence. What is more significant is the contribution made which is unique to any particular denomination. The necessary analysis shows that 88 items came exclusively from the Wesleyan corpus, 69 from the Primitive Methodist books, 13 from the *Methodist Free Church Hymnal* and 12 from *A Collection of Hymns for the use of People called Bible Christians*. These contributions are put into perspective when it is realised that 60 hymns were drawn from the *Church Hymnary*.

The Wesleyan emphasis is overwhelming. For instance, hymns 539 to 568, a run of 30 texts, all come from *Wesleyan Methodist Hymn Book*; 569 does not, then the following seven texts also come from the same book. Within this run of hymns from 539 to 576, 29 items are also found in the *Methodist Free Church Hymnal*. Significantly, the only denomination with unique contributions is Wesleyan Methodism, offering two. No texts within this block are contributed by the Primitive Methodist hymnals at all.

An argument in favour of the use of the *Wesleyan Methodist Hymn Book* could have been the fact that this book had the widest circulation of any hymn book within Methodism at the time of Union, being used by the Methodist New Connexion societies within the United Methodist Free Church as well as the Wesleyans. Two extremely significant consequences proceed from the decision. Firstly, it immediately precluded any structural alteration, and lessened the likelihood that innovative content would be included. This decision was made in spite of the pressure of changes in context and culture between 1904 and 1932 that have already been noted. Secondly, the groups whose hymnals had been used less freely were likely to experience a sense of alienation, unless it could be demonstrated that their small contribution had moved the book substantially in the direction of their cultural or theological position. The analysis of contributions of unique material provided above suggests that this criterion was not met in the editing of this book.

The *Methodist Hymn Book* was not a completely new book in spite of the efforts of those promoting it to present it as such. This book was directly derived from the *Wesleyan Methodist Hymn Book* and there is little present to disguise this fact. If this was solely a matter of the continuation in use of a popular hymn book, suitably revised, then it could be regarded as innocuous. What it demonstrates is the degree of influence of a single, admittedly numerically dominant group, within the process of defining the style and culture of the new denomination.

An indication of the degree to which the *Methodist Hymn Book* was innovative, in spite of its parentage, could be gauged by the contributions of new material (compared with the existing corpus of the *Wesleyan Methodist Hymn Book*) from all sources but particularly from *Songs of Praise* (which was regarded as breaking new ground)[595] and the *Primitive Methodist Hymnal Supplement* (the most recent Methodist hymnal prior to Union). Such an examination indicates that only 22 items from *Songs of Praise* were included compared with 60 from the *Church Hymnary* (a rather more conservative collection, which nevertheless still received Bradley's criticism of discarding useful Victorian material),[596] while contributions of novel material from the Primitive Methodist hymnals amounted to 37 texts. The total number of items from other sources outside the Methodist corpus amounted to 170.

Comparison of the *Methodist Hymn Book* with the *Church Hymnary* and *Songs of Praise* is pertinent. The *Church Hymnary* was in effect a revision of an original book that had first appeared in 1898. The committee charged with the revision was broadly based and developed an international, if colonial, flavour with the involvement of representatives of the Presbyterian Churches of South Africa, Australia and New Zealand. The draft of the collection was approved in 1925 by the General Assemblies of the contributing churches. A survey of the contributing authors indicates that only 16 died after the end of the First World War and before 1927, and of those still alive at the time of publication (24) all but one, Ernest Dodshun,[597] had lived the greater part of their lives in the Victorian era.

In contrast *Songs of Praise* brought together texts from 45 authors who were still living at the time of the publication of the revised and enlarged edition of 1932. Additionally a further six authors are

---

595 Bradley, *Abide with me*, p. 224.

596 Bradley, *Abide with me*, p. 226.

597 Author of 'What service shall we render thee', a text which presents the Lordship and laws of Christ as an antidote for war. In the future which is anticipated the nation's battle cry will be 'brother-hood'.

represented who died between the end of the First World War and the date of publication. What is of even greater significance is the quality of the authorship that was included. While the book sometimes reads like the home counties of the 1930s at prayer, there is much of quality here that has stood the test of time, but which only found its way into other hymnals at a much later date. 'Morning has broken' took a further 50 years before finding its way into the Methodist corpus.

To examine the *Methodist Hymn Book* in the same way suggests that to be dead was almost a prerequisite for inclusion. Only five authors survived publication, though 16 contributors died between the end of the First World War and the appearance of the book. Even Wilfrid Callin (1886–1951), a member of the committee and a Primitive Methodist, had only one hymn included, while Lilian Cox had none.

It appears that, for the most part, the editors of the *Methodist Hymn Book* were conservative rather than innovative. They are not to be condemned for this, for in the immediate aftermath of the war there was great need and, as Lewis has suggested,[598] inordinate pressure to regain the equilibrium that had been lost. There is comfort to be found in those things that are familiar and safe. Music which had provided a sense of security in the past was easy to hold on to, while the new atonal compositions which, though having their origin before the war were particularly suited to respond to the chaotic, were harder to assimilate and less fitted for hymnody. Following trauma it is often impossible to address pain immediately. It took 50 years before the persecution and extermination of Jews during the 1930s and 1940s began to receive really serious attention. Similarly, the voices of those who had served in the trenches were silent. Those who spoke were often the poets who, paradoxically, addressed the nation from beyond the grave. Light-hearted frivolity helped to assuage guilt and anguish, or at least to bury it. The mood of the twenties was one of 'frenzied partying', which Noel Coward questioned in a contemporary song, 'Poor Little Rich Girl': in lives of leisure the craze for pleasure 'steadily grows. Cocktails and laughter, but what comes after? Nobody knows'.[599] Additionally the pressure to provide a sense of continuity with the historic Methodist Church in its various incarnations was

---

598 Lewis, *Sagittarius Rising*, p. 82f.
599 N. Coward, quoted by Neil Tennant, *Arts and Books*, London, Daily Telegraph, 4 April 1998, p. 1.

enormous. To unite the denominations and at the same time move off in a new direction would have been inordinately difficult to do.

The adoption of the Hymn Book was not immediate.[600] The initial raft of sales has to be examined alongside the reminiscence of those who remember the book's introduction. The intention behind its production, that of furnishing the united Church with hymns and ensuring uniformity of worship within the new denomination, was perceived as threatening by many of those for whom it was produced. In the event this rationalization of resource was difficult to achieve. Societies fought hard to preserve their theological and social integrity. The denominations were still not wholly united at grass-roots level 30 years on. The process that the book had been produced to serve came to a standstill. There was little pressure, in this context, to produce a new hymn book. The *Methodist Hymn Book* remained as the one source of authorised hymnody for the denomination for 50 years.

The Hymn Book as Literature

If we use the tools of those who study literature and apply them to this book we may be able to answer a further question: put simply, was the book any good? The book may have been a lineal descendant of the *Wesleyan Methodist Hymn Book*. It may not have reflected to any great extent the spirit of the age in which it developed, but, objectively, was it a book of quality and, again, what does this have to say about the emerging denomination?

How sparse and pale is the imagery, how lacking in inventiveness the style. The book was, as has already been observed, that of another generation and, if analysed historically critically would be placed between 1880 and 1916. There is little evidence of any conscious realignment of attitudes or ideas dependent on Darwin, Freud or Schopenhauer. While D. H. Lawrence was already demonstrating the influence of Nietzsche, the *Methodist Hymn Book* contains nothing that recognises this movement in intellectual and theological thought, even in a vein that might seek to repudiate it. The mood is English,

---

600 Over Christmas 1933 some 70, 000 books were dispatched but this only amounted to 7.6 per cent of the possible market for the book responding. The uptake of the book thereafter would be expected to reduce exponentially.

colonial, late Victorian at best, with the exception of a few texts which are cognisant of the change in thinking and sensibility which had taken place over 50 years, sometimes with evolutionary guile, at others with revolutionary cataclysm. It is illuminating to reflect that the editors of the *Primitive Methodist Hymnal Supplement*, writing in 1912, spoke of the need to understand that after a quarter of a century the hymn book that they were seeking to amend 'was felt by many to be no longer completely adequate'.[601] These were the very people least well placed to influence the production of the new book and determine the direction of the united denomination.

It would be fair to assume that informed editors would operate with an understanding of intellectual movements current to their time. Auden found Freudian criticism liberating.[602] Only one text in the entire corpus of the *Methodist Hymn Book* ('And art Thou come with us to dwell', 259) operates within an obvious understanding of this mode of thinking, and this was first published in 1869.[603]

A Marxist critique looks at literature to try to determine the degree to which it maintains a view of a dominant hierarchy and the extent to which it is liberating, painting an egalitarian, democratic picture. When the *Methodist Hymn Book* is subject to such analysis evidence is presented of a book that comprises texts that were ideologically right wing, preserving feudal contextual structures in which to provide expression for religious truths. It might be argued that such analysis of an avowedly religious work is inappropriate, yet the flourishing of liberation theology in the twentieth century gives the lie to this and Holloway, writing in the present century, acknowledges its value.[604] The discovery that such analysis lays bare might be anticipated, yet Marxist critics recognise that non-socialist writers (for example, Balzac and Sir Walter Scott) could transcend their own ideological limitations.[605] Such criticism here exposes the cultural containment of the editors and, in consequence, the texts they have seen fit to include.

New Historicism is a method of analysis which assumes that in history there has always been a tendency for power to be vested in the most dominant members of a group. Applied to literature it looks for

601 *Primitive Methodist Hymnal Supplement*, p. iii.
602 M. Drabble (ed.), *Oxford Companion to English Literature*, Oxford University Press, 5th edition, revised 1995, p. 376.
603 Watson and Trickett, *Companion to Hymns & Psalms*, p. 255.
604 Holloway, *Doubts and Loves*, p. 207.
605 *Oxford Companion to English Literature*, p. 636.

evidence of such centralised power, or alternatively the sharing of power democratically throughout a group. Applied here it is clear that the Wesleyans played the part of the establishment within the Editorial Committee. The structure that they offered provides apparent security until it is challenged. When this happens it begins to break down. Culturally the collapse of authoritarian structures in society was witnessed in the 1960s. A similar collapse has been observed within the church with the prevalence of 'death of God' theology and the willingness of minorities to challenge received opinion. Arguably, the initial breakdown of Methodism following the death of John Wesley was symptomatic of a similar, and in this instance, effective challenge. At the time of Methodist Union, and shortly after, such a challenge would not have been easy to mobilise, even if the dominance of Wesleyanism was admitted. The whole movement was towards conciliation not disintegration and challenges to hierarchical authority would have been greeted with great suspicion and quickly snuffed out.

That is not to say that resistance was absent. Cultural Materialism looks for ways in which less powerful members of a group react against an establishment by going their own way. In Methodism such action has found its expression in those movements, both radical and evangelical, that have not relied solely on authorised material for their worship. Such movements disregard the dominance of the powerful being confident in the rightness of their cause. Hymnologically their influence began to be detected in the 1950s with the increased use of evangelical chorus books and continued in the charismatic and evangelical hymnals of the 1970s. Alongside these the *Methodist Hymn Book* continued to remain in dominant use in mainstream Methodism.

The theory known as Structuralism states that things are related to the words that we use to name them. We use the word 'book' to name things we recognise as 'books'. In addition each name is related to every other name within a structure. The argument was then made that the link between the name and the object was actually tenuous, it was the structure that mattered. Names were arbitrary – 'a rose by any other name would smell as sweet'. The consequence was an increasing uncertainty over our ability to be sure of the meaning of language. When this theory was related to religious language the uncertainty was compounded. Wittgenstein recognised that language used metaphysically, that is to describe those things outside of normal sensory experience, was bound to follow a circular pattern. We name that which is greater than anything of which we can conceive 'god'. 'God' is that which is greater than anything of which we can conceive. It was suggested that it was impossible to provide a philosophical proof of God but only a circular re-presentation of belief. Even greater ambiguity presented itself with the onset of post-structuralism. This stated that meaning was impossible to tie down but was a matter of the inter-relatedness of words, the meaning of which could never be certain. In spite of this the philosopher Wittgenstein retained a theological belief.

What is the point of this theory for our study? It is helpful in two ways. Firstly, it underlines the dependency of texts on those who wrote and subsequently chose them. They chose the words to describe theological concepts and ideas. They defined the inter-relatedness of the words. Outside of their arbitrary choice the words could mean something else. Secondly, the uncertainty of definition which post-structuralism identified has been symptomatic of the uncertainty, the lessening of the regard for hierarchy and the sense that individual choice is paramount, that truth is relative. This has come to be known as post-modernism. If this is a true reflection then it means that the texts of the *Methodist Hymn Book* have become increasingly less accessible to those who lived in the latter half of the twentieth century. Even if only intuitively, thinking people have sensed that the texts have no tangible link with the world that they inhabit today, and that any link that they might once have appeared to have is increasingly difficult to substantiate. Putting it another way, when using these texts the reader, or singer, breathes his or her own meaning into the language and we are forced to an interpretation, *in vacuo*, in which what is being expressed bears little, if any, relation to the reality in which the singers worship or live, and perhaps is quite detached from the original intention of the author. We are entering a fantasy world disguised as a world of faith, but that world of faith is a tautological construction.

It was this vacuum that the writers of the hymn explosion[606] sought

---

606 Beginning in the early 1960s Fred Kaan and Brian Wren found that the hymns available to them did not match the experience of the congregations they were called to pastor. They began to write material reflecting their own twentieth-century experience yet taking the form of classical hymns. Fred Pratt Green joined this process and at the beginning of the

to fill. Starting from an understanding of the needs of congregations they began to fashion hymns that spoke out of the contexts of work and worship in which church members found themselves from day to day. Their language became less metaphysical, more concrete. Often their words spoke of protest.[607]

The contents of the *Methodist Hymn Book* and other books like it were being challenged. At the time of the composition of the book this would not have been likely to be anticipated by the editors.

Structural criticism had begun to challenge the understanding of the text as a plain description of reality. In many of the hymns of the *Methodist Hymn Book* the detachment is self-evident. Realism is, for the most part, lacking, the tone is Romantic, in the technical sense, but without the radical motivating force that characterised much of early nineteenth-century literature.

Practical Criticism is concerned with the interpretation of meaning and the judgement of the quality of poetry. I. A. Richards,[608] on whose research this method was based, noted the insensitivity of students to the poetry of John Donne, D. H. Lawrence and Gerard Manley Hopkins, while G. A. Studdert Kennedy was widely praised. The application of this technique to the hymn book demonstrates that while poetry has been included and its quality, in an objective sense, is beyond reproach,[609] such material is not always accessible, often using archaic language. The more *avant-garde*, that which is linguistically readily accessible, was often sentimental or theologically conservative. This suggests that the texts that are likely to have lasting currency because of their quality are those that are least accessible, then and now. The most accessible are those which are either held in a particular theologically linguistic strait-jacket, or which are excessively sentimental or banal. Such hymns do not last long beyond the confines of the religious community that has spawned them or collected them.

Placing the *Methodist Hymn Book* against the backdrop of this brief critical survey shows it to be necessarily linked to the decline of

---

twenty-first century his hymns are found in most mainstream hymn books. These authors are now regarded as the dominant writers contributing to the 'hymn explosion' of the late twentieth century.

607 See 'Sing we the song of high revolt', Fred Kaan's interpretation of the Magnificat in *Hymns of the City*, revised edition, ed. John Vincent, Sheffield, Urban Theology Unit, 1998.

608 *Oxford Companion to English Literature*, p. 838.

609 Which in this study has been styled scholarly following Adey.

formal religion in the twentieth century, which was hitherto based on an assumption of the intrinsic interdependence of metaphysical and material reality and the reliability of the words used to describe them. The decline of the *Methodist Hymn Book*, and the difficulty in offering anything that might replace it, are only symptomatic of the same idiomatic change.

Feminist Criticism[610] began in the late 1920s and came into its own in the 1960s and 1970s. To read back such criticism to the period under review is, however, telling. As Marxist criticism can understand those of an opposite persuasion transcending their own belief system in their writings, so it is possible to gauge whether editors and authors of another generation were taken along with the cultural flow of their times or were, consciously or subliminally, swimming against the tide.

The patriarchal nature of the primary biblical texts is acknowledged, yet worship has always involved men and women. While we would not expect in the cultural *milieu* that generated the *Methodist Hymn Book* to find use of the feminine pronoun, hints of inclusivity might be expected to be detected, especially as the Primitive Methodist Church had ordained women to the ministry. Attention is immediately drawn to the composition of the Editorial Committee that had but one female representative. Contemporary women writers are sparsely represented when compared with, say, *Songs of Praise*. The Editorial Committee have in no way demonstrated a move towards inclusivity, except in two texts. The second stanza of 'As helpless as a child who clings / Fast to his father's arms' (508) begins, 'As trustful as a child who looks / Up in his mother's face', while the concluding verse opens with the words, 'As loving as a child who sits / Close by his parent's knee'. The use of the image of the mother, perhaps alluding to Psalm 131, is noticed. For this alone the text is moving against the patriarchal expectations of its day.

Jean Ingelow wrote many poems and, as in the work of Herbert, this is demonstrated in the dexterity with which the text 'And didst Thou love the race that loved not Thee?'[611] (149) was crafted. The rhetorical question with which the hymn begins is a skilful device that sets the scene. A sequence of questions follow which serve to underline

---

610 For an analysis of the manner in which such criticism can be applied to liturgy and hymnody see Wootton, *Introducing a Practical Feminist Theology of Worship*.

611 The text was taken from a poem entitled 'Honours – Part II' which, in its original form, had over 80 verses. Ingelow, *Poems*, p. 18.

the paradox and contradiction of incarnation which leads the author to the understanding that this man Jesus was both God and kinsman, 'loved, but not loved enough'. Ingelow traces six means by which Christ might visit her. This coming, for which she prays, needs must be swift, 'lest this heart should [. . .] Die ere the Guest adored *she*[612] entertain'. There is a sense of poignancy for Ingelow. Reflecting on the obvious, she never saw Christ's earthly presence, yet would not wish to 'miss Thy heavenly reign'. Here is an evangelical presupposition that those who die having not accepted Jesus on earth will not see him in heaven. This text was extant in Primitive Methodism, reflecting, perhaps, that denomination's affirmation of women.

The only occurrence of the word 'humankind' occurs in 'All humankind beneath Thy sun' (982) but this line is preceded by 'Father of men, in whom are one', thus suggesting that the choice of 'humankind' is a device to maintain the metre rather than a conscious use of inclusive language or a reaction to patriarchal structures. A more positive exhibition of inclusivity would not only have felt personally threatening, but would have been likely to have been resisted from the standpoint of the male being perceived as invested with divine definition. This pattern, as the century unfolded, became explicit in those who sought to resist the ordination of women.

In summary, modern criticism begins to provide tangible and salient reasons why the *Methodist Hymn Book* should have fallen into disuse. This is not to condemn the book or its editors out of hand. In the context in which they were working, with the denominational pressures to which they were subject, it is arguable that they could have done little more than they did. Immense changes were taking place around them. Not only was Methodism in a decline that would continue to the end of the century but the metaphysical basis of reality which had been useful and sufficient in the nineteenth century was being swept away. Theologically two streams began to be discerned. The first was a reactionary strand that sought to regain a traditional faith which would have been recognisable by those living at the beginning of the twentieth century. The hymnody of this movement, both charismatic and evangelical, was rooted in popular folk music of the 1960s. The second is a movement towards 'Godless' Christianity which has yet to find, if it ever will, its hymnody but which would be

---

612 My italics.

more comfortable using the radical hymns of late twentieth-century writers like Brian Wren.

The fact that the *Methodist Hymn Book* did not fall into disuse can be deduced from the evidence that it was used by a relatively closed, and consequently shrinking, group of people who anticipated adoption of the book by those who joined them and were oblivious to the fact that, even at its publication, it represented an age which had passed. The very features that were necessary to cement the relations between the uniting denominations were also to work counter to their long-term vitality and mission.

Here is a Victorian hymn book that survived into a post-modern world and even into the twenty-first century.[613] It can further be deduced that the book itself, and the attitude of the church to it, only served to illustrate a deeper malaise which, following Methodist Union, and perhaps even prior to it, had characterised its constituency, that of a conservative and reactionary *modus operandi*.

---

613 John Ware notes that he knows of 'one village chapel that insists on using the old *Methodist Hymn Book*, even though it has a supply of *Hymns & Psalms*'. *Methodist Recorder*, 26 September 2002.

Concluding Comments

This book has uncovered something of the workings of the committee responsible for compiling and editing the *Methodist Hymn Book*, and has given a new insight to the way in which a seminal project was prosecuted at the time of Methodist Union. This has not only begun to answer questions about the *Methodist Hymn Book* itself but has also provided fresh insights into the extent of the Wesleyan domination of the process of that union. A number of salient facts have been uncovered.

The process of ecumenical conversation from which the *Methodist Hymn Book* derived had brought together denominations of widely differing numerical strengths. In addition the attitude to church government of the uniting churches was different. The combined strength and authoritarian structure of Wesleyanism resulted in an Editorial Committee that was to suffer, or benefit, depending on your interpretation, from strong Wesleyan influence. This can be seen to be emblematic of the manner in which the denomination developed subsequently.

As a consequence of this influence the fact that the committee did not consult as widely as it might have done is not surprising. When the response of correspondents to the religious press is examined it is those who are not from a Wesleyan background who are most surprised by, and out of touch with, the process that had been in hand for some time. The bulk of the committee came to their work with a sense of 'knowing best' what the Church needed. Outside influences were reduced to a minimum and, when they were apparent, they were deemed an irritant.

The age of the bulk of the committee members, their cultural background and their experience during the opening years of the twentieth century gave rise to an attitude that was inherently conservative in the choice of material and the manner of its presentation. There was an unwillingness to adopt anything that was new or untried. This was allied to a sense of clinging to that which felt familiar and secure. The book they produced had a late Victorian/Edwardian feel. For the denomination there was an added sense of the need to consolidate a union that had been many years in the making. This was not a time for further innovation.

Finally, the influence of Luke Wiseman must be mentioned. As a competent composer this influence might have been demonstrated by the presence of his compositions within the book. These are few. The pressure that he exerted was subtle and his hand can be discerned in executive decisions and the manner in which he enabled the Wesleyan domination of the committee to have full effect. While he was clearly admired by the other committee members there is evidence of occasions when he could have been more even-handed. That was neither in his nature, nor the expectation of the denomination of which he was a representative. Even within the context of the Methodist Conference his response to criticism was that of a person who expected to have his own way.[614] In addition he was well beyond the peak of his intellectual agility as the book came into existence.[615] The outcome of the combination of these factors was a Hymn Book that was, as we have seen, inherently conservative and Wesleyan in feel. Wiseman was later to become President of the Methodist Conference.

Within the limited scope of this book, four particular questions related to the Hymn Book itself have been addressed:

1. *To what degree was the Methodist Hymn Book really a new hymn book?*

The evidence which has been uncovered shows clearly that the *Methodist Hymn Book* was not, strictly speaking, a new book. The dominance of the Wesleyan Methodist Church in the process of Union resulted in an imbalance of representation within the Hymn Book Committee. The process of the committee was undemocratic and the manner in which consultation of the various Connexions took place was flawed. The whole process was effectively insulated from the Primitive Methodist and United Methodist Churches by a combina-

---

614 MARC 29/261.
615 Davies, George and Rupp, *A History of the Methodist Church in Great Britain*, Vol. 3, p. 340.

tion of the operation of the church press, and the members' own cultural expectations of the manner in which a process such as this would proceed.

It is not unfair to characterise Wesleyan Methodist government as a benign ministerial oligarchy. That of Primitive Methodism and the United Methodist Churches was far more democratic. This had significant consequences for the process of Methodist Union and for the genesis of the hymn book which was to be the outward sign of their unity. The cultural expectations of the membership of the different denominations has been shown to have influenced, not only their attitudes to one another, but also the way in which they understood the necessity to be involved in the process of the production of the hymn book. The members of the denominations that ran on democratic lines seem to have waited in the expectation that matters relating to the book would, at some stage, be divulged. They exhibit either a great sense of trust or one of utterly culpable disinterest. The responses in the religious press when they realised what was happening indicate that it was the former. The Wesleyans, on the other hand, anticipated the need to make comment and to seek to have information made available from an early stage.

The operation of the committee, under Wesleyan domination, assumed that it had delegated powers and that consultation was not a necessary part of the process of editing the hymn book. When information was being generated as part of the editorial process it was regarded as confidential. As those from outside requested elucidation of this process and its results, information was presented slowly and was inadequate to answer the questions that were being asked. The twenty-first-century western culture is one of monitoring, transparency and accountability. From this perspective it is not easy to understand that the process that has been uncovered was likely to have been totally acceptable to the Wesleyan Methodists, and that criticism of it would have been greeted with some degree of disbelief. The expectations of the other denominations might well have been regarded as impertinent. When reference was made to the preferred hymnody of the other partner denominations it was often voiced in a derogatory tone. This underlines the conclusion that wider consultation would almost certainly have resulted in a different book, and perhaps one more representative of the uniting denominations. Its longevity would, nevertheless, probably have been the same as this does not seem to have been a consequence of the content or quality of the book itself.

In this context it was highly unlikely that the committee would look very far beyond Methodism for either editorial guidance or material. This further limited the scope of the editors and their ability to offer hymns that would engage with the world and the experience of people outside the Church.

Consequently the book that was produced derived almost directly from the *Wesleyan Methodist Hymn Book* of 1904. It was not new. What we see was an inherent conservatism that seems to have found its way into the fabric of the denomination. *Hymns & Psalms*, produced in 1983, was not a particularly radical book, yet over 20 years on some Methodists still look back to the *Methodist Hymn Book* with a sense of affectionate loss. The impact which this conservatism has had on Methodism during the last part of the twentieth century still remains to be determined.

2. *Why did the book last so long?*

Was this because of its inherent excellence? From the point of view of the researcher the way the committee worked has generated much frustration. There is a lack of reference in the archive relating to the criteria that the committee used at most stages of the preparation of the book. There are no clearly stated aims that could be easily inter-preted in terms of preference in relation to material. To speak of 'canons of literary merit'[616] without specifying what those canons might be is presumptuous. If such criteria had been present it would have been possible to judge more fairly the degree to which the com-mittee had met them, and the extent to which it had acceded to other pressures. It would also be anticipated that such suspension of criteria would not go without notice in the committee minutes, thus providing another useful insight into the genesis of the book.

A further frustration is provided by the absence of lists of submitted texts, or the texts themselves, in order that a judgement could be made as to the sort of material that was included and excluded. Neither is there any indication of the detailed editing decisions relating to indi-vidual texts except in two cases. It is difficult, if not intellectually dangerous, to make judgements from the absence of evidence.

---

616 *Methodist Recorder*, 1 December 1932, p. 14.

If, as is argued here, the book was not novel, its longevity raises an even greater question. The suggestion has been posited that it was, in a large part, reactionary. The query remains, therefore, as to the degree to which it is nonetheless a book of quality when compared with other tomes of the same period. Watson makes the following statement: 'At least Dearmer [the editor of *Songs of Praise*] was engaging with the world. Other books of this period such as the *Church Hymnary* of 1927 or the *Methodist Hymn Book* of 1933 were much more concerned [. . .] to be of service to the church.'[617] That was their intent and it also provides their epitaph. While the intention behind *Songs of Praise* was ecumenical it was mainly used in educational establishments and, to a lesser degree, in the Anglican Church. It is arguable whether *Songs of Praise* served a constituency within the Church of England, which had already begun to adopt the *English Hymnal*, or went to form that constituency. The intentional detachment from any particular denomination provided editorial freedom.

This resulted in the inclusion of novel material, old and new, ranging from English lyric poetry to material finding its first publication. 'It was', as Watson remarked, 'a highly original venture'.[618] His observation that 'Dearmer would have been better with a committee to keep an eye on him'[619] is right if the inappropriate of use of certain texts was to be avoided; but such constraint might well have resulted in a much less innovative book. Wakefield observed that '*Songs of Praise* was bitterly assailed during the neo-orthodox revival in theology' (1935–55).[620] Meanwhile 'hymnody [became] more aware of the world in which we live and of its urban culture'.[621] In the 1960s the death of God was proclaimed and *Honest to God* was published.

Romanticism gave way to realism. The human Christ was emphasised while the hero-Christ was sidelined. At last the Church was catching up with pre-Union theologians like Findlay.

In a less ecclesiastical, more humanist context, *Songs of Praise* might have been expected to have some hope of survival. What is clear is that the manner in which the *Methodist Hymn Book* and the

---

617 Watson, *The English Hymn*, p. 529.
618 Watson, *The English Hymn*, p. 524.
619 Watson, *The English Hymn*, p. 525.
620 G. S. Wakefield, *Bulletin of the Hymn Society of Great Britain and Ireland*, Vol. 6, No. 12, 1968–69, p. 241.
621 Wakefield, *Bulletin of the Hymn Society of Great Britain and Ireland*, Vol. 6, No. 12, p. 245.

Church Hymnary sought to respond to denominational expectations was, in the end, a contributory reason for the decline of those denominations in subsequent years. There is little evidence here of an awareness of the way in which the world had evolved or a willingness to respond to such change. What *Songs of Praise* demonstrated was that, however imperfectly, such a response could be made without compromising aesthetic principles.

The *Church Hymnary* was replaced in 1973, while *The Methodist Hymnal* of the United States of America was superseded in 1966.

Part of the reason for the survival of the *Methodist Hymn Book* was its utility as a preachers' Hymn Book. It was easy to use. The layout lent itself to planning a preaching service. The sections followed through from awe to adoration, from invocation of the spirit to the gospel call and the response of the people. Other material contained in the book was supplementary. Nevertheless, the judgement has to stand that while the *Methodist Hymn Book* has served the Church with varying degrees of facility, its longevity cannot be attributed to its perfection as a hymn book. The reasons for its survival have to be found elsewhere and have more to do with the denomination than the book.

3. Did Methodist Union in some way paralyse the new Church in such a way that the replacement of the book became a very low priority?

The continued use of the *Methodist Hymn Book* up to 1983 and beyond owed itself to one main fact, apart from the usefulness of the book to preachers.

The initial enthusiasm for unity burnt itself out, if it ever really caught fire at all, in the lives of many ordinary Methodists. Methodism was beset by increasing introspection and inertia. Formal Union had taken place in 1932 but even in 2000 denominational memories remained and defined the life of many churches.[622] Organisationally the dominance of the Wesleyan denomination at Union had stamped

---

622 'Town Church' in Northwich had been formed by the union of Station Road Wesleyan Methodist Church and Bourne Primitive Methodist Church. While I was minister there from 1982 to 1985 the two congregations still sat on opposite sides of the church. Similarly members of Kingsleigh Methodist Church in Leigh, Lancashire still defined themselves as ex-King Street and ex-Leigh Road as late as 2000.

everything that would subsequently be known as Methodism with its seal. This in itself need not have been entirely unhelpful, but the nature of the denomination at that time was such that it was incapable of absorbing the new insights and vigour that the coalition of denominations might have generated. Its authoritarian and less than democratic structures made it difficult for influences outside the establishment to have any great effect and the body politic itself was ageing. The fact that the hymn book was outdated even at the time of its publication, that another war had passed, that space had been conquered, ceased to matter.

Methodism had been in decline for many years. In some ways the Union of 1932 was a response to that decline. Since Union the decline has not slowed down and in such a context the generation of a new hymn book was not a priority for the Church. Mere survival was of greater importance.

4. *Was there simply no new material to warrant the production of a new book?*

While the period from 1900 to 1950 produced little in the way of new hymns since then much new material has become available. The Second World War put another gulf between those outside, and on the fringe, of the churches and those within. The hymns that would work in nostalgic terms for life-long members of the Church were no longer accessible to others. During the 1950s the Twentieth-Century Church Light Music Group began to provide elegant and thoughtful texts that addressed the issues of late twentieth-century society. Albert Bayly provided a bridge between the traditional and the *avant-garde*. Following in their wake authors like Fred Kaan and Brian Wren, seeking to write in ways that ordinary people could understand, and addressing issues with which they could identify, began a movement of writing which has become known as the 'hymn explosion' (see p. 214f.).[623] In the late 1960s and 1970s charismatic hymnody came to prominence and evangelical hymnody experienced a revival. Over a period of 30 years much new material was generated, yet the lethargy

---

623 A proliferation of texts which has progressed so far, not only in quantity but in subject matter and style, as to put into question even what might be defined as a hymn in any traditional sense.

of Methodism was such that the church had to wait until 1983 for a new hymn book.[624] The motivation for the publication of *Hymns & Psalms* was more to acknowledge 50 years of Union than to recognise the lack of utility of a book now half a century old. As a consequence many churches continued to use the *Methodist Hymn Book* even after the publication of the new book, and in some societies when a new book was bought *Hymns & Psalms* was not considered.[625] While part of this decision might be attributed to the content of *Hymns & Psalms*, it was also due to a conservatism that did not want to see the end of the *Methodist Hymn Book*. This influence surfaced in the production of *Methodist Hymns Old and New* in 2001.[626] Many congregations held on to what they knew, to what was familiar: a collection of hymns that had lasted almost unchanged for nearly 80 years. In 2002 the book was still in use.[627]

The End of an Era or the Opening of a New Chapter?

Finally, we must conclude that the *Methodist Hymn Book* of 1933 was not really new, being a direct lineal descendant of the *Wesleyan Methodist Hymn Book* of 1904, and that its longevity in use was due, in part, to the book's usefulness to preachers. It has been shown that new hymns were beginning to be available from 1950 but an earlier replacement of the book was precluded by the state of Methodism during the period to 1983. A door has been opened on a subject that requires further consideration and research. At the outset the limitation of this book to the study of words was acknowledged. Similar work should be accomplished in relation to the archive material relating to the tunes of the *Methodist Hymn Book* and the process of music choice, arrangement and editing.

Of necessity an overview has been provided of the hymns within the book. This has been necessary to set the scene. Lysons has hinted at the need to apply tools other than those of the hymnodist to the subject:

---

624 *Hymns & Psalms*, 1983.
625 For example, Ince Methodist Church, in the Leigh and Hindley Circuit in Lancashire, purchased *Songs of Fellowship* rather than *Hymns & Psalms* during the late 1990s and continued to use the *Methodist Hymn Book* as their main hymn book as this was more widely available to preachers.
626 *Methodist Hymns Old and New*, Stowmarket, Kevin Mayhew, 2001.
627 *Methodist Recorder*, 26 September 2002.

'The sociological significance of hymns has received insufficient attention.'[628] Further work in this area should be attempted. An in-depth
analysis of the literary-critical material presented by the *Methodist
Hymn Book* remains to be undertaken, together with a detailed comparison of the manner in which different sections of the pre-Union
hymn books have developed in the *Methodist Hymn Book* and
beyond. The analysis of *Hymns & Psalms* beckons.

Aside from these academic issues lessons that can be learned
from an analysis of the different cultural expectations of the uniting
denominations at this time could help those involved in ecumenical
discussions at the beginning of the twenty-first century. Where two or
more denominations enter into conversation, if great care is not taken,
it is likely that the culture of the strongest group will swamp that of
the other constituents. This can result in the loss of variety, and of
particular gifts and traits, that are necessary to survival and helpful in
mission. To borrow an illustration from biology, those organisms that
are least specialised generally adapt best to changing conditions.
Those that exhibit great specialisation cannot survive when the
environment that they have specialised in order to colonise changes or
disappears. The Methodist Church, following Union, became a
narrower institution and was less able to cope with the changes of the
last half of the twentieth century than it might have been.

There is much to be done and much to be learned that can inform
the Church's understanding of itself and the choices it makes in future
of the hymns that it sings. Methodism is considering the publication of
a new hymn resource that may perhaps be updated from year to year.
This raises the question, 'what should Methodists sing?'

The Report of the Board of the Methodist Publishing House to the
Methodist Conference of 2004 states that there have been authorised
hymn books in Methodism since the earliest days.[629] The report goes

---

628 Lysons, *A Little Primitive*, p. 202.
629 'Perhaps more than other Christian traditions, Methodists sing their theology [. . .]
The words we sing influence our thinking, sometimes almost subversively. Our hymns are an
important means of transmitting our tradition. They carry much of our theology. What we
sing is what we believe.
'There have been authorised hymn books in Methodism since the earliest days. John
Wesley's own *Hymns for the Use of The People Called Methodists* (the 'Large' book of
1780) served the Wesleyan tradition throughout the nineteenth century, albeit with supple-
ments. The other traditions published hymn books very early in their lives. The first
Collection of Hymns for the Use of the Methodist New Connexion (also a supplement to the
1780 book) dated from 1800 whilst 1824 probably saw the publication of both a *Large*

on to argue that 'If a hymn or song is included in an authorised collection, leaders of worship are entitled to assume that it is consistent with our doctrines and most congregations use authorised hymn books as their normal book.' Use of such books has rarely been mandatory.[630] The report concludes that 'to dispense with authorised or recommended hymnody would be a major break with our tradition and should not be entertained without serious and lengthy consideration'.

All this may be true, but we are now entering the twenty-first century and Methodists have signed a Covenant that will, almost certainly, deepen their relationship with the Church of England.

It is imperative that if there are things which are formative for our denominations, things that are foundations of our faith and our theological understanding, they should be taken with us into any new relationship and not denied. For Methodists beliefs are likely to be expressed in hymns. The wide range of material that is now so easily available to us makes the task of discernment even more important. New hymns will be written, framed in a language which is dynamic, using metaphors that are contemporary to express age-old truths. Statements of faith may be modified as understanding and knowledge grow. Yet the hymns that are sung ought to continue to be in keeping with doctrine.

Ecumenical debate simply underlines what should be, for Methodists, a profound imperative, to believe what they sing. Authorised hymnody still has a place for Methodists. Now, more than ever before, Methodists need to learn from the choices made by their forebears.

Hymnbook for the use of the People called Primitive Methodists (following earlier smaller collections in 1809, 1819 and 1821) and a *Collection of Hymns for the use of the People called Armenian Bible Christians.*' From the Report of the Board of the Methodist Publishing House to the Methodist Conference of 2004.

630 'The 1805 minutes of the (Wesleyan) Conference record the instruction: "Let no book of hymns be henceforth used in our chapels except the hymn-books printed for our Book-Room." But it is not clear for how long, if at all, this instruction applied.' From the Report of the Board of the Methodist Publishing House to the Methodist Conference of 2004.

Bibliography

Primary Documents

Two box files held in the Collection of the Methodist Archives and Research Centre of the John Rylands Library of the University of Manchester (Catalogue information: MAW MS.29[Ref. 1–300] MAW MS.30[Ref. 301–] 1934 HYMN BOOK COMMITTEE) contain 411 documents related to the *Methodist Hymn Book* of 1933. Prior to this research the material had not been catalogued or sorted. A catalogue is now held in the Library.

Methodist Hymn Book, Methodist Conference Office, London, 1933.

Secondary Documents

Alexander, C., ed., *Alexander's Revival Hymns*, London, Morgan and Scott, nd.

Baptist Hymnal, London, Marlborough, 1882.

Bonner, C., ed., *Child Songs*, London, The Pilgrim Press, J. Curwen & Sons Ltd, Methodist Youth Department, 1st edition 1908, reprinted 24 times up to 1963.

Bridges, R., Milford, H., ed., *The Small Hymn Book* – word book of the *Yattendon Hymnal*, Oxford, Oxford University Press, 1920 (MAR 215G.14); *Yattendon Hymnal*, ed. Bridges, R., Wood, H. E., printed H. Daniel, 1899.

Christian Endeavour Hymnal, 18th edition, London, Christian Endeavour Union of Great Britain and Ireland, 1925.

A Collection of Hymns for the use of People called Bible Christians, London, Bible Christian Book-Room, 1889.

A Collection of Hymns for the Use of The People Called Methodists, London, Wesleyan Methodist Church, 1889.

Church Hymns, London, SPCK, nd.

Congregational Hymnary, London, Congregational Union of England and Wales, nd.

Crusaders' Hymnal, London, Epworth Press, 1926.

Davies, W., *Hymns of the Kingdom*, London, Oxford University Press, 1923.

Dearmer, P., Vaughan Williams, R., Shaw, W., *The Oxford Book of Carols*, London, Oxford University Press, 1928 (23rd impression 1956).

Dearmer, P., Vaughan Williams, R., Shaw, W., ed., *Songs of Praise*, London, Oxford University Press, 1925; *Songs of Praise*, enlarged edition, 1931.

English Hymnal, London, Oxford University Press, nd.

Fellowship Hymn Book with Supplement, London, Holborn Publishing House, 1927; Supplement, London, Holborn Publishing House, 1927.

Golden Bells, Children's Special Service Mission, 1925.

Horder, W. G., ed., *Worship Song*, London, Novello and Co., c.1905.

Hunter, J., *Hymns of Faith and Life*, 1896.

Hymns Ancient and Modern, London, Clowes, 1916.

Hymns & Psalms, Peterborough, Methodist Publishing House, 1983.

Hymns of Consecration and Faith, London, Marshall, 1902.

Ingelow, J., *Poems*, 6th edition, London, Longman, Green, Longman, Roberts & Green, 1864.

Joyful Songs, London, Methodist Publishing House, nd.

Martineau, J., ed., *Hymns of Praise and Prayer*, London, Longmans, Green, Reader and Dyer, 1874.

Martineau, J., ed., *Hymns for the Christian Church and Home*, London, Longmans, Green and Co., 1887.

Methodist Hymn Book, The, London, Methodist New Connexion Book-Room, 1904.

Methodist Hymn Book, London, Novello, 1933.

Methodist Hymnal, New York, Eaton & Mains, 1905.

Methodist Hymnal, The, The Board of Publication of the Protestant Methodist Church, Nashville, The Methodist Book Concern, 1932.

Methodist School Hymnal, London, Wesleyan Methodist Sunday School Department, nd.

Oxford Hymn Book, Oxford, Clarendon Press, 1908.

Primitive Methodist Hymnal, London, Primitive Methodist Publishing House, 1886.

Primitive Methodist Hymnal Supplement, London, Primitive Methodist Publishing House, 1912.

Public School Hymn Book, London, Novello, 1919.

Redemption Songs, London, Pickering and Inglis, 1929.

Sankey, I. D., compiler, *Sacred Songs and Solos*, London, Marshall Morgan Scott, 1921.

School Worship, London, Congregational Union of England and Wales, 1926.

Sharp, J. A., *The New Temperance Hymnal*, London, Robert Culley, 1909.

Simon, M. S., compiler, *Wintersdorf Hymnal*, Isbister and Co, 1893.

Stainer, J., Froude, H., ed., Edinburgh, *Church Hymnary*, 1901; *Church Hymnary*, revised, London, Oxford University Press, 1930.

Students' Hymnal, the English section of *Hymns of the Kingdom*, Davies, W., ed., London, Oxford University Press, 1923.

Tiplady, T., *Hymns from Lambeth*, London, Epworth Press.

United Methodist Free Church Hymnal, London, United Methodist Free Churches' Book-Room, 1889.

Wesley, J., *A Collection of Psalms and Hymns*, printed by Lewis Timothy, Charles Town, 1737 (Meth.Arc / MAB BOHI G6).

Wesleyan Methodist Hymn Book, London, Wesleyan Conference Office, 1904.

Westminster Hymnal, London, Burns, Oates & Washbourne, 1912.

Winkworth, C., *Lyra Germanica*, London, Longmans, Green, 1901.

Other sources

A New History of Methodism, ed. Townsend, W. J., Workman, H. B., Eayrs, G., London, Hodder and Stoughton, 1909, Vols I and II.

A Plain Account of Christian Perfection as believed and taught by the Reverend Mr. John Wesley, from the year 1725, to the year 1777, from *The Works of John Wesley* (1872 ed. by Thomas Jackson), Vol. 11, p. 366–446, further editing by George Lyons for the Wesley Center for Applied Theology at Northwest Nazarene College (Nampa, ID).

Adey, L., *Class and Idol in the English Hymn*, Vancouver, University of British Columbia Press, 1988.

Annandale, C., *The Student's English Dictionary*, London, Blackie, 1911.

Baker, F., *Charles Wesley's Verse*, 2nd edition, London, Epworth Press, 1988.

Berger, T., *Theology in Hymns?* Nashville, Kingswood, 1995.

Bett, H., *The Hymns of Methodism*, 3rd edition, London, Epworth Press, 1945.

Bradley, I., *Abide with me*, London, SCM Press, 1997.

Bridges, R., *Poetical Works of Robert Bridges*, London, Oxford University Press, reprinted 1959.

Buchan, J., *The Thirty-Nine Steps*, Ware, Wordsworth Editions, 1993.

Bulletin of the Hymn Society of Great Britain and Ireland, Vol. 6, No. 12, 1968–69.

Cupitt, D., *The Sea of Faith*, 2nd edition, London, SCM Press, 1994.

Currie, R., *Methodism Divided*, London, Faber & Faber, 1968.

Davies, R., George, A. R., Rupp, G., *A History of the Methodist Church in Great Britain*, Vol. 3, London, Epworth Press, 1983.

Davies, R., George, A. R., Rupp, G., *A History of the Methodist Church in Great Britain*, Vol. 4, London, Epworth Press, 1988.

Drabble M., ed., *Oxford Companion to English Literature*, Oxford University Press, 5th edition, revised 1995.

Foreman, A., *Christian History*, Wigan, Independent Methodist Bookroom, 1932.

Hancock, C. P., *A Hymn Lover's Diary*, Leominster, Orphans Press, nd.

Heitzenrater, R. P., *Mirror and Memory, Reflections on Early Methodism*, Nashville, Kingswood, 1989.

Holloway, R., *Doubts and Loves*, Edinburgh, Canongate, 2001.

Houghton, H., *The Handmaid of Piety*, York, The Wesley Fellowship, Quacks Books, 1992.

Hymns & Psalms, Peterborough, Methodist Publishing House, 1983.

Hymns and Songs, London, Methodist Publishing House, 1969.

Hymns of the City, revised edition, ed. John Vincent, Sheffield, Urban Theology Unit, 1998.

Kent, J., *The Age of Disunity*, London, Epworth Press, 1966.

Lewis, C., *Sagittarius Rising*, Harmondsworth, Penguin, 1977.

Lloyd, G., *Charles Wesley: A New Evaluation of his Life and Ministry*, unpublished PhD thesis, Liverpool, 2002.

Lysons, K., *A Little Primitive: Primitive Methodism from Macro to Micro Perspectives*, Buxton, Church in the Market Place Publications, 2001.

Lysons, K., *Robert Wilfrid Callin, Parson, Padre, Poet*, Buxton, Church in the Market Place Publications, 1996.

Mankin, K., *How they sang on the way to Zion – An Examination of the Major Hymn books of the Main Methodist Traditions during the period 1875–1890 and their Relationship to Church and Society*, unpublished MPhil book, Council for National Academic Awards, 1992.

Manning, B. L., *The Hymns of Wesley and Watts*, London, Epworth Press, 1942.

Marsh, C., *Unmasking Methodist Theology*, London, Continuum, 2004.

McLoughlin, W., *Revivals, Awakenings, and Reform*, Chicago, University of Chicago Press, 1978.

Methodist Hymns Old and New, Stowmarket, Kevin Mayhew, 2001.

Methodist Recorder, many editions.

Methodist Service Book, London, Methodist Publishing House, 1975.

Methodist Times and Leader, many editions.

Methodist Worship Book, London, Trustees for Methodist Church Purposes, 1999.

Milburn, G., *Primitive Methodism*, London, Epworth Press, 2002.

Naughton, B., *Neither Use Nor Ornament*, Newcastle upon Tyne, Bloodaxe Books, 1995.

Newport, K. G. C., *The Sermons of Charles Wesley*, Oxford University Press, 2001.

Newton, J., *Heart Speaks to Heart*, London, Darton, Longman and Todd, 1994.

Nuelsen, J. L., *John Wesley and the German Hymn*, trans. T. Parry, S. H. Moore and A. Holbrook, Keighley, Holbrook, 1972.

Orrell Circuit Plan of Public Services, 21 July to 13 October, 1935.

Outler, A. C., *The Works of John Wesley*, Vol. 2, Sermons II, Nashville, Abingdon, 1985.

Outler, A. C., *The Works of John Wesley*, Vol. 3, Sermons III, Nashville, Abingdon, 1986.

Paxman, J., *The English*, London, Michael Joseph, 1998.

Pratt, A. E., *A Study of Frederick Faber's Hymns on the four Last Things in the Context of his Hymnody as presented in the Collection of 1861*, unpublished MA book, 1997.

Pratt, A. E., *Blinded by the Dazzle*, London, Stainer & Bell Ltd, 1997.

Proceedings of the Wesley Historical Society, Vol. 51, Part 1, 1997.

Proceedings of the Wesley Historical Society, Vol. 51, Part 3, 1997.

Rattenbury, J. E. *The Eucharistic Hymns of John and Charles Wesley*, London, Epworth Press, 1948.

Rattenbury, J. E., *The Evangelical Doctrines of Charles Wesley's Hymns*, London, Epworth Press, 1941.

Routley, E., *Christian Hymns Observed*, Oxford, Mowbray, 1983.

Sassoon, S., *War Poems*, London, Faber & Faber, 1983.

Spinney, B., *Bulletin of the Hymn Society of Great Britain and Ireland*, Vol. 17, No. 1, 2000.

Spinney, B. F., *Tuned for Praise*, 2nd impression, Southampton, 1999.

Stevenson, J., 'British Society 1914–45', *The Penguin Social History of Britain*, Harmondsworth, Penguin, 1990.

Telford, J., *The Methodist Hymn-Book Illustrated*, London, Epworth Press, 1934.

Towlson, C. W., ed., *A Mightier Music*, London, Epworth Press, 1934.

Turner, J. M., *Conflict and Reconciliation, Studies in Methodism and Ecumenism in England 1740–1982*, London, Epworth Press, 1985.

Turner, J. M., *Modern Methodism in England, 1932–1998*, Peterborough, Epworth Press, 1998.

Vickers, John A., ed., *A Dictionary of Methodism in Britain and Ireland*, Peterborough, Epworth Press, 2000.

Wainwright, G., *Doxology*, London, Epworth Press, 1980.

Walker, A. H., *How to Receive and Use the New Methodist Hymn Book*, London, Epworth Press, 1933.

Ward, H., Wild, J., *The Way of Peace*, Oxford, Lion, 1999.

Warson, G. R., *Jesus Wants Me for a Sunbeam, A musical history of Anniversary Services at Bicester Methodist Church, 1872–1968*, self publication, 2002.

Watson, J. R., *The English Hymn*, Oxford, Clarendon Press, 1997.

Watson, R., Trickett, K., *Companion to Hymns & Psalms*, Peterborough, Methodist Publishing House, 1988.

Wesley, J., *Explanatory Notes upon the New Testament*, London, Epworth Press, 1976.

Wesley, J., *The Letters of John Wesley*, ed. Eayrs, G., London, Hodder and Stoughton, 1915.

Wesleyan Methodist Church, *Minutes of Conference*, London, Wesleyan Conference Office, 1932.

Whitaker's Almanack, J. Whitaker and Son Ltd, London, The Softback Preview, 1997.

Williams, Patricia A., *Doing without Adam and Eve, Sociobiology and Original Sin*, Minneapolis, Fortress Press, 2001.

Wootton, J., *Introducing a Practical Feminist Theology of Worship*, Sheffield Academic Press, 2000.

Works of John Wesley, Vol. 7, *A Collection of Hymns for the Use of The People Called Methodists*, ed., Hildebrandt, F., Beckerlegge, O. A., Oxford University Press/Nashville, Abingdon, 1983.

Works of John Wesley, Vol. 11, ed. Jackson, T., 1872.

Wren, B., *Praying Twice*, Louisville, Kentucky, Westminster John Knox Press, 2000.

Appendix 1

Contents of the uniting denominations hymn books compared

The layout depicted below follows as nearly as possible that of the respective hymn books with sections placed adjacent to each other for comparison. Underlining and italics indicate sectional headings.

Summary of contents of *The Methodist Hymn Book* (1904)	Summary of contents of the *Primitive Methodist Hymnal* (1886)	Summary of contents of the *Primitive Methodist Hymnal Supplement* (1912)	Summary of contents of the *United Methodist Free Church Hymnal* (1889)	Summary of contents of *A Collection of Hymns for the Use of People Called Bible Christians* (1889)
The Glory of God Adoration and Worship The Holy Trinity The Divine Attributes Creation and Providence	*God the Father* His Being and Attributes His Works His Providence His Grace His Praise	*God the Father* His Glory and Praise	*God the Father* His Nature and Perfections His Works in Creation His Providence His Mercy and Grace	*The Triune God* *God the Father Almighty* His Existence, Perfections and Praise His Wisdom and Goodness in Creation and Providence His Grace in Redemption

The Lord Jesus Christ –	*God the Son*	*The Lord Jesus Christ*	*The Lord Jesus Christ*	*Our Lord Jesus Christ*
His Person, Name and Praise	His Incarnation and Advent	His Advent	His Divinity and Glory	His Godhead and Praise
His Incarnation	His Life, Work and Example	His Life and Passion	His Incarnation and Advent	His Names and Titles
His Life, Teaching and Works	His Sufferings and Death	His Resurrection and Ascension	His Example and Teaching	His Incarnation and Birth
His Sufferings and Death	His Resurrection and Ascension	His Praise and Glory	His Passion and Death	His Life and Example
His Resurrection and Ascension	His Priesthood and Intercession	His Kingdom	His Resurrection and Ascension	His Sympathy and Love
His Priesthood, Kingship and Second Advent	His Kingdom and Reign		His Intercession and Reign	His Vicarious Sufferings and Death
His Kingdom on Earth	His Names and Praise			His Resurrection and Ascension
				His Intercession and Reign
				His Second Coming and Judgment
The Holy Spirit: His Person and Work	*God the Holy Spirit*	*The Holy Spirit*	*The Holy Spirit*	*The Holy Spirit: His Person and Work*
			His Regenerating and Sanctifying Grace	
			His Work as Teacher and comforter	
	The Holy Trinity		*The Holy Trinity*	
			Divine Worship	

			Praise and Prayer The Lord's Day Morning Evening	
The Word of God: The Holy Scriptures	*The Holy Scriptures*		*The Holy Scriptures*	*The Sacred Scriptures*
The Gospel Call – Exhorting Sinners to Return to God Invitations and Warnings The Pleasantness and Excellence of Religion Formal and Inward Religion Mourners Convinced of Sin Backsliders Convicted and Recovered	*Man* His Fallen Condition His Redemption Warnings and Invitations	*The Gospel*	*The Gospel Message* *Evangelistic Services* Invitation to the Sinner Exhortation to Repent Salvation Through Faith Rejoicing in Forgiveness	*The Gospel and its Invitations*
The Christian Life Faith, Pardon and Regeneration Joy and Thanksgiving: For Believers Rejoicing Peace: For	*Christian Life* Its Experience Repentance and Turning to God Justification by Faith Regeneration and Adoption Consecration	*The Christian Life* Experience Trust and Guidance Discipline and Obedience Service	*The Christian Life* Contrition and Longing for God Faith and Consecration Adoption and Sonship Love and	*The Christian Life* Repentance and Faith Pardon and Regeneration Sanctification and Growth Consecration and Service

Believers
Trusting
Love: For
Believers in
Communion
with God
Temptation
and Conflict:
For Believers
Fighting and
Watching
Discipline and
Resignation:
For Believers
Suffering
Aspiration
and Hope:
For Believers
Praying
Consecration
and Holiness:
For Believers
Seeking Full
Redemption
The Graces of
the Christian
Character
Service and
Influence: For
Believers
Working
Pilgrimage,
Guidance and
Perseverance

and Holiness
Steadfastness
and Growth
in Grace
Declension
and Recovery
Its Privileges
Support and
Guidance
Communion
with God
The
Communion
of Saints
Anticipations
and Hopes
Its Duties
Work and
Watchfulness
Trust in God
Contentment
and
Resignation
Prayer and
Supplication
Mutual
Forbearance
and Love

*The Holy
Scriptures*

Holiness
Light,
Guidance and
Growth
Thankfulness
Affliction and
Resignation
Conflict and
Courage
Watchfulness
and
Steadfastness
Declension
and Recovery
Humility
Prayer (see
also Prayer
Meetings)
Service and
Giving
Hope and Joy

Declension
and Recovery
Watchfulness
and Prayer
Communion
with God
Joy and
Triumph
Suffering and
Conflict
Trust and
Courage
Guidance and
Protection
Patience and
Resignation
Hopes and
Anticipations
Death and the
Glory of
Heaven

The Church

The Lord's
Day
The Sanctuary
and Its
Worship
Privileges and
Security of
Christ's
Church

*Christian
Institutions*

The Ministry
The Church
Baptism and
the Lord's
Supper
The Sabbath
Public
Worship

*The Church
and Its
Ordinances*

Divine
Worship
The Lord's
Supper

*The Church
of Christ*

Character,
Unity and
Fellowship
Reception of
Members
Recognition
of Ministers
Prayer

*The Church
of Christ*

Its Unity and
Fellowship
Its Security
and
Blessedness
Reception of
members
Its Ministers

Christian Fellowship
The Church in Prayer
The Sacraments: Baptism and the Lord's Supper
Lovefeast, Covenant Service, Recognition of New Members
Ministers and Teachers
Foreign Missions
Meeting and Parting
The Church Militant and Triumphant

Family and Private Devotion

Time, Death, Eternity

Human Life: Vicissitudes, Sickness, Old Age
Death
Judgement
The Future State

Family Religion

Children and Young People
Family Worship

Hymns for the Young

Temperance Hymns

Meetings (see also Prayer)
Baptism
The Lord's Supper
Lovefeast
Watch-Night Service
Covenant service

Death, Resurrection and Judgment

Heaven and the Life Hereafter

Christian Missions

New Year

Seasons of the Year

Flower Services

Special Intercessions

Christian Ordinances and Institutions

The Lord's Day and Worship
General Hymns
Select Psalms
Prayer and Class-Meetings
Baptism of Infants of Adults
The Lord's Supper

Christian Missions

Harvest Thanksgiving

Special Occasions	*Various Occasions and Seasons*	*Special Occasions and Seasons*	*Special Occasions*	*Special Occasions*
Morning and Evening	Places of Worship	Marriage	Marriage	Marriage
Opening and Closing of the Year	Missions	Summer	Laying Foundation and Memorial Stones	Burial of the Dead
The Seasons and Harvest	Sabbath Schools	Harvest	Opening Services	Laying of Memorial or Foundation Stones of Chapels
Christian Philanthropy and Temperance	Commencement and Close of the Year	Winter	Hospital Sunday and Benevolent Institutions	Opening of a Place of Worship
Marriage	Harvest Thanksgiving	Old and New Year	Burial of the Dead	Laying the Foundation of a School
For Travellers	National Hymns			Opening of a New Schoolroom
For the King and Nation	Mariners and Travellers			Opening of an Organ
	Marriage and Home			Hospital Sunday
	Morning and Evening	*Morning and Evening*	*Travellers by Land and Sea*	General Charities and Almsgiving
				Flower Services
			Parents and Family Worship	For those at Sea
			Services for the Young	
			Private Devotion	
	The Future State			*Times and Seasons*
			Temperance Services	
	Death and the Resurrection			Morning
	The Judgment			Evening
	Final Rewards			Spring
				Summer
				Autumn and Harvest

	Miscellaneous Hymns			Winter The Old and New Year
				The Church in the House
				Children's Services
				Revival and Evangelistic Services
				Temperance
		National and Civic Hymns	*National Hymns*	*National Hymns*
		Death and the Future		The Throne Prayer and Humiliation Thanksgiving
		Additional Tunes		
		Lord's Prayer and Vespers	*Dismissal Hymns and Doxologies*	*Benedictions and Doxologies*
Ancient Hymns and Canticles, etc.			*Psalms and Canticles* [including selections from the New Testament and Ancient Hymns of the Church]	

Appendix 2[631]

Note: The following texts appeared in the draft submitted to Conference in 1932 but were omitted from the final collection:

As the bridegroom to his chosen (SW 103[208]), Infant holy, infant lowly (E 63), O pilot our bark (StO 299), Take time to be holy (YLC 84), How far is it to Bethlehem? (SP 426), God, who created me (ChHy 673), And did those feet (ChHy 640, included in verses) Lord Jesus, when first thou cam'st to man (SP 293, 562).

A blank in all columns indicates that the source was not specified in the draft documents.

Key: AM, *Ancient and Modern*; AU, *American Union Hymnal* (1885); BC, *A Collection of Hymns for the use of People called Bible Christians*; CanH, *Hymnary of United Church of Canada*; CBE, *Chorale Book for England*; CEH, *Christian Endeavour Hymnal*; ChHy, *Church Hymnary*; C, *Congregational Hymnary*; EH, *English Hymnal*; F, *Fellowship Hymn Book with Supplement*; Fr, *Free Church Council Hymn Book*; GL, *Girls' League*; HT, *Hymns for To-day*; HK, *Hymns of the Kingdom*; JS, *Joyful Songs*; LG, *Lyra Germanica*; MFCH, *Methodist Free Church Hymnal*; MH, *Methodist Hymnal*; MSH, *Methodist School Hymnal*; N, nominated (new); NPH, *New People's Hymnary*; O, *Oxford Hymn Book*; OC, *Oxford Book of Carols*; PH, *Pilgrim Hymnal*; PM, *Primitive Methodist Hymnal*; PMS, *Primitive Methodist Hymnal Supplement*; PSH, *Public School Hymn Book*; RS, *Redemption Songs*; SSS, *Sacred Songs and Solos*; SW, *School Worship*; SP, *Songs of Praise*; StO, *St. Olave's Hymn Book*; SSH, *The Sunday School Hymnal*; W, *Wintersdorf Hymnal*; WS, *Worship Song*; WMHB, *Wesleyan Methodist Hymn Book*; Y, *Yattendon Hymnal*; YLC, *Young Life Campaign*.

In the table: WMHB, Wesleyan Methodist Hymn Book; PM, Primitive Methodist Hymnal; PMS, Primitive Methodist Hymnal Supplement; MFCH, Methodist Free Church Hymnal; BC, A Collection of Hymns for the use of People called Bible Christians.

---

631 Original index of the *Methodist Hymn Book* provided by Stainer & Bell Ltd.

MHB	First Line	WMHB	PM	PMS	MFCH	BC	Other
001	O(h) for a thousand tongues to sing	1	142		306	76	
002	All people that on earth do dwell	2	772		172	674	
003	Before Jehovah's awful throne	3	1		171	675	
004	From all that dwell below the skies	9	776		813	686	
005	Let all the world in every corner sing				188		
006	Eternal power, whose high abode	5	2		1	18	
007	O heavenly king, look down from above	12			683		
008	O worship the king	4	13		184	680	
009	O(h) worship the Lord in the beauty of holiness		796			608	
010	Now thank we all our God	19	458				
011	With gladness we worship, rejoice as we sing			192	210	623	
012	Praise, my soul, the king of heaven	13	67		189	679	
013	Praise the Lord, ye heavens, adore him	10	66		196		
014	Praise the Lord who reigns above	26					
015	Praise to the living God!						AU
016	Raise the psalm: let earth adoring	25	68			671	
017	Meet and right it is to sing	11	62		514	22	
018	Let us with a gladsome mind/ For his mercies aye endure	21	39		176	696	
019	Praise, O praise our God and king. For his mercies still endure	938	895				
020	Come, O come, in pious lays						PSH 280

MHB	First Line	WMHB	PM	PMS	MFCH	BC	Other
021	The God of Abraham praise/ The God who reigns on high/ Though nature's strength decays	374/ 376	43/ 44		205/ 206	25	
022	Come, let us all unite and sing						CEH 14
023	King of glory, king of peace						SP 285
024	O God, my strength and fortitude	14					
025	Round the Lord in glory seated/ Lord, thy glory fills the heaven		69			24	
026	Ye holy angels bright						ChHy 39
027	Angels holy, high and lowly			7			
028	All creatures of our God and king/O praise him, O praise him (Draper)						ChHy 13
029	All things praise thee, Lord most high				174		
030	From glory to glory advancing, we praise thee, O Lord						SP 236 (496)
031	God reveals his presence	22					
032	Lord of all being, throned afar	23	51		45	21	
033	Infinite God, to thee we raise	30	200		166	10	
034	Immortal, invisible, God only wise			1			
035	For the beauty of the earth/ Gracious God, to thee we raise	24	64		200	66	
036	Holy . . . Lord God almighty! Early		201		160	5	
037	Hail! holy, holy, holy, Lord!	34				3	
038	Father of heaven, whose love profound		191				
039	Father, in whom we live	33	193				

MHB	First Line	WMHB	PM	PMS	MFCH	BC	Other
040	We give immortal praise	29	196			14	
041	God is a name my soul adores	37					
042	O God, thou bottomless abyss!	38			6		
043	There is a book, who runs may read	85	23		23	41	
044	The spacious firmament on high	75	17		18	632	
045	My soul, praise the Lord! O God						O 252
046	I sing the almighty power of God	874	22			34	
047	Father of all! whose powerful voice						
048	High in the heavens, eternal God	79	30			643	
049	Thy ceaseless, unexhausted love	67	42		312	57	
050	The Lord's my shepherd, I'll not want	86		135	34		
051	The God of love my shepherd is						
052	O love of God, how strong and true	70	7			54	
053	God is love, his mercy brightens		15				
054	My soul, repeat his praise	90				678	
055	Lord God, by whom all change is wrought	52			3		
056	Sweet is the memory of thy grace	80			225	699	
057	In all my vast concerns with thee	50			11		
058	The Lord Jehovah reigns	41	24		20	26	
059	Good thou art, and good thou dost	82	46		43	32	
060	Ere God had built the mountains	60				65	

MHB	First Line	WMHB	PM	PMS	MFCH	BC	Other
061	Earth, with all thy thousand voices	8					
062	O love, how deep, how broad, how high!			53			
063	Eternal depth of love divine	69					
064	Praise to the Lord, the almighty, the king of creation!						ChHy 22
065	O God of God, in whom combine	63					
066	O God of all grace	64					
067	O God, of good the unfathomed sea	36			4		
068	None is like Jeshurun's God	676	380		580	464	
069	This . . . is the God we adore	389			212		
070	All my hope on God is founded						ChHy 448
071	We come unto our fathers' God	96		272	966	566	
072	Begin, my soul, some heavenly theme	57	8		38	46	
073	My God, how wonderful thou art	54	9		187	23	
074	Praise to the holiest in the height	62	230		190	55	
075	Father, whose everlasting love	65	223		309	48	
076	The king of love my shepherd is	72		134			
077	What shall I do my God to love, my loving God to praise?	66			465		
078	How shall I sing that majesty			2			
079	Praise ye the Lord! 'Tis good to raise	48	3		14	701	
080	Thee will I praise with all my heart, and tell	88	424			626	
081	Not what these hands have done				315	286	

MHB	First Line	WMHB	PM	PMS	MFCH	BC	Other
082	Hark, the glad sound! the Saviour comes	139	75		64	110	
083	Of the Father's love begotten			47			
084	All glory, laud and honour	860		45			
085	Come, let us join our cheerful songs	97	150		179	63	
086	Strong Son of God, immortal love		86				
087	Jesus comes with all his grace	116					
088	We know, by faith we surely know	120					
089	Christ, of all my hopes the ground	108				84	
090	Object of my first desire		506				
091	All hail the power of Jesus' (Jesu's) name	207	143		49	59	
092	Jesus! the name high over all	98	145		63	92	
093	To the name of our salvation		162				
094	None other Lamb, none other name	520		99			
095	Jesus, sun and shield art thou		159			91	
096	Join all the glorious names/ Jesus, my great high priest	101	132		68	93	
097	O filial deity	115	346				
098	Thou hidden source of calm repose	107	519		226	102	
099	How sweet the name of Jesus sounds	109	146		209	86	
100	One there is, above all others, well deserves	872	638			98	
101	Rest of the weary			132	618		
102	Immortal love, for ever full	118		168	126	87	
103	O Lord and master of us all	119				88	

MHB	First Line	WMHB	PM	PMS	MFCH	BC	Other
104	Thou great Redeemer, dying Lamb	100				101	
105	Jesus, the first and last	121					
106	Jesus (Jesu), the very thought is sweet						ChHy 421
107	O Jesus (Jesu), king most wonderful		148			71	
108	Jesus (Jesu), the very thought of thee	110	360		182	70	
109	Jesus (Jesu), thou joy of loving hearts	111		57	732	746	
110	Jesus (Jesu), lover of my soul	106			51	277	
111	Jesus, these eyes have never seen		359		59	69	
112	I bless the Christ of God				52		
113	When morning gilds the skies	105		254			
114	Let earth and heaven agree	99	155		352	144	
115	My heart and voice I raise	102	156		50	185	
116	Sing we the king who is coming to reign						F 38
117	Hark! . . . the herald-angels sing	122	79		79	111	
118	O(h) come, all ye faithful	123		24	78	114	
119	Angels from the realms of glory		80		80	105	
120	Christians, awake, salute the happy morn	124	82		77	108	
121	All my heart this night rejoices				75		
122	Brightest and best of the sons of the morning	127	83		67	107	
123	Still the night, holy the night						ChHy 49
124	See amid the winter's snow						ChHy 51
125	O little town of Bethlehem			23			

MHB	First Line	WMHB	PM	PMS	MFCH	BC	Other
126	Give heed, my heart, lift up thine eyes						PH 100
127	Cradled in a manger, meanly						
128	A virgin most pure, as the prophets do tell						O 53
129	While shepherds watched their flocks by night	131	74		73	117	
130	It came upon the midnight clear	132	76		72	112	
131	The first nowell the angel did say						ChHy 45
132	As with gladness men of old	128		21	65	106	
133	From the eastern mountains			74			
134	Glory be to God on high, and peace	134			161	109	
135	Stupendous height of heavenly love	137					
136	The maker of the sun and moon						SP 54
137	In the bleak mid-winter						ChHy 50
138	Love came down at Christmas						ChHy 52
139	The race that long in darkness pined					116	
140	God from on high hath heard						C 84
141	To us a child of royal birth	126					
142	Let earth and heaven combine	133					
143	Good Christian men, rejoice with heart						ChHy 58
144	My song is love unknown			48			
145	What grace, O Lord, and beauty shone		88				
146	Jesus, who lived above the sky					904	
147	When the Lord of love was here						ChHy 85

MHB	First Line	WMHB	PM	PMS	MFCH	BC	Other
148	We saw thee not when thou didst come	117	646				
149	And didst thou love the race that loved not thee?			29			
150	And my heart shall rejoice, Lord Jesus						
150	Thou didst leave thy throne and thy kingly crown	138		26			
151	Who is he, in yonder stall?						ChHy 77
152	What means this eager, anxious throng				333	968	
153	Jesus, thy far-extended fame	140	350		92	328	
154	I heard the voice of Jesus say	361	502		311	313	
155	Heal us, Immanuel! Hear our prayer	145				599	
156	O thou, whom once they flocked to hear	143					
157	Jesus calls us; o'er the tumult	286		156		357	
158	Thou say'st, take up thy cross		410				
159	One who is all unfit to count						ChHy 406
160	Thou art the way, to thee alone	113	499			100	
161	Tell me the old, old story	150		87	331	962	
162	Thou art my life; if thou but turn away						O 306
163	Dear master, in whose life I see						ChHy 460
164	Behold a little child						ChHy 76
165	Forty days and forty nights thou wast						ChHy 79
166	It fell upon a summer day						ChHy 80

MHB	First Line	WMHB	PM	PMS	MFCH	BC	Other
167	Fierce raged the tempest o'er the deep	146	925		89	423	
168	Lord! it is good for us to be	144			83		
169	My Saviour, thou thy love to me	415					
170	O(h) the bitter shame and sorrow	568		100		953	
171	Jesus, I will trust thee, trust thee with my soul			95		940	
172	With glorious clouds encompassed round	151	94		387	161	
173	Would Jesus have the sinner die?		237		106	162	
174	I met the good shepherd						W 63
175	Weep not for him who onwards bears						ChHy 94
176	Man of sorrows, what a name	169		31			
177	Ah, holy Jesus (Jesu), how hast thou offended						SP 61, 99
178	When my love to Christ grows weak					159	
179	Plunged in a gulf of deep despair	152	227			149	
180	There is a green hill far away	869		33	917	913	
181	Lamb of God, whose dying love		737				
182	When I survey the wondrous cross	164	225		107	158	
183	In the cross of Christ I glory		102		96	143	
184	The royal banners forward go						SP 88, 130
185	At the cross her station keeping						ChHy 99
186	O love divine! what hast thou done!	160			101		

MHB	First Line	WMHB	PM	PMS	MFCH	BC	Other
187	O come and mourn with me awhile	162	91		97		
188	All ye that pass by	161	95		99	136	
189	Throned upon the awful tree					155	
190	O perfect life of love						ChHy 102
191	God of unexampled grace						
192	Ride on, ride on in majesty	154	92			150	
193	Behold the Saviour of mankind	158	93		100	137	
194	Go to dark Gethsemane	156	98		104	140	
195	He dies! the friend of sinners dies	171	90		113	169	
196	We sing the praise of him who died		139			157	
197	Beneath the cross of Jesus			34		394	
198	Never further than thy cross			37	667	145	
199	Jesus keep me near the cross				416	941	
200	O Jesus, my hope	519					
201	There is a fountain filled with blood	332	328		108	153	
202	O sacred head, once wounded	163	97		102	147	
203	How shall a sinner find	320					
204	Christ the Lord is risen today, Hallelujah! Sons	170	107		111	164	
205	Jesus Christ is risen today		109			171	
206	Christ is risen! alleluia (hallelujah), risen our victorious		115				
207	Christ the Lord is risen again	174					
208	The day of resurrection	178	113			173	
209	On wings of living light	177					
210	Christ Jesus lay in death's strong bands				117		

MHB	First Line	WMHB	PM	PMS	MFCH	BC	Other
211	Low in the grave he lay						
212	Welcome, happy morning – age to age shall say			40			
213	Thine be the glory, risen conquering Son						N
214	Awake, glad soul, awake, awake		106		112	163	
215	The strife is o'er, the battle done		137				
216	Jesus lives, thy terrors now/ Jesus lives! no longer now	175			115	172	
217	Ye humble souls that seek the Lord	172		39	114	177	
218	The foe behind, the deep before						
219	God is gone up on high, with a triumphant	185			123	165	
220	God is ascended up on high						OC 127
221	Hail the day that sees him rise	181	108		118	166	
222	Our Lord is risen from the dead!	176	105		121	639	
223	See the conqueror mounts in triumph	187	135				
224	The golden gates are lifted up	182			122		
225	Christ, above all glory seated!		124				
226	Look, ye saints, the sight is glorious!		161		124	184	
227	Conquering prince and Lord of glory						CBE 63
228	Hail, thou once despised Jesus	189	235		95	167	
229	Ye faithful souls, who Jesus know	179	399		507	344	
230	Rejoice and be glad! The Redeemer hath come	384		55			

MHB	First Line	WMHB	PM	PMS	MFCH	BC	Other
231	Away with gloom, away with doubt						SW 92, 197
232	Entered the holy place above	192			119	180	
233	Jesus, to thee we fly	191					
234	Not all the blood of beasts	166	231		105	146	
235	I know that my Redeemer lives, what joy			112			
236	With joy we meditate the grace	193	119		523	134	
237	There is no sorrow, Lord, too light	195			635		
238	My faith looks up to thee, thou Lamb	400	330		399	283	
239	Lord Jesus, think on me						SP 64, 106
240	O(h) word of pity, for our pardon pleading						ChHy 97
241	O Son of man, our hero strong and tender						ChHy 146
242	Come, thou long-expected Jesus	198	130		66	179	
243	Jesus, the conqueror, reigns	439	128		572	183	
244	The head that once was crowned with thorns	209	127			191	
245	Hail to the Lord's anointed	206	133		804	659	
246	Earth, rejoice, our Lord is king	212					
247	Rejoice, the Lord is king	213	509		127	190	
248	Jesus (Jesu), the word bestow	222					
249	In the name of Jesus, every			49		60	
250	Salvation! O the joyful sound!	220	41		316	56	
251	Omnipotent Redeemer	216					
252	God is with us, God is with us, so our brave			167			
253	Break, day of God, O break	205		59			

MHB	First Line	WMHB	PM	PMS	MFCH	BC	Other
254	Hark! what a sound, and too divine for hearing						SP 251, 511
255	Wake, awake, for night is flying						ChHy 162
256	There's a light upon the mountains and the day is at the spring						MSH 485
257	O come, O come Emmanuel	197					
258	Thou art coming, O my Saviour		136			203	
259	And art thou come with us to dwell						F 393
260	Mine eyes have seen the glory of the coming of the Lord			73			ChHy 155
261	Light of those whose dreary dwelling	199			489	94	
262	All thanks be to God, who scatters abroad	217			675		
263	See how great a flame aspires	218	838			774	
264	Lo, he comes with clouds descending	200	1009	295	766	199	
265	Lift up your heads, ye gates of brass			68			
266	From north and south and east and west			76		763	
267	Lord, her watch thy church is keeping	204		60		770	
268	Light of the lonely pilgrim's heart	203	836			768	
269	Saviour, we know thou art	224					
270	My heart is full of Christ, and longs	210	138		56	646	
271	Crown him with many crowns	208	129		128	64	
272	Jesus shall reign where'er the sun	767			809	658	

MHB	First Line	WMHB	PM	PMS	MFCH	BC	Other
273	Come down, O love divine						ChHy 191
274	Lord, we believe to us and ours	236					
275	Jesus, we on the word depend	230	170		154	223	
276	When God of old came down from heaven	229	172		135	232	
277	Granted is the Saviour's prayer	234	178			217	
278	Away with our fears, our troubles	239	180				
279	O Holy Spirit, God						SP 601
280	I want the Spirit of power within	250			146	324	
281	Go not, my soul, in search of him			4			
282	Spirit of wisdom, turn our eyes	251					
283	Our blest Redeemer, ere he breathed	235	186		159	226	
284	Father, if justly still we claim	233			144	578	
285	O breath of God, breathe on us now	243		81			
286	Holy Spirit, hear us, help us			220	932		
287	Holy Ghost, my comforter	237				220	
288	Holy Spirit, truth divine				138		
289	Spirit divine, attend our prayers	254	171		134	228	
290	Gracious Spirit, Holy Ghost	579		82		216	
291	Gracious Spirit, dwell with me	252	185		129	215	
292	Come, Holy Spirit, heavenly dove	246	176		140	922	
293	Creator Spirit, by whose aid	228	190		136	212	
294	Come, holy celestial dove	342					
295	Spirit blest, who art adored	253					
296	Holy Spirit, pity me	249	179				

MHB	First Line	WMHB	PM	PMS	MFCH	BC	Other
297	Come to our poor nature's night	238	184		158		
298	Lord God the Holy Ghost					224	
299	Come Holy Ghost, all-quickening fire, come and in me				142	318	
300	Breathe on me, breath of God	244		80			
301	On all the earth thy spirit shower	223	169		145	579	
302	Father of mercies, in thy word	255	207		290	235	
303	O Word of God incarnate	267	212		300	244	
304	Father of all, in whom alone	257			294		
305	Come Holy Ghost, our hearts inspire	256	209		153	590	
306	Come, divine interpreter	260					
307	The Spirit breathes upon the word	262				245	
308	Lord, thy word abideth	268					
309	Break thou the bread of life	263		182			
310	When quiet in my house I sit	264	811		304	246	
311	Thy faithfulness, Lord, each moment we find	273				262	
312	Behold the Lamb of God, who bears	283					
313	Praise the Lord! Praise the Lord! Let the earth hear his voice						
313	To God be the glory! great things he hath done						
314	Come, let us sing of a wonderful love			84			
315	Hark! the gospel news is sounding		262		355		
316	We have heard a joyful sound			93			

MHB	First Line	WMHB	PM	PMS	MFCH	BC	Other
317	Whosoever heareth, shout, shout the sound						
318	Souls of men, why will ye scatter		261				
319	Weary souls that wander wide	277	257		327	264	
320	Art thou weary, art thou languid	293	402		90	247	NPH 148
321	Lord, I hear of showers of blessing	331	313		364	944	
322	Sinners Jesus will receive						CH 31
323	Come, sinners, to the gospel feast	270	243		318	249	
324	Come, ye sinners, poor and wretched	280	264		321	251	
325	O come, ye sinners, to your Lord	276					
326	Sinners, obey the gospel word		245		324	259	
327	Sinners, turn! Why will ye die?	274	259		326	260	
328	Come unto me, ye weary	287	255		308		
329	Ye neighbours and friends of Jesus draw near	284			334	266	
330	O Jesus (Jesu), thou art standing	288				256	
331	Behold me standing at the door					919	
332	Behold! a stranger at the door		246			248	
333	Come, let us, who in Christ believe	291	342		341	923	
334	There were ninety and nine that safely lay	149		94	103		
335	Pass me not, O gentle Saviour					955	
335	Saviour! Saviour! hear my humble cry						
336	In loving-kindness Jesus came						SSS 373

MHB	First Line	WMHB	PM	PMS	MFCH	BC	Other
337	God loved the world of sinners lost						
338	Rescue the perishing, care for the dying			174	959	977	
339	Come, O thou traveller unknown/Yield to me now; for I am weak	449/450	516		379/380	395/396	
340	Come, O thou traveller unknown/Yield to me now; for I am weak	449/450	517			395/396	
341	When shall thy love constrain	321	298		367	300	
342	Come, let us to the Lord our God				558	372	
343	Wherewith, O God, shall I draw near	351	269		386	302	
344	Jesus, the sinner's friend, to thee	307	278				
345	Drawn to the cross which thou hast blest		321		396	271	
346	O Jesus, full of truth and grace						
347	Come, O thou all-victorious Lord	305	279		365		
348	Saviour, prince of Israel's race	309			609		
349	Jesus, if still the same thou art	310	324				
350	With broken heart and contrite sigh	316	277		373		
351	I hear thy welcome voice					932	
352	Oppressed with sin and woe		299		366		
353	Just as I am, without one plea	317	322		407	281	
354	No, not despairingly						MH 453
355	Weary of earth and laden with my sin/O great absolver, grant my soul may wear	356	438			297	
356	Great God of wonders! All thy ways	68	47				

MHB	First Line	WMHB	PM	PMS	MFCH	BC	Other
357	Jesus, in whom the weary find	333					
358	Depth of mercy! can there be	308	433		344	925	
359	Out of the depths I cry to thee	514					
360	Happy the man that finds the grace	295	338		419		
361	Where shall my wondering soul begin?	358	336				
362	Author of faith, eternal Word	345	326		400	307	
363	Spirit of faith, come down	346	329		131	611	
364	Ah! whither should I go	325	297		370	269	
365	God of my salvation, hear	355	309			273	
366	Jesus! Redeemer, Saviour, Lord	352	283				
367	Day after day I sought the Lord	357					
368	Arise, my soul, arise	363	331			306	
369	Thee, Jesus, thee, the sinners' friend	353	318			296	
370	Jesus (Jesu), thy blood and righteousness/Jesu, be endless praise to thee	370/771	327		98		
371	And can it be that I should gain	360	337		443	305	
372	The God of love, to earth he came	349					
373	Lord, I was blind: I could not see		276			314	
374	Jesus hath died and hath risen again						
375	Now I have found the ground wherein	362	644		441	316	
376	Thou great mysterious God unknown	303	349		446		
377	How can a sinner know	359	344		357	312	
378	Eternal sun of righteousness						
379	The people that in darkness lay						

MHB	First Line	WMHB	PM	PMS	MFCH	BC	Other
380	I will sing the wondrous story			111			
381	I am not skilled to understand						ChHy 698
382	Let him to whom we now belong	593	406		657	360	
383	Being of beings, God of love	427			214		
384	My soul, through my redeemer's care	528			445	684	
385	Jesus, I fain would find	589					
386	O thou who camest from above	588	487		663	366	
387	My God I know, I feel thee mine	537	362		464	332	
388	My Saviour! how shall I proclaim	365					
389	Great God, indulge my humble claim	511	339		202	652	
390	Give me the faith which can remove	563	702		707	350	
391	Thy life was given for me	330					
392	I bind unto myself today						ChHy 506
393	I give my heart to thee, O Jesus					354	
394	Just as I am, thine own to be			218			
395	Saviour, while my heart is tender	882				909	
396	Lord, in the fullness of my might	883		101			
397	Lord of life and king of glory						ChHy 652
398	When thy soldiers take their swords	749					
399	What shall I render to my God	373					
400	Take my life, and let it be	566	377		429	369	

MHB	First Line	WMHB	PM	PMS	MFCH	BC	Other
401	God's trumpet wakes the slumbering world			162			
402	Faith of our fathers, living still			165	578		
403	My heart is fixed, eternal God			114			
404	How blest is life if lived for thee		489				
405	God be in my head						SP 239, 501
406	My God, I am thine	368	507		363	415	
407	How happy are they who the Saviour obey	382					
408	My God, the spring of all my joys	369	493		685	417	
409	The glory of the spring, how sweet					847	
410	Come, ye that love the Lord	291	58		197	412	
411	Head of thy church triumphant	386	633			413	
412	Worship, and thanks, and blessing	465			183		
413	When all thy mercies, O my God	92	32		35	45	
414	We thank thee, Lord, for this fair earth		1037				
415	Sing praise to God, who reigns above	383			199		
416	Life and light and joy are found						SW 179, 284
417	Come, thou fount of every blessing	377	163		194	451	
418	Awake, our souls! away, our fears!	385	402		577	436	
419	Happy are they, they that love God!						ChHy 440

MHB	First Line	WMHB	PM	PMS	MFCH	BC	Other
420	O what shall I do my Saviour to praise	367	523		682		
421	I am so glad that our Father in heaven						CanH 480
422	Blessed assurance, Jesus is mine						
423	I've found a friend, O(h) such a friend!			108		938	
424	O bless the Lord, my soul! Let all	89				677	
425	My God, my king, thy praise I sing		60		5		
426	Ye servants of God, your master proclaim	388	795		307	83	
427	Through all the changing scenes of life	17	620		25	642	
428	I'll praise my maker while I've breath	59	71		177	700	
429	God of my life, through all my days	378	53		674	50	
430	Jesus (Jesu), thy boundless love to me	414	391		450	359	
431	Love divine, all loves excelling	426	385		452	331	
432	Hark, my soul, it is the Lord	417	412			927	
433	Thou hidden love of God, whose height	531	392		395		
434	O love divine, how sweet thou art	416	387		469	130	
435	Love is the key of life and death						MSH 396
436	It passes knowledge, that dear love of thine				453		
437	My Jesus, I love thee, I know thou art mine			113	359	946	
438	Jesus (Jesu), my Lord, my God, my all, hear me		423				

MHB	First Line	WMHB	PM	PMS	MFCH	BC	Other
439	O Saviour, I have nought to plead						ChHy 425
440	Far off we need not rove	53					
441	Riches unsearchable	296					
442	Happy the heart where graces reign	577			456		
443	Loved with everlasting love						ChHy 434
444	Beloved let us love: love is of God						WS 384
445	Thee will I love, my strength, my tower	421			467	407	
446	My God, I love thee; not because	418		115			
447	O love, who formedst me to wear			54			
448	O love that wilt not let me go			97			
449	O Lord, enlarge our scanty thought						
450	Now let us see thy beauty, Lord			17	462		
451	I lift my heart to thee, Saviour divine	431	378		444		
452	What shall I do my God to love, / My Saviour and the world's, to praise?	425				342	
453	O my Saviour, hear me					951	
454	I would commune with thee, my God		494		624	399	
455	As pants the hart for cooling streams	510	500		608	645	
456	For ever here my rest shall be	532	367		405	740	
457	Thou shepherd of Israel, and mine	423	521		57	409	

MHB	First Line	WMHB	PM	PMS	MFCH	BC	Other
458	Long did I toil, and knew no earthly rest				690	478	
459	To the haven of thy breast	468					
460	Talk with us, Lord, thyself reveal	422	495		715	406	
461	O(h) for a closer walk with God	343	431		603	377	
462	I hunger and I thirst		734				
463	O Jesus Christ, grow thou in me			104			
464	Jesus, the all-restoring Word	516	369		460	374	
465	Open, Lord, my inward ear	424			475		
466	My soul, there is a country						ChHy 463
467	My spirit longs for thee				389		
468	Nearer, my God, to thee	430	557		402	403	
469	That mystic word of thine, O sovereign Lord		522				
470	Still with thee, O my God		804		267		
471	O God, my God, my all thou art	429			470		
472	Come in, O(h) come! The door stands open now						MSH 313
473	My heart is resting, O my God	432	663		217	483	
474	Still, still with thee, when purple morning breaketh			256	266	833	
475	I need thee every hour, most gracious Lord	456				935	
475	I need thee, O I need thee						
476	From trials unexempted	451				386	
477	Son of God, if thy free grace	344			582		
478	Jesus, my Saviour, brother, friend	445	580		600	390	
479	Fainting soul, be bold, be strong						

MHB	First Line	WMHB	PM	PMS	MFCH	BC	Other
480	Ah! Lord with trembling I confess	448			589		
481	Hark, how the watchmen cry!					440	
482	Hark 'tis the watchman's cry		599		587		
483	Surrounded by a host of foes	434			581		
484	Soldiers of Christ, arise	433	592		563	430	
485	I'm not ashamed to own my Lord, or to	460		110			
486	Arm of the Lord, awake, awake! Thine	219	829		796	434	
487	Come on, my partners in distress	471	420		560		
488	Oft in danger, oft in woe	454	597			427	
489	Workman of God! O lose not heart						
490	Fight the good fight with all thy might			154	566		
491	Christian, seek not yet repose	453			592	385	
492	I the good fight have fought	631			575	442	
493	Love of love, and light of light						Y 97
494	A safe stronghold our God is still	466			561		
495	Who puts his trust in God most just						MSH 340
496	Eternal beam of light divine	474	654		530	475	
497	To the hills I lift mine eyes	399	632				
498	Rock of ages, cleft for me	168	311		110	151	
499	O(h) safe to the rock that is higher than I			131	349	952	
500	Peace, doubting heart! my God's I am	467	478		544	428	
501	Peace, perfect peace, in this dark world of sin?	404		148	413	487	

MHB	First Line	WMHB	PM	PMS	MFCH	BC	Other
502	Omnipotent Lord, my Saviour and King	436	483				
503	God moves in a mysterious way	488	36		27	30	
504	Leave God to order all thy ways	406					
505	O thou to whose all-searching sight	476	441		517	426	
506	My spirit on thy care	398				641	
507	Commit thou all thy griefs	480	37		31	472	
507	Give to the winds thy fears	481	38		554	473	
508	As helpless as a child who clings		623		449	435	
509	The Galilean fishers toil		589		586		
510	Away, my needless fears	482	625		579		
511	Begone unbelief, my Saviour is near	492	482			469	
512	Lord, as to thy dear cross we flee		405		85	119	
513	Who fathoms the eternal thought?	820		143			
514	He that is down needs fear no fall						ChHy 557
515	Thy way, not mine, O Lord	484	456			490	
516	Trust and obey, for there's no other way						
516	When we walk with the Lord						SSS 141
517	Simply trusting every day				351	959	
517	Trusting as the moments fly						
518	Jesus (Jesu), priceless treasure						SP 276, 544
519	Thee, Jesus, full of truth and grace	469	447		524	431	
520	I bring my sins to thee	402					

MHB	First Line	WMHB	PM	PMS	MFCH	BC	Other
521	I am trusting thee, Lord Jesus	403	635		414	931	
522	I could not do without thee	405	305		415	441	
523	I will not let thee go, thou help in time of need	491					
524	My God, I thank thee, who hast made	379	570		186	37	
525	Through the love of God our Saviour		636				
526	O Jesus (Jesu), I have promised	412	414			365	
527	Sometimes a light surprises	479	40		37	420	
528	In heavenly love abiding	409	417				
529	O blessed life! the heart at rest		400				
530	Oft I in my heart have said	397					
531	Light of the world, thy beams I bless		461				444
532	Let everlasting glories crown	300			297	241	
533	Prayer is the soul's sincere desire	507	665		627	392	
534	Jesus, thou sovereign Lord of all	698	673		625		
535	From every stormy wind that blows	702	777		719		
536	My God, is any hour so sweet		810		626	402	
537	'Tis not to ask for gifts alone						MSH 357
538	What a friend we have in Jesus					133	
539	Lord, teach us how to pray aright	505				715	
540	Come, my soul, thy suit prepare	506	669		621	711	
541	Pray, without ceasing pray	499					
542	Jesus, my strength, my hope	503	374		597	391	
543	Hear thou my prayer, O Lord	509					
544	Eternal light, eternal light	51	65		10	17	

MHB	First Line	WMHB	PM	PMS	MFCH	BC	Other
545	O disclose thy lovely face	515	510		378		
546	Come, Saviour Jesus, from above	526	486		454	346	
547	The thing my God doth hate	527			425		
548	All things are possible to him	551	395				
549	Lord, that I may learn of thee	572			616		
550	O(h) for a heart to praise my God	529	365		421	334	
551	O Lord, how happy should we be	508	471			486	
552	Jesus, all-atoning Lamb	565	376		458		
553	Come Holy Ghost, all-quickening fire come, and my	535	396				
554	O come and dwell in me	538			463	333	
555	When, my Saviour, shall I be	574			391		
556	Deepen the wound thy hands have made	540			409		
557	What is our calling's glorious hope	555	364		482		
558	Saviour from sin, I wait to prove	543	390		479		
559	Come, O my God, the promise seal	560	404		428		
560	Jesus hath died that I might live	558	366		459	325	
561	Father of Jesus Christ, my Lord	536			346	310	
562	God of all power, and truth, and grace	548			486	319	
563	Lord, I believe a rest remains	552	358		420	330	
564	Father, I dare believe	557			410		
565	I know that my Redeemer lives, and ever	544	357		457	323	
566	God of all-redeeming grace	592			654		

MHB	First Line	WMHB	PM	PMS	MFCH	BC	Other
567	In full and glad surrender	569			426		
568	Since the Son hath made me free	547	347			340	
569	Thine for ever, God of love		375		430	468	
570	Holy, and true, and righteous Lord	549					
571	Blessed are the pure in heart, they	576					
572	Behold the servant of the Lord! I wait	594	397		649	345	
573	O God, what offering shall I give	564	398		640	364	
574	Father, Son, and Holy Ghost, one in three	562	382		642		
575	Servant of all, to toil for man	584			639		
576	Be it my only wisdom here	582	421		591		
577	O loving Lord, who art for ever seeking						RS 8
578	A charge to keep I have	580	373		588	383	
579	Saviour, thy dying love thou gavest me			36	439		
580	Dismiss me not thy service, Lord	606	606		652	347	
581	Ye servants of the Lord		594				
582	Brightly beams our Father's mercy						
582	Let the lower lights be burning						
583	How blessed, from the bonds of sin	607					
584	Thou, Jesu, thou my breast inspire	595					
585	Rise up, O men of God						ChHy 344
586	Stay, master, stay upon this heavenly hill			197	671		

MHB	First Line	WMHB	PM	PMS	MFCH	BC	Other
587	O Lord of every lovely thing						JS 63
588	Awake, awake to love and work						Fr 4
589	Go, labour on, spend and be spent	698	579		646	351	
590	Forth in thy name, O Lord, I go	586	940		648	349	
591	Believe not those who say			119			
592	I hoped that with the brave and strong	816			952		
593	O'er the harvest reaped or lost						RS 79
594	Lord, in the strength of grace	561			668	361	
595	God of almighty love	585			641	352	
596	Make me a captive, Lord						ChHy 464
597	Teach me, my God and king				661	886	
598	Holy Lamb, who thee confess	600					
599	Sow in the morn thy seed	225	596		662	777	
600	O master, let me walk with thee	605		159			
601	They who tread the path of labour						F 91
602	Father, I know that all my life	602	463		653	476	
603	Jesus, let all thy lovers shine						
604	Fill thou my life, O Lord my God	567		193	221		
605	Jesus, the gift divine I know	590			88		
606	Come all whoe'er have set	613	716		739	497	
607	O God of Bethel, by whose hand	95	35		24	39	
608	Captain of Israel's host, and guide	611	643		493	450	
609	Saviour, like a shepherd lead us			12			
610	Leader of faithful souls, and guide	610	476		773	458	

MHB	First Line	WMHB	PM	PMS	MFCH	BC	Other
611	Lead us, heavenly Father, lead us	625	466		500	460	
612	Lead, kindly light, amid the encircling gloom		479		487	459	
613	Lead us, O Father, in the paths of peace		427		501	461	
614	Heavenly Father, thou hast brought us	629					
615	Guide me, O thou great Jehovah	615	467		490	453	
616	Through the night of doubt and sorrow	628	571			512	
617	Brightly gleams our banner	887				890	
618	O happy band of pilgrims		601				
619	Forward be our watchword	619	611			500	
620	Who would true valour see						ChHy 576
621	Jesus, the good shepherd is	394					
622	Show me the way, O Lord			10		467	
623	I dared not hope that thou wouldst deign to come	626		121			
624	Jesus, still lead on	622	454		499		
625	I to the hills will lift mine eyes						HK 71
626	I want a principle within	443	588		595	389	
627	How happy every child of grace	618			802	503	
628	Ye that do your master's will						Y 94
629	All as God wills, who wisely heeds		622				
630	O(h) grant us light, that we may know						
631	Walk in the light; so shalt thou know		497		488		

MHB	First Line	WMHB	PM	PMS	MFCH	BC	Other
632	Be thou my vision, O Lord of my heart						ChHy 477
633	O king of mercy, from thy throne on high	623					
634	Will your anchor hold in the storms of life						SSS 128
635	Jesus (Jesu), my truth, my way	411			498		
636	Light of the world, faint were our weary feet	627					
637	The sands of time are sinking	633		284			
638	To God, the only wise	616					
639	Christ, who knows all his sheep						SP 158
640	Sunset and evening star	819		287			
641	While ebbing nature grieves	817					
642	When on my day of life the night is falling						ChHy 589
643	When this passing world is done		383		512	343	
644	Thou judge of quick and dead	840	1007		769	204	
645	That day of wrath, that dreadful day	845	1003				
646	Day of wrath! O day of mourning!	844	1013		1040		196
647	Lord, it belongs not to my care	824	974		431	479	
648	Away with our sorrow and fear	848	574		775		
649	There is a land of pure delight	850	1017		782	546	
650	Jerusalem, my happy home, name ever	853			784	534	
651	Hark . . . my soul! Angelic songs are swelling		1032		793	502	

MHB	First Line	WMHB	PM	PMS	MFCH	BC	Other
652	Brief life is here our portion/ Jerusalem the golden	851/ 852	561/ 563			755/ 785	519
653	Sweet place: sweet place alone!	854					
654	The homeland! the homeland!			291			
655	Jerusalem, my happy home, when shall I			290			
656	Around the throne of God in heaven	888	864			889	
657	For those we love within the veil						ChHy 218
658	For ever with the Lord!	856	551		776	499	
659	O day of rest and gladness	640	763		231	606	
660	This is the day of light	639	760			617	
661	Come, let us with our Lord arise					591	
662	Sweet is the sunlight after rain	641				613	
663	Light of light, enlighten me						
664	O(h) how blest the hour, Lord Jesus	265					
665	Sweet is the work, my God, my king	636	752		230	668	
666	We rose today with anthems sweet	642	750		250		
667	The day thou gavest, Lord, is ended	645		264	289	615	
668	Angel voices ever singing	658	791		170		
669	Dear Lord and Father of mankind	416		19		474	
670	Jesus, thou soul of all our joys	656			220		
671	Sing alleluia (hallelujah) forth in duteous praise		1031		1039		
672	Saviour, blessed Saviour	621	164		198	510	
673	Summer suns are glowing	939		20	839	848	

MHB	First Line	WMHB	PM	PMS	MFCH	BC	Other
674	O love divine! whose constant beam						
675	Jesus, where'er thy people meet	703	773		213	602	
676	Great is the Lord our God	652	820		208	649	
677	We love the place, O God	657	790				
678	Lord of the worlds above	648			242		
679	Pleasant are thy courts above	650	536		243	664	
680	Glad was my heart to hear	655	786				
681	God of mercy, God of grace	716	718			656	
682	God of pity, God of grace	667				597	
683	Lo, God is here! Let us adore	653	794		173	603	
684	Jesus, stand among us in/In Thy risen power						ChHy 248
685	Stand up and bless the Lord, ye people		787		211	612	
686	Lift up your hearts! We lift them, Lord, to thee			8			
687	I bow in silence at thy feet						N
688	O God our Father, who dost make us one			199			
689	At even ere the sun was set	916	754		251	588	
690	Our day of praise is done	646	759		254		
691	Saviour, again to thy dear name we raise	644	769		256	609	
692	O Saviour, bless us ere we go	643					
693	Lord, dismiss us with thy blessing	799	1048		975	998	
694	Lord, thou hast been our dwelling place in every generation	813		271			
695	Praise, Lord, for thee in Zion waits	7	52		175		
696	Children of the heavenly king	680				496	

MHB	First Line	WMHB	PM	PMS	MFCH	BC	Other
697	Blest are the humble souls that see			139	480		
698	Abide among us with thy grace	717		58			
699	Great is our redeeming Lord	672					
700	Who in the Lord confide?	677	711		583	689	
701	The church's one foundation	679	717			561	
702	Christ is our corner-stone	661	823			791	
703	City of God, how broad and far			61			
704	By the holy hills surrounded	674					
705	God is the refuge of his saints	668	705		28		
706	Glorious things of thee are spoken	673	722			562	
707	O thou not made with hands						
708	We love thy kingdom, Lord	299					
709	And are we yet alive	785	533		693	708	
710	Brethren in Christ, and well beloved	691				567	
711	How pleasant, how divinely fair	649	771		246	662	
712	Blest be the dear uniting love	791	676		970		
713	Let us join – 'tis God commands	742	539				
714	He wants not friends that hath thy love						ChHy 225
715	For the might of thine arm we bless thee						ChHy 212
716	Thou God of truth and love	692	681				
717	Help us to help each other, Lord						
718	Jesus, we look to thee	789			700	714	
719	See, Jesus (Jesu), thy disciples see	790			713	719	
720	Christ, from whom all blessings flow	689	679			553	

MHB	First Line	WMHB	PM	PMS	MFCH	BC	Other
721	Jesus, united by thy grace	690			699	559	
722	Lift up your hearts to things above		546				
723	O God of our forefathers, hear				447		
724	Jesus (Jesu), Lord of life and glory, bend				219		
725	Lord, in this thy mercy's day		739		332		
726	Saviour, when in dust to thee	157	312			292	
727	Jesus, with thy church abide	718					
728	O God of mercy, God of might				651	753/818	
729	Lord of our life, and God of our salvation	811		16			
730	Father of everlasting grace	707					
731	O Christ our God, who with thine own hast been						PSH 174
732	Sweetly the holy hymn			255	262	721	
733	Jesus, sun of righteousness		943				
734	Jesus (Jesu), meek and gentle					278	
735	When the weary, seeking rest	666	670		216	622	
736	Shepherd divine, our wants relieve	699	666		716	582	
737	Jesus (Jesu), to thee our hearts we lift	706	425				
738	Revive thy work, O Lord				147	957	
739	Our Father, hear our longing prayer				617		
740	Father of all, to thee						F 171
741	We have not known thee as we ought						MSH 314
742	Thy kingdom come, on bended knee			69			

MHB	First Line	WMHB	PM	PMS	MFCH	BC	Other
743	Not for our sins alone						AM 528
744	O happy day that fixed my choice	747	354		749	950	
745	All praise to our redeeming Lord	681	532		694	707	
746	I am thine, O Lord, I have heard thy voice				362	930	
747	All thanks to the Lamb	786	724		705		
748	Come, and let us sweetly join	740	537		740		
749	Come, let us use the grace divine	745	1042		746	864	
750	O God, how often hath thine ear	746	887		748		
751	See Israel's gentle shepherd stand	720	727		723	730	
752	Blessed Jesus (Jesu), here we stand	723					
753	Friend of the home, as when in Galilee						C 280
754	Stand, soldier of the cross	725	733				
755	Lord Jesus (Jesu) Christ, our Lord most dear						ChHy 304
756	Bread of the world, in mercy broken	738		202		736	
757	Spread the table of the Lord						N 21
758	I am not worthy, holy Lord						C 296
759	And now, O Father, mindful of the love						ChHy 320
760	Saviour, and can it be						O 155
761	Jesus, we thus obey				726	747	
762	In memory of the Saviour's love	733	730		728	744	
763	According to thy gracious word	736	729		725	733	

MHB	First Line	WMHB	PM	PMS	MFCH	BC	Other
764	Author of life divine						ChHy 317
765	Come, thou everlasting Spirit	730			150	739	
766	Be known to us in breaking bread	734					
767	Come Holy Ghost, thine influence shed				736		
768	O bread to pilgrims given		736			752	
769	Bread of heaven! on thee I feed	737				735	
770	Jesus, to thy table led		738				
771	Victim divine, thy grace we claim	727	744			755	
772	Here, O my Lord, I see thee face to face	735	745			743	
773	By Christ redeemed, in Christ restored	739	743				
774	O God of love, to thee we bow						ChHy 325
775	The voice that breathed o'er Eden	960	935		861	785	
776	O Father, all creating	961		246			
777	O perfect love, all human thought transcending	962		245			
778	How beauteous are their feet	751	693		815	767	
779	Come Holy Ghost, our souls inspire	751	188			207	
780	Master, speak, thy servant heareth	763		155	944		
781	Lord, speak to me, that I may speak	762	583		504	362	
782	Shine thou upon us, Lord	761					
783	Shall I, for fear of feeble man	459	683			447	
784	What shall we offer our good Lord	597			218		

MHB	First Line	WMHB	PM	PMS	MFCH	BC	Other
785	Jesus, if we aright confess						
786	Lord, grant us, like the watching five	765					
787	Lord of the harvest, hear	752			814	573	
788	Disposer supreme, and judge of the earth	757					
789	Forget them not, O Christ, who stand						C 535
790	Look from thy sphere of endless day	764	833			769	
791	Jesus, thy wandering sheep behold!	753					
792	Lord, if at thy command	756					
793	Lord of the living harvest	760				574	
794	Eternal Son, eternal love	43					
795	O church of God, arise						StO 241
796	Lord, thy ransomed church is waking	780					ChHy 374
797	Once again, dear Lord, we pray						
798	Far round the world thy children sing their song						ChHy 373
799	The fields are all white						ChHy 362
800	Saviour, quicken many nations	768			817		
801	From Greenland's icy mountains	770	845		805	762	
802	The heavens declare thy glory, Lord	774	202		19	630	
803	Thou, whose almighty word		840		820	781	
804	Spread, O spread, thou mighty word	783	211		821	779	
805	Christ for the world, we sing!	781		63			

MHB	First Line	WMHB	PM	PMS	MFCH	BC	Other
806	Let the song go round the earth						GL 17
807	And let our bodies part	792	695		696		
808	Speed thy servants, Saviour, speed them	784	848		822	778	
809	I cannot tell why he, whom angels worship						HT 6
810	Father, let thy kingdom come		837				
811	Thy kingdom come, O God!						SP 415
812	God is working his purpose out, as year succeeds to year						ChHy 380
813	The Lord will come and not be slow		885				
814	Head of thy church, whose Spirit fills	772			672		
815	Hills of the north, rejoice		841				
816	The Son of God goes forth to war	806		175		448	
817	Fling out the banner, let it float			67			
818	Happy the souls to Jesus joined	801			673		
819	Forth rode the knights of old						SW 76
820	Who is on the Lord's side?		600		924	371	
821	Stand up, stand up for Jesus!	462	602		562	368	
822	Onward, Christian soldiers	455	610		569	446	
823	Our life is hid with Christ in God						
824	Come, let us join our friends above	805	870		794	520	
825	The saints of God! their conflict past	809				544	
826	O God, to whom the faithful dead	804					
827	Their names are names of kings				584		

MHB	First Line	WMHB	PM	PMS	MFCH	BC	Other
828	Ten thousand times ten thousand	859		293		201	
829	Hark! the song of jubilee		847		806		
830	Hark! the sound of holy voices	810		292			
831	Give me the wings of faith to rise	803	545		800	526	
832	For all the saints, who from their labours rest	807	608		791	523	
833	What are these arrayed in white	802	1028		792	536	
834	Above the clear blue sky				919		
835	When, his salvation bringing	861	862		'		
836	Hosanna, loud hosanna		861				
837	Children of Jerusalem	862					
838	Jesus high in glory, lend a listening ear	870		210	931	902	
839	There's a friend for little children	871		214		915	
840	God, my Father, loving me						SP 357
841	Jesus, friend of little children			200			
842	Gentle Jesus, meek and mild	879		208		893	
843	In our dear Lord's garden						C 660
844	Jesus (Jesu), tender shepherd, hear me	885					
845	God make my life a little light				940		
846	Lord, when we have not any light						F 293
847	O Jesus, we are well and strong						SW 83
848	Hushed was the evening hymn	876		215		898	
849	Father, lead me day by day			226			
850	Looking upward every day			227			
851	All things bright and beautiful	875		225	923		

MHB	First Line	WMHB	PM	PMS	MFCH	BC	Other
852	All things which live below the sky						MSH 167
853	A little child may know						SSH 1
854	It is a thing most wonderful			206		901	
855	I love to think, though I am young					899	
856	I love to hear the story	867		217			
857	God has given us a book full of stories						SW 43
858	Tell me the stories of Jesus						MSH 62
859	Once in royal David's city	863		205	926	906	
860	Away in a manger, no crib for a bed						ChHy 657
861	O come, little children						G 3
862	Wise men seeking Jesus						MSH 212
863	The shepherds had an angel						SP 439, 372
864	Remember all the people						369
865	I think when I read that sweet story of old	866		216		900	
866	When mothers of Salem their children brought to Jesus			213			
867	Day by day we magnify thee	892		204			
868	Lord and Saviour, true and kind						F 449
869	Praise to our God, who with love never swerving						ChHy 676
870	Lord, behold us with thy blessing/Lord, dismiss us with thy blessing, thanks					997	ChHy 677/678

MHB	First Line	WMHB	PM	PMS	MFCH	BC	Other
871	In our work and in our play, Jesus, ever						
872	We bless thee, Lord, for all this common life			13			
873	Thou gracious God, whose mercy lends	897					
874	Away with our fears! The glad morning	896		954			
875	O happy home, where thou art loved the dearest	899		244			
876	Omnipresent God, whose aid	913					
877	How do thy mercies close me round!	912	649		36	455	
878	O God, our help in ages past	812	972		750	666	
879	God save our gracious King/ Queen	971	910		969	982	
880	God bless our native land	972	911	277		985/ 984	
881	Lord, while for all mankind we pray	976	908			989	
882	Rejoice, O land, in God thy might						EH 475
883	Judge eternal, throned in splendour			282			
884	Before thy throne, O God, we kneel						F 343
885	Rejoice today with one accord		914				
886	O Lord, stretch forth thy mighty hand						
886	To thee, our God, we fly					992	
887	God of our fathers, unto thee						AM 708
888	O King of kings, O Lord of hosts	975		283			
889	God of our fathers, known of old			269			

MHB	First Line	WMHB	PM	PMS	MFCH	BC	Other
890	Lift up your heads, ye mighty gates				193	253	
891	King of the city splendid			281			
892	Eternal ruler of the ceaseless round						ChHy 489
893	O ye who taste that love is sweet						ChHy 358
894	Father, who on man dost shower						ChHy 349
895	Where cross the crowded ways of life						F 344
896	Now praise we great and famous men						SW 267, 372
897	What service shall we render thee						ChHy 644
898	Once to every man and nation						SP 178, 309
899	Father, in heaven, who lovest all						
899	Land of our birth, we pledge to thee						ChHy 647
900	I vow to thee, my country, all earthly things above						SP 188, 319
901	God the all-terrible, king, who ordainest			280			
902	All glory to God in the sky	979			676	178	
903	O God of love, O king of peace		907				
904	Behold the mountain of the Lord	221	834		811	757	
905	Ring out the grief that saps the mind						

MHB	First Line	WMHB	PM	PMS	MFCH	BC	Other
905	Ring out, wild bells, to the wild sky						SP 348, 633
906	Lord Christ, when first thou cam'st to men						
907	Almighty Father, who dost give						ChHy 491
908	Life of ages, richly poured						SP 290
909	When wilt thou save the people?			279	981		
910	These things shall be; a loftier race	980		78			
911	O brother man, fold to thy heart thy brother						ChHy 485
912	Turn back, O man, forswear thy foolish ways						SP 197
913	With the sweet word of peace				974		
914	God be with you till we meet again	800		200			
915	Father, who art alone	964			893		
916	Holy Father, in thy mercy						ChHy 629
917	Eternal Father, strong to save	967	926		888		
917	O hear us when we cry to thee						
918	O love divine, that stooped to share	497	1035			425	
919	Thine arm, O Lord, in days of old	953	1045		877	813	
920	Thou to whom the sick and dying	950		152	878	814	
921	From thee all skill and science flow	951					
922	O thou, before whose presence	955					
923	We give thee but thine own	949		180	638	821	

MHB	First Line	WMHB	PM	PMS	MFCH	BC	Other
924	Christ, whose glory fills the skies	904	944			829	
925	The star of the morn has risen						H 11
926	My Father, for another night						PSH 9
927	O timely happy, timely wise	901	941		261	832	
928	Morning comes with light all-cheering	908					
929	Come, my soul, thou must be waking						
930	O Lord of life, thy quickening voice			253			
931	Awake, my soul, and with the sun	900	938		256	828	
932	O splendour of God's glory bright						
932	Our mind be in his keeping placed						
933	At thy feet, O Christ, we lay						
934	All praise to him who dwells in bliss	928					
935	Father divine, I come to thee			96			
936	O gladsome light, O grace						SP 50
937	Hail, gladdening light, of his pure glory poured			257			
938	Father, in high heaven dwelling		961		279		
939	The sun is sinking fast		950		288		
940	The radiant morn hath passed away	921	960		276	845	
941	Lord Jesus, in the days of old						MSH 517
942	Sun of my soul, thou Saviour dear	910	947		272	843	

MHB	First Line	WMHB	PM	PMS	MFCH	BC	Other
943	Glory to thee, my God, this night/All praise to Thee, my God, this night	909	945		269	835	
944	Now the day is over	884	951		941	905	
945	The night is come, wherein at last we rest	925					
946	Now all the woods are sleeping						LG 228
947	Ere I sleep, for every favour	926					
948	Abide with me, fast falls the eventide	911	963		271	834	
949	Behold us, Lord, a little space	603	780		717	710	
950	Blessed (blest) are the pure in heart			117			
951	The day is past and over	915	954		275	844	
952	God the Father, be thou near	918					
953	O Lord, who by thy presence	914					
954	Another year is dawning		883		831	860	
955	Onward, then and fear not						
955	Standing at the portal				825	874	
956	Come, let us anew our journey pursue	930	877		745	863	
957	Father, let me dedicate		882				
958	O God, the rock of ages	815		15	12	871	
959	Sing to the great Jehovah's praise	931	872		824	873	
960	Join, all ye ransomed sons of grace	936	673		743		
961	Across the sky the shades of night	937	885		742		
962	Come, ye thankful people, come	942	901		851	849	
963	All good gifts around us						

MHB	First Line	WMHB	PM	PMS	MFCH	BC	Other
963	We plough the fields, and scatter	941	898		860	858	
964	To thee, O Lord, our hearts we raise	944	902		859	857	
965	The spring again is here						SW 44, 149
966	Earth below is teeming					850	
967	Now the year is crowned with blessing	945					
968	Yes, God is good – in earth and sky		5				
969	O Lord of heaven and earth and sea	948	70		178		
970	Hear us, O Lord, from heaven, thy dwelling-place	947					
971	A gladsome hymn of praise we sing				912		
972	Here, Lord, we offer thee all that is fairest		1051		846	823	
973	Rejoice for a brother deceased	831	998		887		
974	God of the living, in whose eyes	833		294		527	
975	When the day of toil is done	858	567			514	
976	Now the labourer's task is o'er	836		288		788	
977	Safe home, safe home in port	835	1026				
978	When our heads are bowed with woe	155	981				
979	Our Father, by whose servants						Sp 107, 194
980	O light, from age to age the same						SP 106, 192
981	Christ is the foundation	662			863		

MHB	First Line	WMHB	PM	PMS	MFCH	BC	Other
982	Father of men, in whom are one						SP 409, 338
983	Be with us, gracious Lord, today	661			868		
984	O thou, whose hand hath brought us	665		185	867		

Appendix 3

Members of the Hymn Book Committee as at Digswell Park Conference House, 7 April 1930.

Biographical material is taken from *A Dictionary of Methodism In Britain and Ireland.*[632]

Address	Forename	Surname	Degree(s)	Notes
Revd	G.	Ayre		Primitive Methodist – absent – no entry
Revd	B. A.	Barber		Primitive Methodist – present – no entry
Revd	E.	Barrett	MA	Primitive Methodist – present – no entry
Revd	Edgar C.	Barton (1873–1953)		Wesleyan – Representing Dr J. Alfred Sharp – Book Steward 1932–48. Educated Woodhouse Grove and Richmond. Malta and Ghana, Inner city mission St John's Square, Clerkenwell 1911–22. Secretary of the First London District from 1914 becoming Chairman in 1932. First Secretary of MCMS in 1935.
Revd	James R.	Batey		Wesleyan – present – no entry
Revd	Henry	Bett (1876–1953)	MA	Wesleyan – absent – Taught Pastoral Theology and Church History at Handsworth. President of Conference 1945. Wrote *Hymns of Methodism in their Literary Relations* (first published in 1913; 3rd enlarged edition 1945).

632 Of 50 members of the Committee listed Vickers mentions only 25. John A. Vickers, ed., *A Dictionary of Methodism in Britain and Ireland*, Peterborough, Epworth Press, 2000.

Revd	Harry	Bisseker (1878–1966)	MA	Wesleyan – absent – Educated King Edward's School, Birmingham and Jesus, Cambridge. Chaplain to The Leys School and Minister in City Road Circuit. NT Tutor Richmond 1910–15. 1919–34 Headmaster of The Leys School.
Revd	J. G.	Bowran (1869–1946)		Primitive Methodist – present – Pupil teacher before training at Manchester PM Theological Institute. Middlesborough and Hexham. Pastor and administrator. Connexional Editor 1916–21. President 1928 and acting President 1929 after his successor's death. Director of Chapel Aid Association from 1925; Chairman 1939–46. Gave Fernley Hartley Lecture on 'Christianity and Culture' (1923). Writer of homely stories under pen name of 'Ramsay Guthrie'.
Mr	T.	Bowran		Primitive Methodist – absent – no entry
Revd	K. Harley	Boyns		Wesleyan – present – no entry
Revd	Edmund	Bromage		Wesleyan Reform Union – present – no entry
Revd Dr	David	Brook (1854–		United Methodist – present – Leading part in negotiations for the 1907 Union and chief UMC advocate of Union in 1932. Chairman of Union Committee of own denomination and member of interdenominational union committee 1922–32. President of UM Assembly and FCFC in 1901.
Revd	R. Lee	Cole (1878–1963)	MA	Wesleyan – present – Irish, educated at Methodist College Belfast. Ministry mainly in Dublin. Preacher and administrator. Educational affairs. Secretary of Irish Conference 1926–32. Keen student of History.
Miss	Lilian	Cox		Wesleyan – present – no entry

Revd	N. M.	Cuthbert		Primitive Methodist – present
Revd	W. T.	Davison (1846–1935)	MA DD	Wesleyan – present – Scholar and author. Educated at Kingswood. Did not take up Oxford Scholarship because of 'his father's dread of the influence of Tractarianism and of *Essays and Reviews*'. Classics tutor at Richmond from 1881. Theological tutor Handsworth 1891–1904. Helped Wesleyans to come to terms with scholarship and thus faced heresy charge. Connexional Editor for one year – which he left with relief. Theological Tutor and Principal Richmond 1909–20. Also Dean of the Faculty of Theology of London University. Editor Methodist Recorder 1883–86. Ecumenist with interest in poetry and music. President of Conference 1901.
Mr	James	Duckworth		United Methodist – present – no entry
Mr	Edward C.	Early (1883–1940)		Wesleyan – present – Local Preacher from prominent Methodist family. Eight other members listed in *A Dictionary of Methodism in Britain and Ireland*.
Sir	Walter	Essex		United Methodist – present – no entry
Revd	P. J.	Fisher (1883–1961)		Primitive Methodist – present – Trained Hartley College and Chaplain in France and Flanders throughout First World War. Member of Faith and Order Committee. Editor of *Methodist Leader* 1930–33. Co-editor *Methodist Times and Leader* 1933–37. Wrote plays, devotional works and poetry.
Mr	Isaac	Foot (1880–1960)	MP	Wesleyan – present – Lawyer and Liberal MP for Bodmin. Minister for mines 1931–32. Vice-President of Conference 1937. Temperance advocate.

Mr	Clement	Gerrard		Primitive Methodist – present – no entry
Revd	Arthur S.	Gregory (1895–1989)	MA	Wesleyan – present – Read Classics at Trinity, Oxford. Assistant Tutor at Handsworth College before entering Circuit work in 1926. Expert on Charles Wesley's hymns. Founder member of MCMS and MSF. Wrote *Praises with Understanding* (1935; revised and enlarged 1949) – 'a notable landmark in Methodist hymnology'.
Revd	A. W.	Harrison (1882–1946)	MC BSc DD	Wesleyan – present – Educated University College Nottingham and Didsbury College. Combatant and Chaplain in First World War. Vice-Principal Westminster College 1921 becoming Principal in 1930. President of Conference 1945. Champion of Methodist Union and devoted student of Bunyan and the Puritans.
Revd	William H.	Heap		Wesleyan – present – no entry
Revd	Henry	Hooks		United Methodist – absent – no entry
Revd	Henry	James		United Methodist – present – no entry
Revd	W. M.	Kelley		Primitive Methodist – present – no entry
Mr	Edmund S.	Lamplough (1860–1940)		Wesleyan – present – Underwriter and deputy-chairman at Lloyds. Vice-President of Conference 1935. Collector of Wesleyana and organist.
Revd	W. F.	Lofthouse (1871–1965)	MA DD	Wesleyan – President of Conference – absent – Tutor Handsworth 1904–65; Principal 1925–1940. President of Conference 1929. Influenced by J. Scott Lidgett and founder of the Union for Social Service. Continual concern was Ethics as a key branch of theology. 'Generally considered the widest ranging Methodist scholar of his time'.

Revd	W. Russell	Maltby (1866–1951)	DD	Wesleyan – present – Trained Headingley College. Warden of the Wesley Deaconess Order 1920–40. President of Conference 1926. Exercised a ministry among students through university missions and conferences.
Revd	J. C.	Mantripp (1867–1943)		Primitive Methodist – present – Connexional Editor 1926–31. Wrote on *The Devotional Use of the MHB.*
Revd	Edward	McClellan (1870–1967)		Primitive Methodist – present – Trained Hartley College. Connexional Editor 1921–26. Wrote extensively. President of Conference 1931. 'One of the last great PM orators'.
Revd	G. A.	Metcalfe		Wesleyan Reform Union – present – no entry
Revd	J. Ernest	Rattenbury (1870–1963)	DD	Wesleyan – present – Closely associated with Central Halls. Helped found the WM Union for Social Service. Led the Wesleyan Methodist opposition to Union in 1932. Founded the MSF. Wrote *The Eucharistic Hymns of John and Charles Wesley* (1948).
Mr	John	Rounsefell	MA BSc	United Methodist – present – no entry but prominent in educational circles. A headmaster.
Revd	R. H. B.	Shapland		United Methodist – President of Conference – absent – no entry
Revd	J. Alfred	Sharp (1856–1932)	DD	Wesleyan – absent – Apprenticed to a carpenter. Trained Didsbury and Handsworth Colleges. Interest in social issues. Connexional Temperance Secretary 1906. Book Steward 1911–32. Wrote on Abraham Lincoln and David Livingstone. President of Conference 1921. President of the Free Church Federal Council 1930. At age of 55 became a Mason and was Assistant Grand Chaplain of the Grand Lodge. Made a Freeman of Shaftesbury in 1921.

Mr	W. S.	Skelton		United Methodist – present – no entry
Revd	C. Ryder	Smith (1875– 1956)	BA DD	Wesleyan – present – Educated Kingswood School. Assistant Tutor Headingley College. Twenty years in English Circuits and Bombay. Tutor in Systematic Theology Richmond, 1920–40. Professor in the University of London and Dean in the Faculty of Theology. Wrote a series of studies including one on *The Bible Doctrine of Womanhood* (1923). President of Conference 1931. Played an important part in the movement towards Methodist Union.
Revd	Henry	Smith		United Methodist – present – no entry
Mr	Stanley	Sowton (1875– 1958)		Wesleyan – absent – Successful Circuit Missionary Secretary. Left banking to join Mission House Staff in 1906. Prolific writer. Reorganised JMA. Sunday School Superintendent at Muswell Hill. Declined to stand as Vice President of the Methodist Conference.
Revd	J. H.	Squire	BA BD	United Methodist – present – no entry
Revd	R.	Strong	MA BLit	United Methodist – present – no entry
Revd	J.	Swinden		Primitive Methodist – present – no entry
Revd	John	Telford (1851– 1936)	BA	Wesleyan – present – Trained at Didsbury College. Connexional Editor 1905–34. Editor, author and publisher. Wrote a companion to the MHB.
Mr	C. W.	Towlson (1889– 1963)	MA DPhil	Wesleyan – present – Brought up an Anglican. Educated Oxford. Taught for 40 years. Became a Methodist Local Preacher. Vice President of Conference 1950. Musical gifts used on the MHB Committee and that of the *School Hymn Book* (1951). President of MCMS. Published *Moravian and Methodist* (1957).

Revd	E. C.	Urwin (1884–1978)	MA BD	United Methodist – absent – Trained at Victoria Park College. Secretary of Temperance and Social Welfare Department 1933–53. Prolific author on temperance subjects.
Revd	J.	Walton (1874–1936)		Primitive Methodist – absent – amateur astronomer.
Revd	F. L.	Wiseman (1858–1944)	BA	Wesleyan – Chairman – present – Served Birmingham Mission for 26 years. President of Conference in 1912 and 1933. Keen interest in hymnody. Composed 11 tunes in MHB. Lectured on *Charles Wesley, Evangelist and Poet*.

Index